DAUMIER: MAN OF HIS TIME

Photographic portrait of Daumier by Nadar
George Eastman House, Rochester, N.Y.

DAUMIER

MAN OF HIS TIME / BY OLIVER W. LARKIN

Professor Emeritus of Art, Smith College

McGRAW-HILL BOOK COMPANY / NEW YORK / TORONTO / LONDON

To the memory of Grace T. Wills, who shared the author's admiration

for the subject of this book.

CONTENTS

Introduction   *ix*

Acknowledgments   *x*

Vignette: Rebellious Young Man   *3*

1: The First Republican Campaign   *8*

2: Daumier's Human Comedy   *31*

3: The Artist   *64*

Vignette: Family Man   *80*

4: The Republican Honeymoon   *83*

5: The Human Comedy, Act Two   *108*

6: Citizen-Painter   *134*

Vignette: Time of Crisis   *157*

7: The Republic Victorious   *161*

8: La Fontaine, Molière and Cervantes   *187*

Vignette: Last Years   *207*

9: Man of His Time and Ours   *210*

Notes   *222*

Index   *237*

List of Illustrations   *245*

INTRODUCTION

It seems unlikely that the writers of biographical novels will ever devote their talents to Daumier. In these characteristic literary products of our day, fact and fiction are cleverly blended and the public's appetite is often sharpened by the vivid description of whatever was neurotic in a man's personality or picturesquely sensational in his behavior. The loves of Goya have thus been served up to us, the pathos of Lautrec among the prostitutes, the self-mutilation of Van Gogh, Modigliani's losing battle with alcohol, and the "agony and the ecstasy" of Michelangelo.

The seventy-one years of Daumier present no turbulent actions, no sexual escapades, no searing emotional crisis, no agony and no ecstasy; the pattern of his daily existence differed in no striking way from that of the thousands of Frenchmen of middle station to whom his drawings gave an instant and enduring life. He said little and wrote less. Out of the few scraps of his writing that have come down to us, and with the help of his friends' comments and anecdotes and their drawn and photographed likenesses of him, I have fashioned a few brief *vignettes* which, placed at intervals here, will help the reader to see him as a person, however mild and inconspicuous.

The man is wholly in his work. My object here is to introduce the general reader to his vast *oeuvre*, not only its superb formal qualities but its expressive content. The idea and the shape, the motivation and the deed are inseparable if one is to understand how this gifted man moves from his first experiments to the mastery of several media and so to his final and most eloquently expressive works. The sources of his themes, his point of view, his attitudes toward the human situation in the political, social, literary and artistic context of his time are relevant to the understanding of what he accomplished.

The stylistic evolution of Daumier as a great lithographer is plainly to be seen in the ten volumes of the Delteil catalogue. I believe that a parallel development in the paintings, although a more complicated one, makes it possible to establish a degree of chronology, an approximate dating for these oils and water colors, a sequence now and then supported by such external evidence as the dates of a few exhibitions and an occasional comment in a diary or a newspaper. To Jean Adhémar goes the credit for having first attempted such a chronology; the one implied in my pages differs considerably from his, and is much closer, I believe, to those of Bernard Lemann and K. E. Maison. The latter's forthcoming *catalogue raisonné* of the paintings and drawings will be a major contribution to the literature on Daumier.

My own book attempts no comprehensive listing of individual works. I have chosen for discussion those prints, paintings, sculptures and drawings which will best illustrate the character of this man's search for the full artistic embodiment of his ideas and feelings. To the notes at the back of the book I have relegated the mention of other works with their present location, also the titles and catalogue numbers of many caricatures, and references to books and articles which will extend the student's knowledge of Daumier and his world. For the convenience of the general reader I have translated French titles into English; in the notes a somewhat different procedure is followed, and works in Continental collections are given their accepted French titles.

The literature on this artist has reached enormous proportions. If I have added one more volume to this swollen flood of words, it is in the hope that, by presenting my Daumier, I may help the reader to find his own.

ACKNOWLEDGMENTS

My effort to put this man's art into words owes much to other Daumierists. Bernard Lemann generously shared with me the results of his own research. Professor Howard Vincent and M. Jean Cherpin, both of whom have discovered new material concerning this artist's life and work, have helped me in letters and conversations. The technical studies of Henri Marceau and the late David Rosen have shed light on Daumier's painting methods. More than any other, Mr. K. E. Maison has exchanged ideas and information with a friendly patience which deserves my deepest gratitude.

My indebtedness to the owners of works by Daumier is indicated in the captions; but a word of special thanks in this connection goes to the Print Department of the Boston Museum of Fine Arts, from whose collection most of the lithographs here illustrated have been taken; also to Anker Larsen, Paul Strand, Rita Roitman, Miss Emilia Lang of the Goldfarb Library at Brandeis University and to my former student Miss Catherine Blanton. Some of the material in my final chapter was presented by me in the annual Katharine Asher Engel Lecture at Smith College in 1962.

Oliver W. Larkin

Northampton, Mass.,
1966

DAUMIER: MAN OF HIS TIME

VIGNETTE: REBELLIOUS YOUNG MAN

In the year of Waterloo Jean-Baptiste Daumier, a glazier by trade and a poet by ambition, quit Marseille for Paris in his effort to exchange putty for the pen; a year later his wife and children joined him there. His son Honoré-Victorin had been born on the twenty-sixth of February, 1808, in the place Saint-Martin in Marseille, a shabby huddle of buildings where neighborly talk was between window and window and where the flavors of the day's cooking lingered. The Street of The Iron Pot in Paris was more cavernous, but a boy of nine could find there the same malodorous intimacies, the same pinched economy and thrift-ridden outlook (Fig. 1). Through streets like this the boy ran errands for the sheriffs of the law courts, a "brook-jumper" observing the flocks of black-robed lawyers who were to stride and gesticulate in his future drawings. There was a brief clerkship in a bookstore of the Palais-Royal. Equally brief was his submission to art-instruction with his father's friend Alexandre Lenoir, founder of a small museum of sculptural fragments salvaged from the Revolution, an ardent classicist who had discovered in the *Leonidas* of David the greatest example of suspended animation in the history of painting. Lenoir now tried to impose on a gifted boy in his teens the correct way to draw from plaster casts and from engravings of Hellenistic sculpture; nonetheless, Daumier's sculptural way of seeing owed something to this teacher.

The pen-struck father meanwhile moved his family constantly from one quarter to another—one Daumier scholar has listed ten lodgings between 1815 and 1832—and with the help of Lenoir sought contacts with men above his station in the hope of advancing his writer's career. A turgid quasi-classical drama on Philip the Second was performed by amateurs and proved that its author was more skilled in mending window-panes than in constructing Alexandrines; his poem *A Spring Morning* was a pale echo of the Abbé Delille:

> Rich in my simplicity,
> A willing stranger to mankind,
> I'd dwell in happy memory
> Of lovely skies I've left behind.

In this precarious household one can only surmise what forces shaped the mind of Honoré Daumier. The contrast between an unworldly father and a sturdy, practically minded mother from Entrevaux in the Basses-Alpes cannot have been lost upon a boy in whom both traits were combined and who was to become both knight-errant and solid citizen, both Don Quixote and Sancho Panza. And it was probably in his father's small library that he discovered the *Odyssey* and the *Iliad*, La Fontaine, Béranger and Rousseau. The miller, his son and the ass, the frogs demanding a king, the cat

3

changed into a woman, these were to be the stuff of future drawings. When he read the crisply worded fable,

> Two thieves were fighting for a prize,
> A donkey newly stolen . . .

an image lodged in his mind for future use with brush and pencil, just as the gods and heroes of Homer and Virgil would come to hilarious life one day in his pictorial travesties.

By what process and how early in life did Daumier come to believe that a democratic republic was the only kind of state worth having, and that kings, aristocrats, political schemers and priests-in-politics were its eternal enemies? We have his own word that he loved the common touch and the simple cadences of Béranger, who said that he had descended from the heights of Pindar to turn into songs the joys, the sorrows and the patriotism of the most numerous class, the lowest of the low. And we can suspect that Daumier came early to realize that his generation had inherited a task left unfinished by the Great Revolution.

Both the elder and the younger Daumier read Rousseau, whose maxims seem to have held their grip early and late on the son's mind: "Might is not right. . . . One has not to obey other than rightful authorities. . . . The less understandable the cult, the more force must be used to impose it. . . . Whenever theological intolerance is established . . . the sovereign is no longer sovereign even in the temporal realm; from then on, priests are the real rulers." And Daumier's lifelong modesty—what one of his friends was to call his heedlessness of glory—may well have derived from his having read in these early years, and taken to heart, the words of the Savoyard priest in *Émile:*

> Good young man . . . if ever your ripened talents give you the power to speak to mankind, never speak to them save as your conscience bids, and do not look for their applause . . . it matters not whether they adore or detest you. What matters to a man is to fulfill his obligations on this earth, and in forgetfulness of self he achieves his own best ends.

By the mid-1820s Daumier knew that whatever he had to say to mankind would be said in the language of art, and was ripening his talents before the live model in one or two of the small academies where students worked without instruction and where he made his first friends in the world of artists, the talented and witty sculptor Auguste Préault and the versatile Philippe-Auguste Jeanron, both of whom were of about his own age and shared his ardently democratic sympathies. In the establishment of Belliard, the maker of lithographic portraits, Daumier began by preparing stones for other draftsmen and in an astonishingly short time was proficient enough to see his own drawings reproduced. Five rather fumbling lithographs published in

1. Street of the Iron Pot, Paris. Photo Anker Larsen

2. Daumier at twenty-two, lithograph by Jean Feuchère
Smith College Museum of Art, Northampton, Mass.

1822 and 1824 with the initials H. D. are attributed to him by one commentator, while another claims that the first print which can be called his own was *On Your Way!* which appeared on July 22, 1830, in the short-lived *Silhouette* of Balzac and Émile de Girardin. In that year Charles Philipon and his brother-in-law founded their illustrated journal, *La Caricature,* and the career of Daumier at twenty-two commenced in earnest.

This is the deceptively mild young man with unruly long hair, upturned nose and a fringe of blond whiskers, whose portrait his friend Jean Feuchère drew in 1830, the mouth hinting at obstinacy, the large eyes quietly observant (Fig. 2). This impudent draftsman must often have wondered, as did his associates, how long he could keep out of jail. The question was answered two years later when Daumier was arrested at the house of his parents, and scribbled a note to his editor that he was "in a most painful position" before being taken to the prison of Sainte-Pélagie. He had gone too far in his litho *The Washermen* and in an earlier drawing, *Gargantua,* boldly signed with his name, which showed the King of France in the act of excreting boodle.

For this high-spirited young rebel, who was allowed to serve half of his sentence in the sanatorium of Doctor Pinel, his nine or ten weeks at Sainte-Pélagie were no tragic ordeal. Had not Béranger preceded him? Its motley population was housed according to political opinions: one section was for the socialists, another for republicans, still another for Bonapartists, and a whole dormitory for legitimists whose aristocratic friends were forever sending them baskets of wine, pastry and game. Through a sky-light one could let down a bottle on a string and pull up a book which a pickpocket had acquired. One could see a fiery editor weaving tapestry, hear a concert that had been arranged by a viscount, or join a chorus in the songs of the Revolution. From his cell Daumier wrote to his friend Jeanron, as one impenitent crusader to another, that he was detained "by a slight indisposition":

Here am I then in Sainte-Pélagie, a charming residence where not everybody enjoys himself. Me, I do find enjoyment here if only to be contrary. I give you my word that I'd make out very well in the Pension Gisquet if, now and then, thoughts of my home and my family didn't ruffle the calm of sweet solitude . . . aside from that, prison won't leave any painful memories with me,—I'm getting four times as much work done in my new boardinghouse as I did at papa's. I'm mobbed by citizens who want their portraits drawn. . . .

H.D.

P.S. Don't write politics because letters are unsealed and read.

1: THE FIRST REPUBLICAN CAMPAIGN

Michelet spoke for the generation of Daumier when he said, "We are the sons of those who, by an heroic national effort, accomplished a world task and established for all nations the Gospel of Equality." For these young men the great names and high principles would always keep the warmth and color which the events of the Revolution had given them, events which they could hear described by men still living or by the new historians. They did not always realize that the dramatic moments of 1789 and of 1792 were the culmination of slow change, and that old French institutions and economic relations, old social and political patterns had crumbled long before the Bastille. A commercial revolution had given the master merchant more importance than the master craftsman; peasant ownership had replaced the feudal scheme of landholding; the new bourgeois could marry into the nobility, buying titles as he bought land, and could make those vital decisions which were to relocate social and political power where economic power already lay.

Behind the great events which marked the triumph of a new class and cleared the way for future achievements were the great ideas. Victory was not suddenly wrenched from the adversary on a material field of encounter, for men had prepared themselves over long generations for the struggle; they had announced their moral and social objectives in terms which were sometimes coldly rational and sometimes fervently idealistic, and had glimpsed long vistas of human betterment which stretched far beyond the horizon of 1789. Voltaire, Diderot, Montesquieu and Condorcet had declared what the program of modern society was to be. Theirs was the revolutionary notion of progress which seemed to justify confidence in the power of man's reason to solve old problems considered by men of the past to be locked mysteries; theirs also was the conviction that every man's pursuit of his own interests would serve the interests of all; theirs too the condemnation of religious prejudice and blind faiths whose propagation had made the Church an obstacle to progress. In these writings one learned that laissez-faire was an economic and moral law, and that the owning of property was a natural right which made the owners the very core of society; but one also read that freedom must prevail in the world of ideas as well as in the material world, the freedom to write, to speak, to assert oneself which enlightens men as to their true nature and the true interdependence of their interests, and thus makes progress a non-violent affair, the inevitable achievement of that essentially wise and noble creature which is Man.

For the philosophers of change, the short-lived Republic of 1792 served as a model for free men. A republic, they believed, was that form of government which made the "social contract" explicit in a written constitution, and was managed by administrators and lawgivers who were the chosen representatives of the popular will; its eternal enemies were those rulers, opportunists and false preachers who kept man from coming into his own. The philosophers had described the new order as though it could be accomplished without one man's meat becoming another's poison; the years since 1792 had demonstrated that an ideal was something to be defended amid harsh realities, its values salvaged in the dust and heat of pitched battle. Gallicans fought to shear of its worldly power a Church too wealthy and too hostile to necessary change, and to give French Catholics a degree of independence from Rome. Partisans of the old régime, having fled the country, tried with the help of foreign kings to unseat the Revolution, whose leaders were forced to defend their work both at home and abroad. In the councils of government there developed the conflict between reformist and revolutionary, between the Gironde and the Mountain, between moderate men who feared centralized power and recoiled when fire had to be fought with fire, and those more realistic spirits who would ruthlessly suppress all attacks, internal or external, against their revolution.

With Napoleon's coup d'état of the eighteenth of Brumaire in 1799 which ushered in the Consulate, men who had dethroned a King lived subject to an Emperor through years of contradiction when those who claimed freedom for themselves denied it to others and when the internationalism of the theorists tried to exist beside the ferocious patriotism bred by foreign attacks upon France. No less contradictory was the Charter which closed this period in 1815, a document which provided, to be sure, that deputies should be elected, but limited them to citizens of a certain age and financial status, and narrowed the electorate to those businessmen, manufacturers and landowners who had managed to climb far enough up the economic ladder to pay substantial taxes. Still more unrepresentative was the Bourbon Restoration of Louis the Eighteenth and Charles the Tenth, whose governments tampered with elections, corrupting voters and falsifying returns, and whose favors to the clergy threatened to restore the old theocracy.

When Paris learned in July of 1830 that the Charter was to be discarded, the free press suspended, the Chamber dissolved and the royalty entrenched in government, a cry of "Long Live the Charter!" was heard in the streets. Young radicals from the schools joined forces with typographers and tradesmen to make what would always be known as the "three glorious days" of revolution. Out of the city's pavements barricades were built in the night of July twenty-seventh, and next morning the bells of Notre Dame tolled to announce that the crowd had taken it over; along the boulevards men sniped from windows upon the occupying troops, whose demoralized flight up the Champs-Élysées on the twenty-ninth marked the triumph of the insurgents. On the thirtieth, King Charles took carriage for Rambouillet and abdication. A week later, Louis-Philippe of the House of Orléans became the Constitutional King of France.

For the republican rebels of 1830, this July Monarchy was a gigantic and bitter anticlimax. Its ruler had been chosen by Adolphe Thiers, who had no faith whatever in popular suffrage; one of its dominant figures was to be Guillaume Guizot, whose advice to his countrymen was "Enrich yourselves"; its leading figures were to be bourgeois citizens of substance who were more concerned with the acquisition of property for exploitation than with its wider and more equitable distribution. The revolutionary philosophers had mined the metal of freedom, and now the men of practical affairs forged from it the special freedoms they needed —freedom from royal or parliamentary control, from the organized pressures of artisans, from the efforts of the small farmer to gain influence in proportion to his vast numbers. Aléxis de Tocqueville described the régime as an industrial company whose every move was planned for the benefit of the stockholders. The Gospel of Equality had become the Gospel of Getting Ahead.

If the builders of the July Monarchy could quote revolutionary scripture in justification of their conduct, so could their opponents. For eighteen years, while the bourgeois settled down to consolidate his triumph, young men with consciences who preferred the religion of democracy to that of success would struggle to give Equality a more substantial meaning than Rousseau had given it, to revive Voltaire's tongue-lashing of the priests and the hatred of Condorcet for war and chauvinism, his insistence that poverty was an evil to be destroyed, his belief in the power of education and the efficacy of universal suffrage. They were aware of the staggering discrepancy between revolutionary promise and bourgeois fulfillment, and impressed by the contradiction between those mighty forces set loose in the world by the crisis of 1789 and the meager, less than humane existence most Frenchmen now led. Daumier's friend Champfleury spoke for them all when he said, "Every young man in 1830 was fired by a last spark of the Revolution." He might have added that the forms of dissent were many and conflicting and that the men who for one reason or another found themselves at odds with the new dispensation were a motley assortment of social theorists, literary and artistic rebels, militant revolutionists and mildly democratic reformers.

No group, for example, more keenly felt the drabness of the French atmosphere than the poets and painters of the Romantic movement, and their revival of the chivalric past, their exploitation of the exotic, their devotion to the heroes and villains of Shakespeare, Goethe and Walter Scott, were in this sense antidotes to present ugliness, a protest of the imagination against the reduction of man's stature to the size of a cog in the social machine, a defiance of conventional dress and deportment, of the stilted routine of respectable offices and drawing rooms. Charles Baudelaire called for the artist who would express in form and color the struggle of the noble, sensitive individual against the moral and spiritual decadence of the bourgeois world; Alfred de Vigny spoke of the everlasting conflict between man's fruitful, insistent inner life and that outer life which blights and repels. Along with this ardent individualism went a mistrust of social collectivities, an above-the-battle posture; and Théophile Gautier was heard to declare that he would surrender all his rights as a French citizen to see the shapely ballerina Julia Grisi getting out of her bathtub.

This preoccupation with the individual soul was not always inconsistent, however, with concern for the general welfare. Social romanticism had no relish for violent change, but it voiced its indignation and its warm sympathy for the victims of injustice and inequality. Romantic poetry, said Lamartine in 1836, felt the dignity of the human vocation and dreamed of a society where all man's freedoms, all his capacities and his virtues would have full play. The Victor Hugo of these years, whose political naïveté and changing loyalties gave him the reputation of an opportunist, saw the poet as a shepherd of the mind whose mission was to transform the mob into the people; his *Autumn Leaves* of 1831 echoed his hatred of oppression in all its forms.

Far more impatient and more politically-minded than the Romantics were the men of the extreme left: Auguste Blanqui the atheist, the believer in revolutionary dictatorship, the tireless organizer of secret clubs where city workmen learned the necessity for direct action in a war between rich and poor; Armand Barbès, who helped Blanqui to stage the May insurrection of 1839; Louis Blanc, whose *Organization of Work* demanded that the State guarantee to all citizens the right to work and who had this to say of Equality: "What good is it to have the right to better yourself if you have not the power?"

To the dissent of the 1830s the visionaries and social dreamers contributed their notions of a better world with slogans which more often stabbed the consciences of individual followers than provided battle cries for the faubourg Saint-Antoine. Pierre Leroux, of an apostolic and tormented temperament, was called a lesser prophet of socialism, and claimed indeed that he was the first to use that term as the opposite of individualism. The disciples of Saint-Simon, whose evangelical rites drew the scorn of the respectable and attracted a lunatic fringe of believers, nevertheless shrewdly analyzed the conflict of classes. In the pages of *La Démocratie Pacifique,* Victor Considérant gave a proletarian accent to the doctrines of Charles Fourier, whose "phalanges" had been designed to get men out of the cities, back to the land; but he cheerfully accepted the régime of Louis-Philippe, placing his confidence in social but not political change. Equally devoted to peaceful persuasion were the followers of Étienne Cabet, whose *Voyage to Icaria* reached five editions before 1848, with its vision of an ideal human association which could be realized only in some oasis of unselfishness, whether Icaria or Brook Farm.

These social dreamers sometimes angered their friends by strategic retreats into prudence. They dwelt, one cynic observed, in the Republic of Plato, adding that platonic affairs produce no children. Less utopian in temper than these, and also more wholeheartedly democratic than most of the Romantics, were those republicans in shirtsleeves whose favorite poet was Béranger, whose historian was Michelet, whose voice among the preachers was Lamennais and, among the politicians, Ledru-Rollin. Old Béranger had said that songs about loving and drinking, about barks of Charon and deceived husbands would never get themselves sung by artisans and soldiers around tavern tables; and scarcely a Frenchman lived in the 1830s who did not know by heart the simple verses in which this poet of the people rhymed his sense of the national destiny, his hatred of kings, his scorn for the black-robed reverend fathers, "half-fox, half-wolf."

Jules Michelet was convinced by the events of 1830 that the mass was the prime mover in historic change, and in *The People* this famous historian teacher recalled that his own childhood had known the dirty, crooked streets of the workmen's quarter, and added, "I have remained people." Michelet reproached his Romantic friends for having too eagerly stressed the abnormal, the ugly, the non-typical, for having considered free love more poetic than family affection, robbery more exciting than work, the prison more picturesque than the shop. Michelet described the forms of modern slavery which had replaced the bonds of the feudal régime—the farmer rooted to his small acre, the worker bound to his machine, the small manufacturer a slave to the big one, the shopkeeper caught up in the whirlpool of competition, the clerk tied to his desk and his inkwell by red tape. And from his classroom he defied the clerical pack in full cry against him: "We have overthrown one dynasty to drive you out, and if need be we shall destroy half a dozen!"

Few preachers could be counted among the democrats, but Lamennais was one of them. While the Ultracatholics were calling the University a cesspool of vice and its teachers the worthy sons of the Reign of Terror, he launched the liberal Catholic movement and "set the red cap on the Cross" in his *Words of a Believer,* a work which brought him excommunication and a burial without benefit of clergy.

Ledru-Rollin, whom his critics called a Danton minus the conviction, eloquently proclaimed his belief in Progress and described the Church as a worm-eaten temple where liberty had always been anathema. When his newspaper, *La Réforme,* was accused of socialism he replied that the "Red Republic" was a phantom; that he did not fear the socialists, although he believed that they offered the wrong remedy, and that the best way to prove them wrong was to restore the nation to life and health. The masses of the present day, he declared, were like the slave-population of antiquity escorting the victor's chariot, or a stepladder to be smashed by the powerful as soon as they had used it in order to climb into power.

Where, in this welter of conflicting opinions, was Daumier to take his stand among tender and toughminded republicans, old veterans and young idealists, the makers of utopias and the makers of barricades? In so far as Romanticism was a passionate denial of the past and a liberalizing force in the realm of art and of society, he was on the Romantic side. But his selflessness would hold him aloof from the more irresponsible elements in an artistic Bohemia which bred so many egos; and it would give him an amused tolerance for the genius-in-frenzy, the long hair and short temper of the artist with a capital A; nor could this child of the middle class share the savage disdain of Gautier "for everything that pleases the bourgeois elected or electable." As for the militant radicals, the inciters to direct action, Daumier never succumbed to the panic which their activities aroused in so many solid citizens. Having a shrewd sense of current realities, he looked upon the visionary prophets of social change with a degree of skepticism; this young man with his feet on the ground sometimes ridiculed but also sometimes respected men with their heads in the clouds. On the whole, it was the democracy of such men as Michelet which most appealed to him; and nearly forty years of drawings were to prove his obstinate belief in a republic, in economic, social and political equality, the right of all Frenchmen to determine who should best represent them, and full freedom of written and spoken opinion.

In the battle which was now to engage him, legislative debate and compromise would not suffice; republicanism needed effective means by which to touch the minds of men. Secret societies were forming in back rooms for stormy debates and pamphlets were drawn up and circulated. Among the workrooms of the faubourg Saint-Marceau, Heine discovered that artisans were reading the speeches of Robespierre and Marat and the works of Cabet and Baboeuf, "writings that smell of blood," and in the foundries he saw half-naked men beat time with their hammers to the tune of songs which seemed to have been composed in Hell. Another means of appeal was the political newspaper: the more moderate spirits read the *Revue Républicaine*, the *Réformateur*, the *Tribune* or the *National*, while the more fiery sheets—the *Moniteur*, the *Homme Libre* and *La Réforme*—spoke a language which the Paris workmen could understand. When Charles Philipon founded his two journals it was with the deliberate purpose of propagandizing through pictures, and his writers and draftsmen dedicated their talents to "warfare every day upon the absurdities of every day." Thereupon, as Thackeray observed, "a most curious contest speedily commenced between the State and Monsieur Philipon's little army."

Philipon, whom someone described as "journalism made flesh," was the supreme tactician of both *La Caricature* and *Charivari*. The former was a slim sheet which sometimes had articles by the mysterious "Count Alexandre de B . . . ," none other than Balzac, and one large picture or several smaller ones. When it announced its own demise in August, 1835, after four years and ten months of crippling fines, confiscations and prison terms, its sister publication *Charivari* was three years old and destined to survive persecution for several decades.

In the pages of these two journals the nimble editor was to refine and enrich the craft of humorous drawing. Although Leonardo da Vinci had drawn deformed heads, they were scientifically observed deviations, caprices quite without humor. It was in the seventeenth century that Annibale Carracci made those *ritratti caricati*, portraits with ludicrously exaggerated features, which recall that the word *caricare*, and its French counterpart *·charger*, means to overload; in these and in the faces of Pietro Ghezzi were emphasized the features which made one man differ from another in defiance of the theory of ideal beauty. For Reynolds in the eighteenth century caricature was the playful exercise of the imagination in one's less conventional moments; for William Hogarth and Thomas Rowlandson it became a species of humorous genre which pleased the middle-class Englishman by describing ordinary life in an appropriate setting, a satire of human behavior which could be coarse in Hogarth and violently patriotic and political in the work of James Gillray. This broader conception took a bland and charming form in the French pictorial satire of the early 1800s, in Bosio's ridicule of fashions and in the "expressive heads" which Boilly drew to explore the variations in human physiognomy with only mild exaggeration.

Caricature had come of age, and the crude image etched or engraved on metal or wood with balloon-shaped quotations issuing like protoplasm from the mouths of its characters had given place to the drawing whose form conveyed its meaning with or without the use of captions. Romantic writers welcomed caricature as a challenge to academic notions of perfect beauty, a reduction to absurdity of man's pretensions to superior wisdom, a genial exposure of the bourgeois. In his essay *The Essence of Laughter* Baudelaire distinguished between the monstrously grotesque as one found it in Goya, and that "relative comic" which amuses men of common sense by less violent means in Molière, Voltaire, and in those caricaturists of his own time whom the poet recognized and praised as truly creative artists.

These artists now possessed a new medium for graphic expression. Ten years before Daumier was born, an inquisitive Bavarian named Aloys Senefelder, in the course of his experiments in relief engraving on stone, had discovered that lines drawn on the stone with a gummy ink could be directly transferred by pressure to a sheet of paper, and thus in 1798 invented the lithograph. Mechanically speaking, lithography is surface printing based on the affinity of grease for grease and the antipathy between grease and water. The drawing is made with a crayon, with a pen, or with a brush dipped in lithographic ink, and consists of greasy areas which are subsequently fixed chemically to the stone's surface. The stone is moistened with water, which affects only the areas which have not been drawn upon, and is then inked with a roller, the ink adhering only to the drawing; it is then placed in the bed of a handpress, a dampened sheet of paper is laid upon it, and the printer squeezes paper and stone together, pulling the sketch from the latter to the former.

When Senefelder died in 1834 several handbooks in France and England had explained every detail of the craft as it was to be practised until steam and photography further modified it, and several establishments were printing lithos there and in Germany, Italy and the United States. Never did invention more completely answer need. Society people made it a hobby, newspaper publishers found it a process which gave their illustrations a maximum of effect with a minimum of expensive machinery, and artists quickly realized how direct a medium it was. One could draw on the stone as though on paper, with the same freedom of touch, the same variety of line and tone, and then see that drawing reproduced in hundreds of prints, each of which was in every true sense an original. By every other process, their work was in some degree changed before it could yield a print. The steel or copper engraving, the etching, the wood engraving were translations and not always faithful ones; but the lithograph, as Joseph Pennell has pointed out, is the drawing itself, "unchanged, actually as the artist made it, multiplied."

Hence the breadth and richness of the stable scenes of Géricault, of Bonington's print of the great clock tower at Rouen, of the seaports and fishermen of Isabey and the plates in Baron Taylor's *Picturesque Voyages*, which were signed by all the great names from Ingres and Delacroix to Harding and Prout. Horace Vernet drew portraits of celebrities,

while the life of the "other half" could be seen in the beggars and pedlars of Carl Vernet, the hunchbacks of Boilly, the clerks and lawyers of
Henry Monnier, and the Bohemian carnivals of Gavarni. Delacroix was
commissioned to illustrate *Faust* in this medium, and Devéria to supplement Victor Hugo, while the glory of Napoleon was kept alive by
Charlet and by Raffet. The former could reproduce a whole battle on a
sheet ten inches by eight, while in the latter's *Nocturnal Review* the
ghosts of dragoons rose out of the mist to salute their commander on his
white charger.

Small wonder that, by the time Daumier made his first efforts on
stone, the department of the Seine alone supported twenty-four lithographic houses, one hundred and eighty presses, and five hundred workmen, and the new vogue was set to music in a ballad:

> Lithography, All hail!
> The fad will n'er grow stale!
> Fair, ugly, big and small,
> The crayon gets them all.
>
> Our streets go on and on,
> A regular salon
> Where, though you've never posed,
> You'll find yourself exposed.

Bending over the polished or grained stone, Daumier learned the feel
of its surface, its crisp response to his stroke; he discovered how to use
a blunt crayon for the darker tones and a thinner and sharper one for
the lighter; how to accent his forms now and then with a pen and to
spread dark areas with a brush. By the slow building up of cross-hatched
tones he managed to convey a sense of atmosphere for his backgrounds,
of texture for a man's silky top hat or timeworn frock coat; he became
deft in picking highlights with a needle or a knife blade, in scraping a
darkened area to suggest the slant of rain and the fall of snow, the
sheen of oily cheeks and noses. His finished sketch must, in the words
of a manual, "look delicate in the light tints, firm in the middle ones,
and rich and powerful in the darker parts." He had to resign himself to
some loss of this brilliance when, for reasons of economy and of speed,
his publisher made a master proof from his original, transferred it to
several other stones and took prints from them all at once, or when the
fine imported Chinese papers gave way to the cheaper and flabbier ones
which were made in France and whose thinness allowed the printing on
the reverse to show through the lighter portions of his print. Only the
trial proofs on thick paper gave back his full effect, and these were to
become collectors' prizes in our time. Occasionally a print was issued

which had been colored by hand, an unfortunate procedure in the case of an artist whose range of greys so richly suggested color.

Daumier was but one of several men recruited by Philipon from among the talented but impecunious; armed with the new weapon of lithography, they now proceeded to exploit its every resource. Of necessity, the squad took over the inherited stock-in-trade of their profession—the symbolic type-character whose antics embody the moral or political behavior of a whole class, the *portrait-charge* whose irregularities of feature were cleverly overstressed, the parody of a famous work of art which brought it up to date, the full pictorial composition whose action revealed a form of behavior to be ridiculed or a wrong to be attacked. There were moments of burlesque when a whole family took shelter beneath the nose of d'Argout or when Daumier personified the *Constitutionnel* by a female monstrously blown up to the point of bursting; for the most part however, Philipon's snipers could bring their shots closer to the mark by avoiding gross distortion.

Some of these fighters deserted, some returned to the ranks, and some were freshly recruited as the years passed and the campaign shifted its terrain and tactics. Their styles were as varied as their personalities, although they worked in close collaboration, borrowing technical devices from one another and exchanging ideas for pictures or for captions. Among these creators of modern caricature, Gavarni worked seldom for Philipon. His superb and rather elegant draftsmanship brought to life the artists and lights-of-love of the Bohemian world, the flutter of plumes on a modish bonnet, the sheen of ribbons and the soft depths of velvet; but this man of conflicting interests scorned the life of the average middle-class citizen whose behavior seemed to him sordid, corrupt and unsanitary, and wished his lithographs to be understood simply as a comedy of manners in crayon. But although he could flatter, as Baudelaire observed, he could also bite, and his comedy turned tragic in the figure of Thomas Vireloque, whose every appearance on the artist's stone was a reminder of the degradation and the misery which this specialist in charm had stumbled upon in the narrower streets of Paris.

Henry Monnier, though he lacked the virtuosity of Gavarni, had a sensitive and painterly touch, a mild irony in the scenes of bourgeois life which he made in the intervals of painting, writing, and improvising those monologues out of which he fashioned Monsieur Joseph Prud'-homme for the professional stage, a creature to be borrowed by his colleague Daumier. More trenchantly political was the unhappy and oversensitive spirit of Charles Grandville, whose animals, dressed and behaving like people, became the models for Tenniel's more famous beasts in *Alice*. Charles Traviès, embittered by extreme poverty and his failure

3. *Lower the Curtain, the Farce Is Ended*, lithograph
Museum of Fine Arts, Boston, Mass.

as a painter, drew his notorious Mayeux from the dregs of society, a
coarse and repellent hunchback portrayed on repeated occasions with a
thin, acidulous crayon. More opulent were the lampoons of kings and
priests by Alexandre Decamps before he became a full-fledged painter.

What united these talents and those of lesser men was Philipon's
announced purpose to keep the republican idea alive in people's minds
by attacking the July Monarchy and all its works, hitting hard and not
always above the belt. For these fighters with pen and crayon, Louis-
Philippe embodied the detested monarchic principle; consequently, the
Louis-Philippe whom one encountered day after day in the drawings of
Daumier and his companions was not the hero who had fought for the
Revolution nor the peaceable elderly man who did his best to be friendly
with those he met on the sidewalks of Paris. To them his mutton-chop
whiskers, jowl, paunch and umbrella personified eternal caution and
shabby compromise. It was Philipon who changed the King's pyramidal
head into a pear, served up endlessly by the whole staff of caricaturists.
Daumier explored this and other transformations: on August 31, 1833,

the monarch was half-pear and half-man, walking the diplomatic tight-rope as the "foremost acrobat of Europe"; three weeks later he became a Chinese porcelain, a fat parlor ornament; in December he rang down the curtain on parliament as a clown who cried, "The Farce is Over!" (Fig. 3). In a less comic mood the artist drew him in May of 1834 in the rusty black of an undertaker hiding his relief under false mourning as the funeral of Lafayette went by, and on other occasions he prayed in a monk's gown beneath a crucified republic, and as a doctor, bled the French nation. Still more relentless was the print where the King stood beside the bed of a political enemy who had died in chains, a fat figure to be recognized even though for reasons of prudence Daumier turned his back to the observer, and declared, "He can now be set free because he's no longer dangerous."

The King's ministers rapidly came and went, but not rapidly enough to escape Daumier's pencil. More than once he traced the dogged, tight-lipped features of Guizot, who enraged the democrats by observing that the unequal distribution of wealth was one of the laws of Providence. More frequently the butt of caricature was the diminutive Louis-Adolphe Thiers, a shrewd lawyer from Aix who had steadily climbed to influence in the 1820s by cultivating the appropriate editors, politicians and financiers, and whose owl-like head with its huge spectacles, barely visible above the parliamentary rostrum, was a sight to tempt any comic draftsman. James Russell Lowell noted his resemblance to Punch, the "firm, round head looking hard enough to go through a wall . . . with a look that says, 'This is the likeness of a man who cannot by any possibility be mistaken.' " He might have been describing the "portrait" of Thiers by Daumier which was published by *Charivari* in June, 1833, when the little man was busily campaigning for a seat in the Academy, courting the daughter of a wealthy Parisian, and deep in a covert struggle to shrink the powers of a King who once remarked, "I've given him a bed in my own chamber, but he's determined to sleep in *my* bed." (Fig. 4). Daumier pursued Thiers year after year as the consummate politician sparred and shifted, using all factions but committing himself to none, guiding the chariot of state in the path of moderation when he could, and devising mischievous ways to stay its progress when others held the reins.

An observant reader of Philipon's two journals could have noted the unevenness of Daumier's contributions, ranging from the rather simple and crudely obvious to those more carefully executed lithos in which every resource of the medium was exploited. He might have noted, in the bust-portraits of the parliamentary leaders, the first of which appeared on April 26, 1832, a new strength and richness which were

4. *Thi* . . . (Thiers), lithograph. Collection Benjamin A. and Julia M. Trustman, Brandeis University, Waltham, Mass.

essentially sculptural. These personalities had in fact been modeled in clay before they were drawn on stone. From the gallery of the Chamber, Daumier had memorized every feature of these "celebrities of the Golden Mean," shrewd men voting the construction of railways in which they owned shares, swappers of jobs for votes, ancient relics of the good old times at sea in a commercial age, lazy men feathering their nests with political pluckings, men growing paunches and losing hair, rising inopportunely to a point of order or contentedly sleeping out the session. In his workroom he pushed and prodded the coarse clay into remembered shapes to make his rogue's gallery of legislative ineptitude, a series of heads some five to seven inches high, to which

5. Bust portrait of Prunelle, bronze
Smith College Museum of Art, Northampton, Mass.

he then added colors to differentiate pink flesh from white neck-cloths
and the black or brown of clothing. No doubt he recalled the lithographs
by Boilly which had tried to show how the emotional makeup of an
individual and even the nature of his occupation were revealed by the
shape of his head and his features. Nor was the sculptured caricature
an invention of Daumier, who had seen the busts and full-length
statuettes in plaster and bronze which Jean-Pierre Édouard Dantan
had begun to fashion in the late 1820s, grotesquely comic effigies of
Alexandre Dumas, Hugo, Liszt and other famous people sold from
Dantan's gallery and reproduced in lithos and wood engravings. But
Daumier's small heads were more vigorously individualized than those

6. *Mr. Prune* (Prunelle), lithograph
Museum of Fine Arts, Boston, Mass.

of Boilly and less obvious in their exaggerations than the statuettes of Dantan Jeune. His clay bestiary—the apelike skull of Dupin, the bulldog phiz of Baillot, the anteater's proboscis of d'Argout—respected the limits of human physiognomy; its power derived from the plausibility of these lips pursed by egotism or greed, these brows knit by vulgar cunning, these jowls grown fat and flabby with gluttony.

Taken together, these diminutive busts were, in the words of Daumier's editor, "a monument which we raise to contemporary folly"; individually, each was a startlingly faithful likeness, a complete and unique characterization. Here were the pinched and supercilious features of Sébastiani, who had served Napoleon and now "had nothing left but his aristocratic pretensions"; here was Judge Hippolyte-Abraham Dubois, dispenser of political justice, his piglike eyes nearly lost in the flabby expanses of his face; here was the ugly aggressiveness of Prunelle, the Mayor of Lyon, half-concealed under a mop of cascading hair (Figs. 5, 6); the slow-witted obstinacy of Odier's tight mouth; the falsely genial smile of Alexandre-Simon Pataille; the cruelly pointed nose of that ruthless prosecutor of the press, Jean-Charles Persil.

Long after Daumier's death, thirty-six of these fragile pieces of unbaked clay which the artist had given to Philipon, their surfaces crumbling and their colors fading, were to be cast in bronze, a medium which gave them a new sculptural force, a wholly different kind of expressiveness than had been their maker's intention. Quite clearly he had thought of them not as self-sufficient sculptures but as memoranda, swift records of things seen which he had before him when he drew on stone the long series of *portraits-charges,* including both busts and full-length seated or standing figures, which appeared in *Caricature* and in *Charivari* at intervals between April, 1832, and November of the following year. In the earlier lithographs the head and shoulders of the victim were accompanied by a fanciful coat of arms, and all of them could be identified under thinly disguised names—*M. Prune, Bataille, Vieux-Niais, Odieux, Guiz . . . , Tu Bois.* The new force and subtlety to be found in much of the man's work in the middle 1830s were the result of this venture into sculpture. Daumier had the forms of Dupin, for example, in his fingertips when his crayon modeled the litho of June 14, 1832, the skull built with planes which cleanly join one another, the hollows dark in proportion to their depth, the most salient shapes glistening where the stone has been scraped white, the textures of soft hair, starched jabot and heavy robe superbly suggested, and the sheen of oily skin drawn taut over bones (Fig. 7).

On subsequent occasions the individuals thus lampooned reappeared in group compositions, of which the finest is *The Legislative Paunch* (Fig. 8), one of a series of large lithographs carefully printed on good

7. *Dup* . . . (Dupin), lithograph
Museum of Fine Arts, Boston, Mass.

paper which appeared under the disarming title of *The Monthly Lithographic Association*. Here Daumier has ranged thirty-five members of the bourgeois legislature in four receding tiers and has used the full gamut from glistening white to rich black to throw them into harsh relief in the light which falls from above them. What might have been a monotonous array has been kept alive by the curving backs of benches, the slight diminution of scale with distance, the breaking of the foreground line by the portly figure of Prunelle, and the variety of pose and gesture as men chat, smile, take snuff, slide into stupor or blow their noses.

The *portrait-charge* was by no means the only form of Daumier's satire. Although much of Philipon's space was given to attacks on individuals, there were issues as well as personalities to be fought. In the field of foreign policy it seemed to democrats that large nations dickered over the fate of smaller ones, and in *The London Conference* Daumier drew the great powers around a table under which lay the chained and helpless body of Poland. His comment on the rival intrigues of France and England in Spain showed Thiers and Montalivet hoisting Louis-Philippe into the saddle of an apprehensive nag under

8. *The Legislative Paunch,* lithograph
Museum of Fine Arts, Boston, Mass.

the title, *Departure for Spain.* These plates and others like them
lashed an opportunism which alternated between reckless defiance
of other nations and shameful appeasement.

Within France a constant war-by-imagery had to be waged against
those Catholic extremists who in the Restoration years had combined
forces with the relics of the nobility to form the extreme right. Under
Charles the Tenth, Béranger had watched the Jesuits returning from
exile and had written,

> Heav'n and the Saints be praised! Amen!
> They're setting up the monks again!

Under Louis-Philippe, in an effort to win religious support for the
monarchy, a new law granted to elementary schools managed by
priests a freedom equal to that of lay institutions, and Daumier was
quick to dramatize this threat to education. Obese and greedy, his
priests of the 1830s murmur as they pass by the starving, "Blessed are
they that hunger and thirst."

The main objective of the republican press in these years, however,
was not the ridicule of little men in big positions nor of the clerical

9. *Rue Transnonain,* lithograph
Museum of Fine Arts, Boston, Mass.

invasion, but rather the maintenance of the very right of republicanism to exist, to organize, to put its ideas before people in spoken, written and pictured form. When legal action was taken in 1831 against the *Tribune* and *Figaro,* repression bred revolt; barricades went up in the streets behind the Hôtel de Ville to cries of "Long Live the Republic!" Within two days order had been restored and Guizot assured the Chamber that riots were dead, clubs were dead, revolutionary propaganda was dead. But the resistance smouldered underground. In Paris and the provinces the Society for the Rights of Man grew to nearly five thousand members. Ten months after Daumier had served his prison term for lampooning the government, he sketched a cell in which a man chained to the wall faces his prosecutor with "Nevertheless, the Republic goes forward." In a litho of October, 1833, a printer of the *National* squeezes Louis-Philippe to a shapeless pulp in his press. And a larger drawing of March, 1834, shows the fat monarch flourishing his umbrella, while in the center foreground a stalwart typographer with clenched fists, sleeves rolled up and cap defiantly cocked, commands all comers to keep off.

One month later the discontent of working people with a régime which blandly ignored them could no longer be contained. When the government moved against the leaders of a general strike at Lyon, riot and bloodshed followed in several large towns and on April 13 in Paris itself, where Thiers as Minister of the Interior rode beside Marshal Bugeaud into the crossfire of the barricaded streets. It was during this brief and unsuccessful insurrection that one wounded officer was killed by a sniper from a window in the rue Transnonain, whereupon his companions made a shambles of the house. Accounts of the affair conflicted, as conservatives disclaimed the responsibility of the government and republicans angrily made of the incident a weapon in their battle with the régime. Out of the massacre of the rue Transnonain, Ledru-Rollin made a fiery pamphlet and Daumier a grim lithograph which drew crowds to the publisher's shopwindow (Fig. 9). Word and picture complemented each other.

The writer had pieced together the gruesome depositions of the survivors:

> A little after five o'clock on the morning of the fourteenth a platoon of light infantry came down the street. . . . They tried to break down the door of our house but couldn't because it's very thick. . . . M. Guitard, my husband and I hurry downstairs to open up . . . the soldiers rush into the corridor . . . and shoot down my husband and Guitard just as they get to the bottom steps. . . . The soldiers reach the second floor . . . a door is opened by an old man, M. Brefford père. He says to the officer, "We're quiet people without arms, don't murder us" . . . he is pierced three times by a bayonet.

Another speaks:

> It was here they killed my baby . . . it was in this corner, under a table where he was hiding, that they killed that respectable M. Bouton with fifty-one shots and bayonet wounds. . . . Madame Godefroy is pushed into the hallway, M. Hû falls dead with his baby beside him. . . .

In Daumier's drawing, as Baudelaire said, only silence and death reign. The troops of law and order have withdrawn and the sprawling corpses lie where they have fallen. The painter David had once made a dead Marat a martyr in a bathtub; Daumier's central figure is a martyr without a name, death in a nightshirt, beside a cheap bedstead and a wrenched bolster. The print would eloquently serve as a warning and a reminder. "In time," wrote the pamphleteer, "the reaction will take place; the people will rise in anger and wrest from kings the cry of remorse that Theodosius uttered after the massacre of Thessalonica —'Would to God I could bring back to life today these dead men who accuse me!' " Years afterward, when Flaubert wanted to explain why one of his characters had become a republican, he described how the young Dussardier had once stood before a grocer's shop in the rue

Transnonain and seen soldiers with bloody bayonets and with human hair stuck to their gunstocks.

Ledru-Rollin had challenged the government to investigate the butchery of April 14 and to punish the guilty; instead, the Chamber of Peers on the day following voted itself the function of a high court to prosecute the leaders of the insurrection. The trials opened at the Luxembourg on the fifth of May, 1835; two days later, Daumier published *The Phantom,* a superb lithograph in which the ghost of Marshal Ney, enveloped in a gleaming white mantle, knocks at the door of justice. That hero of Napoleonic battles who abandoned King Charles to support the cause of the returning Bonaparte, had been condemned for treason and executed in the gardens not far from the palace where this trial of 1835 was to be held. During the July Monarchy there was popular but futile agitation to cancel the old sentence and thus make amends for what one republican leader called "this abominable murder." Daumier's drawing may have been made at an earlier time and now published as a warning that the defendants in the so-called "April trials" could expect no evenhanded justice from the Chamber which had refused to honor the dead Marshal.

From the two thousand men who had been arrested, one hundred and twenty were singled out for indictment. Not until the next January were the most dangerous enemies of the State safely under lock and key. Daumier had been given the assignment of sketching the accused and accusers for *Charivari* and now watched a trial which every day became less legal and more political, as the defendants put the whole conservative government on the defensive in a dialogue which kept the sedate chamber in an uproar:

Cavaignac: I demand the floor in the name of all the defendants.
The President: You cannot have the floor!
The Defendants: Speak, Cavaignac, speak!
Several peers: Monsieur le Président, oblige the defendants to be silent.
M. De Plougoulm: The defendants are to remain seated! (all the accused stand up and shout)
The Procurer-General: The ministry will not permit itself to be intimidated by this uproar. I declare that, if the slightest disturbance is injected into the trial, I shall bring in a verdict of guilt against the defendants.
Several voices: Cut it short! Judge us now, without letting us be heard. That won't take so long.
The defendants (en masse): Condemn all of us! All! All!

Once more Daumier relied on his knowledge of parliamentary physiognomy in a series of lithographed portraits, *Judges of the April Defendants,* half-humorous with Portalis, Gazan and Siméon, wholly

10. *You Have the Floor, Explain Yourself,* lithograph
Museum of Fine Arts, Boston, Mass.

grim in the seated figure of Barbé-Marbois, a sick man in dressing gown and slippers with a tight black cap framing his ruthless mask. The most powerful drawing showed a defendant gripped by his prosecutors, his mouth gagged and his arms pinned down, before a judge with the muzzle of a hyena who snarls, "You have the floor; explain yourself; you're free!" (Fig. 10).

The government, which had not foreseen the risks of the May trials, used the attempt of Fieschi on the King's life to justify its final move to silence the left, the laws of September, 1835. One paragraph paid unintentional tribute to Daumier and his colleagues:

Article 7 of the Charter proclaims that Frenchmen have the right to circulate their opinions in published form. But, when opinions are converted into actions by the circulation of drawings, it is a question of speaking to the eyes. That is something more than the expression of an opinion; it is an incitement to action not covered by article 7.

Henceforth these artists could speak to the eyes but not in political accents. For the time being, republicans had lost their appeal to force, their right to organize and to issue propaganda, had lost their leaders to prison and exile. Philipon's little army was defeated. Two days before the September laws were passed, Daumier fired one parting shot in the final issue of *Caricature*. Three bloodstained and bandaged men who had died on the barricades five years before push up their tombstone, with the words, *They Died for Liberty* carved upon it, sadly look about them, and remark, " 'Twas really not worth the trouble of getting ourselves killed."

2: DAUMIER'S HUMAN COMEDY

After the September laws, as Thackeray wrote, the pigmy Thiers would disappear from Philipon's pages; the syringe of Marshal Soult would be hung up in peace, and the multitudes would no longer take shelter beneath the nose of M. d'Argout. But if the political arena was now closed for thirteen years to the gladiators of the pencil, there was the far more spacious field of French society itself, with its enormously varied types and their behavior to be chastised through laughter. Daumier's satire of that society during these years constitutes between one-fourth and one-third of his total work on stone. His family's frequent shifts of domicile gave the young artist an intimate knowledge of the humbler streets of Paris, a knowledge enriched by prowling among other quarters as this inveterate flâneur stocked his memory with images.

Under a King who also walked the streets like any commoner with top hat and umbrella, the face of Paris and of France was changing. The first public bus line had opened a few years before his accession, and the new railways were dumping provincials on the town. Here and there in the capital new sidewalks invited the stroller, although whole districts still twisted narrowly in half-daylight. In the country itself the large towns were growing larger, and a few of their people aped the modes of Paris while the rest spent their lives in pastoral complacency or outright boredom. In Paris itself could be found restaurants, shops and theaters whose degree of glitter and whose tariff matched the customer's social status and his purse. The playgoer of 1825 could have chosen among a dozen theaters; by 1848 there were nearly twice as many.

As the metropolis grew, each of its sectors assumed the character of one social element, reflecting its taste in architecture, its dress, decoration and furnishing, its accustomed daily routine, its recreational habits, its political or artistic standards. The Latin Quarter on the left bank of the Seine was the home of literary Bohemia; in the faubourg Saint-Germain the old nobility nursed its rancors and its impotence behind closed doors, and lived in fading memory of a régime which the new economic order had swept away forever. Across the river in the faubourg Saint-Honoré lived the legitimists, sworn champions of the exiled House of Bourbon, sworn enemies of the Orleanist "usurper" who now ruled France; here also lived those Napoleonists who had owed their titles and their wealth, and now owed their disenchantment to the man of Saint Helena. Snubbed by men of the past, the men of the present moved into the Chaussée-d'Antin, those bankers, industrialists, railway builders, absentee landlords and owners of forests and coal mines who were the "golden pedestal" of the July Monarchy. In the eastern end of town huddled the artisans of the faubourg Saint-Antoine, anonymous dwellers at the very bottom of the social scale who were as yet scarcely aware of their collective power and who were ignored by their betters except when there were barricades to be built or mass demonstrations to be quickly recruited and as quickly dissolved. From these swarming streets and malodorous alleys came the porters, the pedlars, the strolling musicians, the bill-posters and old clothes men of Daumier under such general captions as *Parisian Types*, and ranging from the sheer comedy of the janitor at the keyhole to the shabby pathos of the man who collects cigar butts, and the tragedy of a "model son" who drags his drunken parent homeward.

Between the western and eastern extremities of society dwelt the middle and lower bourgeoisie, a motley collection of the ambitious and the naïve, the hard-boiled and the sentimental, men whose energy won them admission to more exclusive levels, and the climbers from below who took their places. The man of middle station was indeed a contradiction made flesh. More than a century before, Marivaux had watched the bourgeois in the making, a creature whose effort to imitate the polished manners of the gentry had to be made at the cost of his more natural self, who might own as expensive a house as the nobleman yet show forth his magnificence unnobly; a man who lifted himself on his toes to look taller than he was. He had become a human paradox by Daumier's time, when Michelet noted that he had now accomplished his task of creating a new aristocracy but still gave the impression of being arrested by nature at a moment of half-development, a being who could neither walk nor fly but strutted self-importantly. By energy and ambition he had pushed up from the mass and now, at the moment of success, began to collapse under the weight of his own commonplace pretensions.

Surveying the bourgeoisie of the July Monarchy, the historian Georges Weill differentiated between its upper and its lower strata. Wealth alone gave access to the former, a group united by their hatred for the aristocracy of birth, although men of the old order kept themselves solvent by marrying their children with those of parvenu bankers; united also by the love of regularity, by an equal dislike for irreligion and for clericalism, by tenacity in the struggle of politics, by celebration of the domestic virtues and by charity toward the lower orders provided they kept their place. There was no warmth of sentiment, no feeling for art or for poetry, no true understanding of democracy among these people, who maintained friendly relations with only those of lower status who were qualified by their property to become voters.

Among the middle and lower reaches of this class, a motley assortment of white-collar men, shopkeepers, professionals and petty functionaries whom Daumier knew most intimately, the dominant motive seemed to be the wish for social and economic security; they tended to be liberal in politics, industrious and cautious, and their hope was in the ballot box. Balzac noted their anxiety to achieve an air of distinction, their dream of public honors, their fundamental goodness of heart, shrewd common sense and generosity—a people whose plain virtues could be destroyed by contact with those above them in the social scale.

Faced with so complex and so dynamic a social scene, both the historians and the novelists knew that they could no longer portray the life of their country in terms of conspicuous heroes, of the individual genius, but must rather explore the slow, deep changes in society as a whole from which new human types emerge. But it was the *Human Comedy* of Balzac, rather than the historical works of Mignet, Guizot and Thiers, which best provided a detailed and comprehensive analysis of social types, a recreation of the backgrounds of living, the conflicts between layman and priest, between city and country, between the moral and the material, the successful and the humble—in short, all the forms of modern existence which moulded thought and action.

Balzac had already completed several of the novels which comprise the *Comedy* when this broad title occurred to him. "Does not society," he asked, "make of mankind, in accordance with the milieu in which it acts, as many varieties of men as there are variations in zoology? The differences between a soldier, a workman, an administrator, a lawyer, a loafer, a scholar, a statesman, a business man, a sailor, a poet, a pauper, a preacher are, though more difficult to define, as considerable as the differences which exist between the wolf, the lion, the jackass, the crow, the shark, the seal, the sheep. . . ." Out of his prodigious powers of observation, his laborious documentation and his unremitting craftsmanship came Balzac's mighty ensemble, with its characters whose careers begin in one volume and are developed and cross-related in successive ones, its movement on all social levels, its vast repertory of men and women who are both personalities and types. "A generation," its author boasted, "is a drama with four or five thousand salient characters. This drama is my book."

Daumier, in contrast to his literary colleague, never proclaimed himself the champion of a new approach to social history, and his Human Comedy had no such ambitious purpose, no such deliberate planning. Such continuity as it had consisted in over-all titles—*The*

11. *The Friends,* lithograph, detail
Museum of Fine Arts, Boston, Mass.

Good Bourgeois, for example, under which a series of lithographs
appeared at varying intervals over a period of weeks or even years.
The rapid crayon could not probe individual character so deeply as
the novelist's pen, nor could the settings of human action be described
with the infinite detail of Balzac. On the other hand, Daumier's attitude
toward his subjects was simpler and more consistent; he never accepted
even subconsciously, as Balzac did, the creed of the upper bourgeoisie,
its cult of success, its scorn for those who pushed up from below.

Neither was Daumier's picture of French society all-inclusive.
Among his cast of characters one does not find those aristocrats of
land and title who so fascinated the novelist, nor the new moneyed
nobility who had usurped their places. From the opposite extreme, the
peasant and the workingman appear seldom in his lithographs. The
former, occasionally glimpsed in the series, *Pastorals,* is an uncouth
creature whose life, dominated by the cycle of the seasons, has been
untouched by progress and whose devotion to his small property is
fiercely stubborn. He is Balzac's "tireless sapper, this nibbler who

12. *Don't Meddle with It,* lithograph, detail
Museum of Fine Arts, Boston, Mass.

breaks the soil into separate morsels . . . this unsocial element created
by the Revolution." The city worker, as Daumier could observe him,
was a man whose relation with his employer was no longer personal
or paternalistic but one of conflict. He was learning the power of
organized resistance to those who were now gathering the fruits of
economic change, meeting openly with his kind when the law permitted,
secretly when trade unions were proscribed. Daumier had no trace
of that uneasy fear inspired in the middle class by the man who worked
with his hands. The laborers in his lithos range all the way from ragged
and drunken street-brawlers (Fig. 11) to the typographer who defends
the freedom of his press (Fig. 12), a figure drawn with sympathy
and no condescension, and one who deserves the tribute which Victor
Hugo was to offer in later years—"true, formidable and sincere."

The peasant and the proletarian, however, were the exception and
not the rule in Daumier's satire. It was from the great shifting middle
society, the urban bourgeois class, that Daumier assembled his dramatis
personae. By birth, economic status and social environment he was of

13. *Cholera Morbus,* wood engraving from *Némésis Médicale*

that class; his interest in it was inexhaustible and his total picture of it was astonishingly complete. During the July Monarchy he fully exploited every pictorial device known to caricature: the single figure isolated on the page; the bust-length study of two or more figures; the completely developed composition within a rectangle; and the currently popular scheme known as the vignette, where the theme is not developed to the limits of an enclosing rectangular frame but fades off, as it were, into the page, with interest sharply focused on a lone figure or a small group in action, and a mere suggestion of environment. From time to time Daumier supplied vignettes which he had drawn not on stone but on the woodblock, to be engraved by others for illustrated books. In these chapter headings, tailpieces and text pictures he was one of many draftsmen, among them Alfred and Tony Johannot, Célestin Nanteuil, Jean Gigoux and the Devérias, who made effective use of the vignette.

Although Daumier's penciled line was made stiffer and wirier by the engraver on wood, some of the best of this kind were from his hand. The engraving of a cholera epidemic (Fig. 13), one of thirty which he designed for *Némésis Médicale* of 1840, is a small masterpiece: a fallen victim, a slinking dog and the stark silhouette of a distant hearse evoke the horrors of the plague, and the untouched white paper has the cruel glare of the sun at noon. The drawing makes its own boundaries with a few hints of pavement, a shadowed doorway, a suggestion of rooftops and a hint of cloud. The vignette idea, since it lent itself to movement and dramatic emphasis, was frequently in Daumier's mind when he drew on wood or on stone and even when he made his first attempts at painting. One sees it at work in some of the lithographs of his first great sequence of one hundred drawings of *Robert-Macaire,* published between 1836 and 1838.

When the Macaire series began, the face and figure of this character were already well known by the public (Fig. 14). A talented actor named Frédérick-Lemaître, whose versatility owed something to panto-miming in a popular playhouse, clowning on horseback in the circus and playing the companion of tragedy queens at the Odéon, had been given the leading role in a blowsy melodrama of 1823, *At the Sign of the Turnip.* According to Théodore de Banville the actor was struggling in vain to bring life to the part of a cape-and-dagger bandit when he encountered a nameless fellow in a sidewalk café.

His hair was dressed in windblown style under a shapeless top hat. One eye was covered with a black patch. A voluminous red flannel scarf covered his face from the nose down and hid the place where a shirt ought to have been but was not. From a pocket of what had once been a green coat with silver buttons cascaded a bundle of many-colored rags, the remains of a splendid scarf. The right hand with which he gestured magnificently wore the fragments of a white glove; in his left hand he grasped a huge cane. His red military trousers clung to his shanks, and showed dingy white stockings above a pair of woman's satin shoes. He was as beautiful as a god, as bold as Diogenes, as elegant as a rake, as bland as a baby.

Heaven had put in the actor's path, said Banville, a creature of flesh and bone whom he would bring to life on the stage, a figure destined to become the Cid and the Scapin of modern comedy. A cheap pseudo-tragedy was transformed into an hilarious and terrifying satire, and Robert-Macaire into the very incarnation of the swindler theme. Critics called him the Figaro of the city streets, in whom one could see the image of the century, and Balzac was said to have used him as the model of Vautrin. A second piece, *The Life and Resurrection of Robert-Macaire,* had been produced under the threat of suppression by a government which recognized its implications, when Daumier

14. Lemaître as Robert-Macaire, contemporary photograph

gave the rogue still another life in a series of caricatures longer than any that he ever attempted, in which Macaire's Midas fingers touched innumerable men and women, corrupted a wide range of enterprises and traded upon a gullibility and a thirst for quick profit so universal as to make the supply of victims inexhaustible.

This Macaire of Daumier ranged up and down through the drawing rooms and counting houses of the July Monarchy in an Odyssey of opportunism, of fake advertising, the promotion of nonexistent mines and of mythical real estate, marriages for money, stock-juggling, art patronage and chauvinistic flag-waving (Fig. 15). As early as 1835 the artist had drawn Thiers in the rags and tatters of Macaire; nine years after the long series was ended, he could think of no more appropriate symbol of the times than Robert and his companion Bertrand, whom he represented as statues flanking the Bourse—money-changers guarding the temple.

Since the episodes in this epic of swindling were not the invention of Daumier but of his editor Philipon, who wrote their elaborate captions, one does not find the former at his pictorial best in drawings which often suggest a bored and even perfunctory draftsman. The satire of Daumier needed no verbal explanation and found its richest expression in those scenes of his human comedy, penetratingly observed and genially set forth, where flesh and blood people enact their day-to-day existence—the potbellied Leander swimming in the public bath, the old bachelor and his cat calling it a day, the bank clerk finding love among the wheatfields, the pug-nosed actor spouting Racine, the shopper ecstatically sniffing the melon of his dreams, the jealous National Guardsman deserting his military post to make sure that his spouse is faithful to her domestic one. More often than not the artist's comic point is the discrepancy between complacent bourgeois self-deception and the unlovely actuality.

As one leafs through these years in *Charivari* one finds that Daumier has left untouched no occupation, no habit, no form of odd or ludicrous behavior. Here is the small rentier whose outlook upon life depends on whether his stocks move up or down, whether a change in government conserves or threatens his meager pension, whether the apartments he rents are occupied or empty. (Fig. 16). One caption sums up his horizon, "Two thousand francs in rents, a dog, a cat, canaries, and a glimpse of a garden from his window." In the thirty-nine drawings of *Tenants and Landlords* he has become a proudly strutting creature humbly saluted by his concierge, a space-merchant of smoking fireplaces and leaky roofs who boasts that from one of his windows the tenant can see Victor Hugo getting out of bed.

Here also, standing with empty pockets before a sumptuous display

15. *Ladies and Gentlemen!,* lithograph
Museum of Fine Arts, Boston, Mass.

of food in the window of a restaurant, is one of that innumerable
swarm of white-collared mediocrities, the secretaries, clerks and petty
officials whose lives were spent in assessing taxes, drawing up reports
and digesting editorials for their superiors in the bureaucratic hierarchy,
the functionary so fully portrayed by Balzac as a man who could
mount the administrative ladder only through flattery and self-abase-
ment.

The bourgeois as politician had already been the victim of
Daumier's crayon before 1835 in the persons of Thiers and other conspicuous individuals; now the artist records the struggles of lesser men
to get themselves elected by holding babies or by discussing crops with
farmers. In one of his parliamentary series the falsely affable candidate

16. *The Little Rentier*, lithograph. Collection Benjamin A. and
Julia M. Trustman, Brandeis University, Waltham, Mass.

for office greets the shirtsleeved proprietor of a small shop; on another
occasion we see him as the happy self-seeker who has been elected
and finds with delight that the official newspaper has recorded his contribution to a recent debate in the Chamber—"Hear, Hear!" He is the
politician described by Eugène Briffault:

17. *Sniffing the Merchandise*, lithograph
Museum of Fine Arts, Boston, Mass.

Auguste now knew everything. I had heard him talk humbly, devotedly of the things he wanted to get for his district . . . now he thought only of the happiness, the safety of France; sometimes he went so far as to settle the affairs of both hemispheres.

Another human type whose nature and whose evolution were set forth by Daumier was the shopkeeper—the baker, the tailor, the butcher, the grocer, the druggist, the dispenser of dry goods—each jealously devoted to his own commodity, to the shop which he has probably inherited, and to the family and clerks who serve behind his counter. His customers are steady and well known, his shop narrow and cluttered. Daumier shows us the "grocer-citizen" as he peers from among his pickle jars, kegs of grapes and sugarloafs, an odd person glued to his counter and his scales (Fig. 17). In later drawings, however, we see the type transformed, along with the scene of his activity. The mechanisms

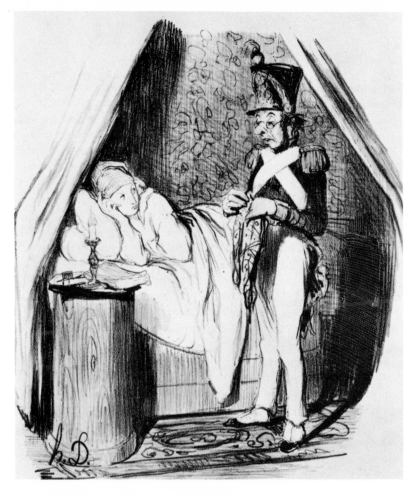

18. *Yes, Dear Friend* . . . , lithograph
Museum of Fine Arts, Boston, Mass.

of marketing have changed, the small specialized shops are assimilated into larger and more handsome establishments; the merchant-speculator recruits a small army of clerks and stands in his doorway planning how to cheat his customers and outsmart his next-door competitor. In *Bigger and Bigger Shops* the artist gives us the long palatial vistas of a dry goods emporium where nattily dressed clerks politely hover; on other pages one sees the shopwindows of Paris become brightly lighted spectacles.

This is the metamorphosis traced with greater detail by Balzac in the novels which he called *Scenes from Parisian Life*, where Guillaume was the small-scale merchant of integrity, while Birotteau was the hireling who bought a perfume shop, built a small factory for the distillation of his carminative water and his Sultana Paste, enlarged his shop, became the prey of speculators, and died a martyr to his own honesty, leaving his assistant Crevel to plunge without scruple into a morass of gambling and of fraud, to emerge as the mayor of his district, a member of the Legion of Honor, and a friend of men in high places from whom he stole his mistresses. Everybody knew that Crevel was a fictional version of a real-life bourgeois named Louis-Désiré Véron, a doctor of medicine without patients, whose druggist-partner Regnault invented a pectoral paste which Véron proceeded to exploit before he became Director of the Opera in 1831, a vain and scrofulous opportunist who personally inspected the half-naked candidates for the roles of odalisques, winning himself the title of "satrap of the ballet." Daumier would not pour graphic venom on the gross and shameless doctor until he had become a political force as editor of the conservative *Constitutionnel;* in the meantime one could recognize him in a litho of 1842, where a sick Véron is being treated with his own medicine, and in a drawing two years later a chemist dispenses a salve which is as good as that of Regnault and much cheaper.

When the grocer, the clerk or the small householder joined the National Guard, that citizen-militia created by Lafayette whose function was to defend law and order, he became the butt for the caricaturists of the day, squeezing his paunch into belt and cross braces, topheavy in his fur bonnet, stumbling over his sword and solemnly pacing his post to the delight of street urchins (Fig. 18). In one of Daumier's lithos he smugly notes that he was born wearing this helmet; in another he preens before a full-length mirror; in his less fatuous moments, he splashes miserably through puddles or crouches yawning before a hot stove in the guardhouse.

While the merchant class throve by its small economies and its unremitting devotion to the counter, the bourgeois who had adopted a profession lived by his wits, none more precariously than the over-burdened schoolteacher who competed with the village priest and was scorned by his rebellious flock and largely ignored by a society which rewarded its politicians but not its educators. The decrepit hero of Daumier's series of thirty-nine plates, *Teachers and Brats,* is the half-droll and half-pathetic schoolmaster described by Eugene Nyon in a black skullcap, a sagging frock coat and black trousers which have turned gray, standing before his class like a manikin used to frighten birds. With a kind of mild ferocity he defies the sullen culprit; with a proud dignity he bestows a prize on the exemplary Alfred, the only member of the class who has not wiped his nose on his sleeve for a whole week.

For one Frenchman willing to endure the humiliations of the teaching profession there were hundreds who flocked into the chambers of the

19. *True, You Have Lost Your Case* . . . , lithograph
Smith College Museum of Art, Northampton, Mass.

law in response to the growing number of clients who preferred to
cheat one another legally. Since childhood Daumier had seen this
species in action, with its billowing robe, white stock and crown-shaped
cap, and now gave it a scathing publicity. The lawyer of these early
lithographs is a mildly comic rascal, not the terrifying and ravenous
creature of the artist's later drawings. The black-robed gentry make
an occasional appearance before 1845 in *Charivari*, but it was in the
thirty-nine prints of *Men of the Law*, begun that year and continued
at intervals to 1848, that Daumier most fully demonstrated its complacent pride and its sly chicanery. A scene in a trial for divorce

20. *This Morning before Sunrise,* lithograph
Museum of Fine Arts, Boston, Mass.

contrasts the spread-eagle posture of the advocate with the smug
stolidity of his client. One lawyer makes it clear that his degree of
oratorical conviction will depend on the size of his fee; another
consoles a hardened offender with the remark, "I couldn't prove you
innocent in this case, but better luck next time!" A third advises his
client to cry a little, even out of one eye; a fourth reminds the weeping
woman whose case he has lost that at least she must have enjoyed
the eloquence of his pleading (Fig. 19). Sweeping down the broad
stairway of the Palais de Justice, advocates who have just torn each
other to verbal shreds in the courtroom genially exchange congratula-
tions. Daumier's variations on his theme are inexhaustible, and his
manner of describing face, action and costume grows simpler and
stronger as he proceeds.

When the satirist turned from the antics of the legal profession to
the frustrations of the world of art, his crayon was more indulgent.
His own friends among artists were young men with reputations yet

to be made; cold-shouldered by their hustling contemporaries, they had to make up in self-confidence what they lacked in security. Their bleak studios, with an inadequate stove and a few battered plaster casts, were not unlike his own. Two painters dance to keep warm in a litho of 1833, *Wood is Dear and Art Goes Badly,* and twelve years later the subject is repeated with variations. Daumier's style has changed in the interval, but not the material state of the two daubers who have burned their last easel. The aspiring but unsuccessful artist appears in more than one drawing with the customary beard and shoulder-long hair; on one occasion he thrusts his foot through his own rejected canvas with the cry, "Ungrateful country, you shall not have my work!" On another page he adds the final touch to his painting while it is being carried into the exhibition on a comrade's shoulders. And Daumier does not forget the bourgeois patron in search of an untruthful likeness, or the householder who measures a canvas with his walking stick and regretfully concludes, "It's half a cane less than what I need."

No aspect of the life around him more fascinated Daumier than the domestic behavior of the ordinary citizen, a theme on which he played a thousand variations. Neither in the back parlor nor in the kitchen did the artist's eye spare the paterfamilias, neither in bed nor in bathtub. Framed by bed curtains, he wears over his nightcap the birthday wreath of flowers bestowed by his spindly offspring (Fig. 20), or reads by candlelight to his enraptured spouse, "We reclined softly on the odorous moss; the moonlight pierced the willow-branches stirred by an evening zephyr. Intoxicated with love, we launched toward Heaven our vows. . . ." Here and elsewhere, romantic pretension and the delusion of superiority are ridiculously at war with the homely physique of the family man, his innate goodness, his honest pride in his repulsive offspring, his cheerful endurance of misadventure. In *The Papas* are set forth the pleasures and torments of paternity; in *The Good Bourgeois* the picnic makers stagger under the weight of lunchbaskets, nap nervously in the shade among lizards and are precipitated waist-deep into swampy water by a passion for forget-me-nots; they are pursued by cows, drenched by thunderstorms and stung by swarms of bees. In a series of sixteen lithos on the railways this urban creature is being transported with many a discomfort and mishap to the open country by a new contraption which he both respects and fears. Among the beauties of nature this rentier or merchant on holiday proceeds in Daumier's *Pastorals* to ogle the planets (Fig. 21), recoil in terror from an oversized toad, or shrewdly estimate the money value of a forest which he has cut down in his imagination. In *Conjugal Mores* a delightful old couple rediscover their initials on the trunk of a tree (Fig. 22); in the second series of *The Hunt* an amateur sportsman plods through mire and falling snow with a gun which backfires or a fishline which he flings into the branches of a tree.

Having returned "refreshed" to the gas lamps and asphalt of his proper sphere, Monsieur Goutout timidly dips his heel into the safer waters of the public bath (Fig. 23), spies through a crack at the amplitude of "fat Fifine," or teaches his drenched and terrified children to swim, in a series of thirty drawings, *The Bathers,* whose protagonists seem cheerfully unaware of their protuberant bellies or their stringy shanks, a series in which Daumier richly displays his knowledge of what overeating does to the paunch and much sitting to the buttocks.

On these occasions the bourgeois housewife is the long-suffering and submissive partner of the family's head. In one drawing, to be sure, a young wife looks down with scorn at her snoring bedmate, but for the most part these women of Daumier play the part to which custom has assigned them, a part defined by Guizot when he declared that women were dedicated by Providence to a life of domesticity. Such notions did not go unchallenged by the Romantic writers, who found them less than chivalrous, nor by those prophets of social change for whom the equality of the sexes was a necessary condition of human progress. Père Enfantin in the 1830s reminded his feminist readers that they could inspire men not as domestic slaves but through their sexual powers, and the idea of emancipation was echoed by the followers of Pierre Leroux, of Fourier and of Cabet, by the editors of the first feminist review and by a flock of literary women, ranging from duchesses to working girls, whose essays and poems kept their cause alive in the new journals. George Sand made the problems of women her central theme in *Indiana* and in *Valentine,* and Flora Tristan's *Emancipation of Woman* was published in 1845.

These bluestockings, lady novelists and hostesses of salons faced the storms of ridicule which are the reformer's lot. The Rosanette of Flaubert, for example, was the woman who believes herself made for maternity and the routine of domestic life; and the novelist etched in acid his portrait of her opponent, Mademoiselle Vatnez, a frustrated spinster who spent her days in peddling her little manuscripts and her evenings in dreaming of a socialist world in which the freedom of the proletariat had been achieved and middle-class marriage reformed or abolished altogether.

Among the most vociferous anti-feminists were the writers and draftsmen of *Charivari.* In a Daumier drawing of 1844 Mademoiselle Vatnez seems to have been anticipated in the person of the skinny poetess who sits at her window, contemplates the night sky, and murmurs, "O moon, inspire me with some little thought that will be just a bit grandiose!" (Fig. 24). In the nearly sixty plates of his three series, *Bluestockings,*

21. *Fruitless Search for the Planet*, lithograph
Museum of Fine Arts, Boston, Mass.

22. *A Souvenir of Youth*, lithograph
Museum of Fine Arts, Boston, Mass.

Divorcing Women, and *The Female Socialists,* his ridicule is directed
not to reform itself but to its sententious high priestesses and silly camp
followers: the literary wife who composes dialogue while her husband
wipes the dishes or feeds the baby; the lowering female Hamlet, skull
in hand, reflecting on the perfidy of man; the authoress of a tragedy
who seethes with fury on a sofa—"Hell and damnation! I've been
hissed!" A group of drunken feminists toasts its emancipation; a socialist wife cries that her husband has destroyed her dignity as a woman by
forcing her to sew a button on his braces. And Daumier turns the joke
upon himself in the last three plates of the bluestocking series with
groups of mannish crusaders who bitterly complain that his caricatures
have maligned them.

It was inevitable that this mocker of self-delusion would find a rich
source for laughter in the make-believe world of the French theater, to

23. *Come, Make the Plunge, Père Goutout,* lithograph
Smith College Museum of Art, Northampton, Mass.

which he owed his Robert-Macaire and from which he would one day
borrow Joseph Prud'homme. He knew at first hand that the playhouses
of the July Monarchy were as varied in their degree of opulence and in
the nature of their repertory as the taste of the patrons to which each of
them appealed. In the rue Le Peletier stood the Opéra, frequented by
the newly rich whose penchant for the spectacular, the lavishly staged,
the musically extravagant piece was gratified by Rossini and Meyerbeer. Here the connoisseurs of ballet could dispute the rival charms of
the voluptuous Ellsler and the chaste Taglioni. In the place de la Bourse
the Opéra-Comique dispensed lighter humors and less ponderous music
with Auber's *Black Domino* and the tuneful pieces of Donizetti. The
Théâtre Italien staged Bellini's operas in elaborate scenery for an elegant clientele as vehicles for the greatest singers of the time—for Tam-
burini and Mario and for Marietta Alboni, whose voice in her prime

24. *O Moon, Inspire Me . . .* , lithograph
Museum of Fine Arts, Boston, Mass.

was compared to the trilling of a ringdove, and whom a critic described
in her decline as an elephant who had swallowed a nightingale. On the
boulevard Montmartre the special appeal of the Théâtre des Variétés
was the excellence of its comic actors, among them that "ineffable buffoon" Odry, praised for mad and pompous improvisations.

The more sober citizens were likely to prefer the Théâtre Français
and the Odéon, twin pillars of the classical repertory. In the former, the
seventeen-year-old Rachel played her first heroine in 1838; the great

colonnade of the latter also sheltered Racine and Molière but on occasion gave new authors a chance to be heard.

From the most literally minded sectors of Paris society came the audiences of the Gymnase and the Vaudeville, content to see their own humdrum woes, not those of ancient gods and romantic heroes, reflected in the playwright's mirror. Eugène Scribe won early and prolonged success with literally hundreds of domestic comedies as sharply observant as they were superficial, peopled with gay colonels, smart widows, foolish husbands, devoted wives and submissive daughters, and duly provided with a moral message. The concoctions of Scribe and of the younger Dumas were the staple of the Gymnase, and the Vaudeville was to produce in 1852 the latter's *Lady of the Camellias.*

Evenings in the family theaters were sedate affairs compared with the boisterous nights of the Théâtre de la Porte Saint-Martin, an old-fashioned playhouse which had been once used for operas and which now echoed to the thunderous climaxes of the elder Dumas and of Victor Hugo. The latter had undergone his bath of fire at the Théâtre-Français, and Daumier may well have been among the youthful rebels who turned the première of *Hernani* on February twenty-fifth in 1830 into a demonstration by the "cavaliers of the future, the defenders of artistic freedom." Gautier has described that famous occasion, when the Romantic squads took possession of the galleries at two o'clock in the afternoon, fortified with chocolate, rolls and garlic sausage, and chanting passages of the coming play to pass six or seven hours before the curtain rose and the storm broke, every mighty metaphor wildly applauded from above and hissed from below by the patrons of an orchestra "paved with academic and classical crania."

The life span of the Romantic theater was relatively short from Dumas' *Henry III* of 1829 to the *Ruy Blas* of Hugo in 1838, but long enough to challenge the neoclassical vogue and the popularity of the comedy of manners. The young writers found the measured pace of Alexandrines too formal, the passions of Racine and Corneille too coldly abstract, the unities of time and place too rigid to contain the movement of life. They held in equal scorn those plays of Scribe which pandered to the coarse and prosaic taste of the middle class and played upon self-satisfaction and sentimentality, providing moral sermons which Gautier found as boring in art as in real life, in a dialogue quite without style or color. An alternative to classical rigor mortis and to domestic stultification had been suggested by the work of that prolific maker of melodramas, Pixérécourt, but his plots were thin, his characters devoid of inner motivation and his effect one of horror more than of tragedy. When the elder Dumas wrote *Antony,* he tried to give his leading character the complexity of a living person. The protagonists of other Romantic dramas drawn from the exotic periods of Italian, Spanish and English history, were brought to life by players whose poetic and exalted speeches called for new histrionic methods—Bocage, Mélingue, Madame George and Mademoiselle Dorval.

No questions of artistic concept or style troubled the audiences of the boulevard du Temple, and when Thackeray noted his boredom with Racine he added that he would rather go to Madame Saqui's or watch Deburau dancing on a tightrope. In the dank and crowded quarter of the Temple a whole street of diminutive playhouses catered to the grisettes, the journeymen, the lower bourgeois families and the working-men in shirtsleeves, and came to be called the Boulevard of Crime in honor of its cutthroat entertainments. Here the sidewalks were lined with barkers, sword-swallowers, clowns and acrobats, the side shows or *parades* of Bobêche and Gallimafré. At the Folies-Dramatiques Le-maître triumphed in the second version of *Robert-Macaire*. In the malodorous darkness of the Funambules, where mushrooms grew in the dressing rooms, famous artists and writers jostled the shabby locals to watch a superb mime called Deburau whom they had discovered, and whose silent art compassed both pathos and the broadest farce. The Cirque Olympique offered historical pageants, with a preference for Napoleonic battle scenes; the Gaîté was the home of blood-and-thunder melodramas; at the Théâtre de Madame Saqui this incredibly aged queen of the tightrope who had once pleased Napoleon made her last appearance in 1839.

In these and other theaters of Crime Boulevard the traveler Thack-eray saw fat old men crying like babies and sucking enormous sticks of barley-sugar, heard the indignant audience growl furiously when a tyrant king sentenced his slave to death and howl its encouragement to the bereaved mother pleading for her child's life. "There is in every one of these boulevard mysteries," he concluded, "a kind of rude moral." In contrast to the profoundly immoral and absurd drama of Hugo, Dumas and the enlightened classes, he found the theater of the ordinary people "absurd, if you will, but good and right-hearted . . . long there-fore may fat grocers blubber over mimic woes, and honest workmen shake their fists. . . ."

The lithographs in which Daumier commented upon the life of the theater, some forty in this period, were far less numerous than his corresponding work during the Second Empire, but demonstrate his fascination with this world of tinsel. For him it was not merely a place of enchantment where people like himself could weep with the hero and laugh with the clown; behind its proscenium he could watch homely and pedestrian creatures try with no great success to transform them-selves into the warriors of antiquity, the queens of Shakespeare and the desperadoes of Dumas and Victor Hugo. As a social satirist he could study the various forms of audience behavior and as an artist he was delighted by the odd tricks which the footlights played on the forms behind them. Several drawings of scenes from plays were published so soon after their respective premières as to indicate that he was sometimes a first-nighter.

Among the artist's friends were a few of the leading actors of the day, whose portraits in action he drew for *Charivari*. Jacques Charles Odry, the skilled farceur of the Variétés, appears in two lithographs of 1836 as Carmagnole in the play of the same title. On July third in 1837 the two sidewalk comedians Bobêche and Gallimafré opened at the Théâtre du Palais-Royal in a *parade* in three acts; two weeks later Daumier showed them in a scene from this entertainment. An exchange of letters proves the acquaintance of the caricaturist with Bernard Léon, whose troubled career took him from one playhouse to another and whose likeness in the role of Mignet was published in 1844. An exhibition of caricatures in 1888 is said by Jean Adhémar to have included a Daumier portrait of Bocage, linked to the artist by their common dislike for Louis-Philippe and doubtless by the latter's admiration for this gaunt and impassioned actor who as a juvenile lead created the part of Antony and in later years performed many of the great romantic roles. His successor in the field, Mélingue, had once studied sculpture, and it was reported that he modeled a statuette during every performance of *Benvenuto Cellini*. This stately thespian became the favorite of the Boulevard houses in a long series of cape-and-dagger pieces, collected the work of Delacroix, Decamps and Gavarni, and often received Daumier at his home in Belleville; a drawing of Mélingue was shown at the exhibition of 1888.

These friendly contacts reminded Daumier of the sometimes ludicrous but often tragic contrasts between the actors' brief and brilliant appearances and their long hard years of poverty, of bitter rivalries, of shining success and resounding failure. In a litho of 1844 an actor of light comedy is resplendent in lace and velvet as he stands in the flattering glow of footlights; two years earlier a down-at-heel player shambles to the stagedoor of the Funambules (Fig. 25), muttering to himself:

> What weather to get passionate in! In a few minutes I'll have to burn with love and cry, "O Zuleika, share my treasure and my throne; come, drink to the full of pleasure and abundance!"—and all this with a pennyworth of fried potatoes in my stomach.

In a drawing of 1847 a rueful Pierrot who reminds us of Deburau is being paid off and dismissed by his manager.

Other caricatures of the 1840s hint at the social distinctions among playhouses and playgoers. One of them presents two well-to-do patrons

25. *The Actor of the Funambules,* lithograph
Museum of Fine Arts, Boston, Mass.

admiring a ballerina at the Opéra; in another a bluestocking rises in
her box at the Odéon to proclaim herself the authoress. Other prints
suggest that Daumier shared the preference of Thackeray for the less
genteel pleasures of the popular theaters. A line of patrons huddles in a
snowstorm before what seems to be one of the shabbier houses of the
Boulevard of Crime in one of the series, *Parisian Emotions,* and snow
falls on the weary spectators who emerge at two o'clock in the morning

from the Théâtre Historique, which was founded in 1847 by Dumas for the production of overlong dramas by himself and Hugo. A whole gallery of simple souls are dissolved in tears in the fifth act at the Gaîté, and on two occasions Daumier takes up his position in the shadowed audience, with a glimpse of the brilliantly lighted stage picture over its heads, a vantage point to which he will return on later occasions in lithos and in paintings. A rough workman in shirtsleeves at the Porte Saint-Martin is moved to inarticulate praise by some unspecified act of slaughter before him; in another playhouse the concentration of the audience is complete, and the caption reads, "The spectacle is a good thing for the people of Paris. . . ."

Among Daumier's most effective theatrical drawings were those in which he lampooned the current effort to reinstate the so-called classical drama, one major engagement in a war between the Ancients and the Moderns which involved not only playwrights but poets, critics and artists, and which in one form or another had been waged since long before Daumier was born. When Marivaux declared that the cult of Homer was a ridiculous idolatry, his irreverence was an eighteenth-century echo of the dialogues of Lucian, written in second-century Athens to attack superstition and to shrink the gods to human proportions. Lucian had described the busy routine of Zeus in his office, receiving the prayers and petitions of mortals through windows in the floor of Heaven. In a like mood Marivaux turned Ulysses into M. Brideron of provincial France and Calypso into a fat woman of forty in his parody of *Telemachus*. Diderot observed that if Cato and Catiline, Brutus and Caesar came back to life, they would not recognize themselves on the boards of the French theaters or the walls of art galleries. For a time, to be sure, the ancients achieved a fresh meaning and a new life when the painter David transformed them into symbols of courage, patriotism and self-sacrifice in the minds of revolutionists who identified the austere virtues of the Roman republic with those of the régime they had established. But in the years which followed Thermidor, Horace and Brutus began to lose their grip on men's minds; David's own art sank to the level of *Leonidas,* and he vainly exhorted his followers, "Quick, quick, leaf your Plutarch!" The new society, concerned with practical and mundane matters, could not understand, as Karl Marx observed, that "the ghosts of the days of Rome had watched over its cradle."

In Hugo's preface to his play *Cromwell* and in Gautier's introduction to *Mademoiselle de Maupin* the young Romantics issued their declaration of war against the stilted heroics, the cramping unities, the moralizing tone of dramas and novels which embodied the caution and the conformism of the bourgeois. For Gautier the coldly correct verses of Casimir Delavigne on Danaë and on the women of Troy were the work

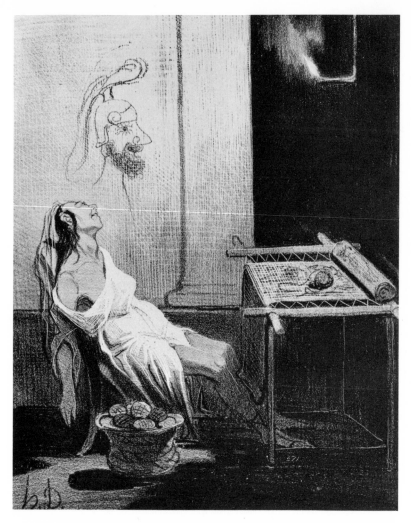

26. *Penelope's Nights,* lithograph
Museum of Fine Arts, Boston, Mass.

of a man whose Pegasus had no wings, who could trot, amble and even
gallop, but not fly. For the editors of the conservative *Constitutionnel*
in the year 1834 the proposed revival of Dumas' *Antony* was a threat
to the public's morals which must be prevented at all cost. Out of this
literary civil war, as *Charivari* called it, came Gautier's brilliant and
sarcastic preface, declaring that art could not be a means of moral im-
provement, that only the useless was beautiful, and that the author was
among those who preferred a Chinese vase to a chamber pot.

The triumph of Romantic drama was as brief as it was boisterous,
and the failure of Hugo's *Burgraves* in 1843 coincided with the success
of François Ponsard's *Lucretia*. Both occasions were celebrated by
Daumier, who pictured a disconsolate Hugo gazing at a comet and ask-

27. *The Handsome Narcissus,* lithograph
Museum of Fine Arts, Boston, Mass.

ing himself why a star could have a queue but not the ticket office of his play; a few weeks later he showed a towering Lucretia with the tiny figures of demoralized Burgraves scampering from under her feet. Ponsard's piece, with the brilliant Bocage playing Brutus, was part of a classical counteroffensive, a rather futile effort to tame dramatic extravagance by means of logic and "good taste." The director of the Odéon proclaimed that a new Racine had been born, and Daumier's friend Préault observed, doubtless with tongue in cheek, that if there had been a Prix de Rome for dramatists, Ponsard would be starting tomorrow for the Eternal City.

This same year saw the triumph of *Phèdre* in the person of Rachel, who in the following years would discipline her impetuous temperament and her scrawny body to become the interpreter par excellence of Racine's heroines. Her admirers wrote that her face and figure acquired the perfection of ancient sculpture and her declamation an overwhelming passion; to Thackeray her effort to untomb Racine could only galvanize the corpse, not revivify it.

On a January night in 1846 at the Odéon one more effort was made to reinstate the ancients by making them the spokesmen of a contemporary message. The play was *Diogenes*, its author an ardently revolutionary republican named Félix Pyat, whom the historian Frank Jellinek has called "the purest romantic terrorist that ever flung a paper bomb." This odd personage explained in one of his prefaces that his plays were written for the people, to reinforce their common sense, intelligence and virtue; and in *Diogenes* the parallel between the decadence and venality of ancient Athens and that of the July Monarchy was made sufficiently obvious. *Charivari*, whose republican and anti-government sympathies swayed their judgment, called the piece piquant and original, and in a lithograph published some three weeks after the première, Daumier presented one of its episodes in which the wrathful Diogenes points a scornful finger at the wastrels and degenerates who have impoverished and betrayed the Athenian citizens.

It was during this period that Daumier made his own comments on the resuscitation of the antique gods and heroes in a series of fifty lithos entitled *Ancient History* and in some twenty caricatures of actors playing the roles of Corneille, Voltaire and Racine. When the first of the ancient history plates appeared on December twenty-second, 1841, *Charivari* mockingly coupled Daumier and Ingres as Siamese twins of beauty, and pretended that the former had just returned from a sketching trip to Greece where he rediscovered the primitive and pure sentiment revealed in the first of this "sublime collection," a drawing of Menelaus strutting before the walls of burning Troy with a plump Helen who thumbs her nose at him—a gesture which, the editors explained, Daumier had seen the moderns make in the presence of the Bavarian King.

In succeeding caricatures the ideal beauty of the ancients was ludicrously modernized by an artist who knew what too much food did to the sagging torso and tight shoes to the feet. The followers of Leonidas handle their spears as awkwardly as the National Guard its muskets. A middle-aged Penelope with pendulous bosom dreams by gaslight in a sleazy nightgown of the absent Ulysses (Fig. 26). Damocles in a restaurant complains to the waiter of the suspended sword which is spoiling his appetite. Alcibiades is a dandy with a monocle, as in Ponsard's play. The doting mother of Achilles dips the squalling infant in the Styx. Narcissus smirks at the reflection of his bony adolescence (Fig. 27),

and Ariadne watches the departing ship of Theseus with the look of a
farmer's daughter abandoned in a hayfield. Daedalus watches the fall of
his son through a telescope. Alexander presents a female model of over-
abundant proportions to a wiry Apelles who probably resembles one of
the artist friends of Daumier. Leander swims the Hellespont in water
wings, Anacreon's banquet takes place in one of the more elegant cafés
of Paris, Cornelia's "jewels" are the snuffling brats of an ill-managed
bourgeois household, and Sappho a dishevelled bluestocking. The whole
hilarious parody is in the tradition of Lucian's dialogues and Marivaux's
travesties, and when it was completed, *Charivari* remarked that, whereas
David had glimpsed the beauty of antiquity and Ingres had sought for
it, Daumier had found it. And Baudelaire, for whom the heroes of the
Iliad were but pigmies compared with those of Balzac, decided that
Ancient History was the best answer to the famous question, "Who will
deliver us from the Greeks and from the Romans?"

The twenty-one lithographs in which, as his editors put it, Daumier
lent his support to the resurrection of tragedy by drawing the most
beautiful types and most striking scenes of the classical theater, appeared at intervals from 1838 to 1841, the longest series being the fifteen
plates of *Tragical-classical Physiognomies.* In all of them the artist
found in the effect of stage lighting new possibilities for grotesque exaggeration, as it cast the shadow of un-Roman noses upward on the
brow, shadowed the upper lips which spouted sonorous phrases and gave
the breasts of heroines a monstrous rotundity. Beneath the peplum, the
oriental turban and the shining breastplate these are the buck-toothed,
chinless, potbellied and exophthalmic nonentities of bourgeois Paris. The
falseness of Agamemnon's beard is sharply defined against his jawbone;
the laurel wreath of Caesar clamps his wig firmly to his homely skull; the
toga lays bare the scrawny neck which a modern cravat would hide, and
the Adam's apple of Orestes keeps time with his Alexandrines (Fig. 28).
In *The Cid*, Rodrique screws his pudgy features into the semblance of
heroic courage (Fig. 29); in *The Death of Caesar* a band of super-
numerary Romans has obviously been recruited from among stagestruck
clerks and grocers. On every page mediocrity of mind and body is at war
with the exalted phrases being launched over the footlights. The classical
reaction begun by Rachel was incomplete, a note in *Charivari* explained,
adding that Daumier could claim the glory of having finished it.

When the last drawing of the series *Tragedy* was published in February of 1848, the curtain was about to ring down on the first act of
Daumier's Human Comedy, and its author would turn to other tasks.
His crayon had set moving on a stage a few inches square not only the
principals of the social plot but literally thousands of lesser characters
—errand boys, waiters, midwives, ragpickers, catchers of cats for rabbit

28. *Yes, Since I Find So Faithful a Friend,* lithograph
Museum of Fine Arts, Boston, Mass.

29. *Rodrigue, Have You Courage?,* lithograph
Museum of Fine Arts, Boston, Mass.

stew and fishers in the muddy Seine. He had caught the fright of a man about to be touched for a loan, the shapes of mouth and eye which distinguish the lover of oysters from the man who prefers ice cream; he had discovered in the public bathhouse and under the actor's Roman cuirass every roll of fat, every withered muscle and knobby joint which occupation, routine and appetite had wrought in the people of his time. Nobody had revealed with so much affection and so much understanding, as Baudelaire contended, every small stupidity, every petty pride, every enthusiasm and every despair of a type at once so commonplace and so eccentric.

Daumier has lived intimately with him, has spied upon him day and night, has penetrated the mysteries of his bedroom, has consorted with his wife and children; he understands the form of his nose and the construction of his head, he knows the spirit that animates his house from top to bottom. . . . Look through Daumier's works and you will see parading before your eyes all that a great city contains of living monstrosities in all their fantastic and thrilling reality. . . .

3: THE ARTIST

In the year of Daumier's birth Jacques-Louis David gloomily prophesied that the themes of antiquity to which he had given urgent contemporary meaning would be abandoned by painters within a decade: "All these gods and heroes will be replaced by knights and troubadours singing under the windows of their ladyloves in the shadows of old castles." So long as Frenchmen had accepted the Roman Republic as the model for the one they were fighting to establish and found in the austere patriotism of Brutus the qualities they needed for their task, David's blend of classical formality with trenchant realism in the *Horatii* and in the dead *Marat* symbolized revolution and demonstrated the power and responsibility of the artist as a citizen. When revolution was followed by reaction the Davidian ideals and practices lost their point; the master descended to the banalities of *Mars and Venus* while his disciples tried in various ways to loosen what one of them called his Spartan discipline.

The disillusions and uncertainties of the Restoration years were not conducive to art with a civic purpose, but rather to the defiant cultivation of the individual vision by artists loyal only to their art. The young and discontented had caught a glimpse of new horizons in the Louvre, which held Rembrandt's *Christ at Emmaus*, Rubens' *Life of Marie de Medici* and his turbulent *Kermesse*, Titian's *Deposition*, the Veronese *Wedding Feast*, and Tintoretto's *Susanna* and his study for the *Paradise*. Many painters hopeful of commissions and purchases from a régime which had its own reasons for encouraging royal and saintly subjects turned from the stodgy present to the picturesqueness of the middle ages and produced the knights and troubadours foreseen by David; still others worked within the limits of the bourgeois mentality, its pleasure in descriptive detail, its preference for the homely and sentimental anecdote or the speaking likeness. The citizen who wandered rather dazedly through the labyrinth of the Salon most admired the art which made least demands on his imagination. Some fifty years before, Diderot had expressed in his reviews that same zest for the material, the tangible, the fully realized actuality when he condemned the frivolous and aristocratic cupids and Venuses of Boucher, praised the tear-jerking homilies of Greuze, and stood entranced before Chardin's domestic scenes, his apples and peaches: "It is the very substance of natural objects, it is air and light themselves that you have at the tip of your brushes."

For fifteen years this confusion and cross-purpose gave the Salons of the Bourbon period the atmosphere of a vast and crowded marketplace for competing ideas and practices, a pictorial Babel in which no single voice was clearly heard, no single movement could sharply define itself or dominate the others. In 1817 the *Cupid and Psyche* of David and the *Clytemnestra* of Guérin kept company with those gestures toward royal approval, Gros' *Departure of Louis the Eighteenth* and Gérard's *Entry of Henry the Fourth into Paris*. Two years later the Salon walls held less of mythology and more of Jeanne d'Arc and of Saint Louis; the King said a few nice words about Girodet's *Pygmalion* and the critics found none for the sleek odalisque of Ingres; Géricault's *Raft of the Medusa* was thoroughly contemporary in subject, starkly dramatic in conception and fundamentally realistic in execution. In 1822 the *Dante and Virgil* of Delacroix had to contend with four hundred and forty historical or anecdotal canvases, two hundred and fifty genre scenes, three hundred landscapes, eighty still lifes and nearly a thousand portraits. A critic of the time referred to the *Dante* as a "frightful mishmash"; another was to hail it as the first clear signal of the romantic revolution.

By the mid-twenties one spoke of the battle sharply joined between the worshipers of Homer and those of Shakespeare, the latter having acquired the vague name of Romantics in spite of the diversity of their styles and the fact that Delacroix was the only man of major gifts among them. For the Salon of 1824 Xavier Sigalon contrived a *Locasta Giving to Narcissus the Poison Destined for Britannicus* which was praised by conservative critics for its good taste and its lack of exaggeration. In the same exhibition hung the *Massacres of Scio* by Delacroix, whose drama was an interior one, and whose tragic, brooding atmosphere reminds one of the verse of Hugo:

The Turks have passed this way. All is ruin and sorrow.

Comment on the *Massacres* ranged from the verdict "absurd and barbarous" by critics who could see in it only a careless surrender of form to expression, to the tempered admiration of more liberal commentators who felt its somber power but winced at its breadth and brusqueness of execution. In the Salon of 1827 one could die with Sardanapalus or with Queen Elizabeth. The Delacroix had some of the swirling dynamics and boldly expressive colors which he so admired in Rubens, while the Delaroche was a carefully documented and nerveless tableau vivant. The most resounding success of the show, however, was a concoction by Eugène Devéria called *The Birth of Henry the Fourth*.

Daumier was twenty-two and had made his first contacts with the world of art and artists when the revolution of 1830 seemed for a few exhilarating moments to hold the promise of political, social and artistic liberation, and then quickly fizzled to an anticlimax of eighteen years' duration. The Salon, to be sure, now became an annual event, with some thirty thousand Parisians flocking to the opening day and more than a million surveying its enormous display in the two-month period. Every newspaper of importance published reviews by politicians, literary critics and poets whose printed comments now gained the power to make or break a reputation, tempting the weaker artists toward compromise and conformity but driving the bolder ones to defiance. Yet the painters found fewer purchasers, public or private. The new King's taste inclined to overlarge scenes from the national past; a commission to decorate the Chamber of Deputies in 1830 was awarded to a nonentity; the members of the Institute who now served as jurors for the Salon managed to suppress all forms of pictorial innovation, serving as true representatives of those citizens who, when they ventured to become patrons, usually demanded portraits of themselves.

In this stuffy atmosphere of the July Monarchy rebellious painters, poets and musicians proclaimed the success of their own insurrection. Delacroix, Hugo and Berlioz in that crucial year of 1830 had each shattered the old forms which could no longer contain the thought and feeling of contemporary man. *Liberty on the Barricades* shocked the observer less by its theme than by the power of its forms, the nervous vibration of its colors, its stark confrontation of the beautiful with the ugly. *Hernani* destroyed the hallowed unities of time and place, the measured pace of tragic verse, and Berlioz called its author a daredevil who risked death to explode a mine under the old restraining barriers to expression. In the *Fantastic Symphony* invariable rhythms and conventional blocks of harmony gave place to astonishingly fresh sonorities, to a passionate and driving movement, to the tender and melancholy evocation of feelings too intimate and too mysterious for words.

These were perhaps the "bouquet of masterpieces" which, as Théophile Gautier recalled in later years, renewed every aspect of the arts. "What ardor," he wrote, "what enthusiasm, what devotion to art, what horror of vulgar success bought at the price of bourgeois concession!" Yet these rebels of 1830 had to recognize that theirs was a palace revolution which had not disturbed the massive complacency of a public which still preferred the picturesque Italian brigands of Léopold Robert, the expiring monarchs of Delaroche, and a *Defense of Clichy* which Horace Vernet produced at the rate of three square feet a day. Inevitably the more sensitive painters nursed their distrust of mass opinion and took refuge in the smaller municipality of art from the tyranny of current conventions. The morbidly sensitive Delacroix saw his *Liberty* scorned by all but a few critics, bought by the King as a gesture of appeasement toward his republican opponents, hung for a few years in a remote corner of the Louvre and then rolled up and consigned to an attic, an experience which confirmed the painter's haughty detachment from what he once called "the vain pasturage of the common run of men." And Gautier spoke for the rancorous and alienated minority when he proclaimed as a doctrine what had been implicit before—the complete autonomy of a work of art, its power to move us by means peculiar to itself, its glorious independence of practical or moral usefulness; in short, the principle of art-for-art's sake.

Gautier could thus define Romanticism in his own anarchic terms, but there were other romanticisms in the 1830s, other artists who saw a parallel between the liberation of art and the struggle for freedom and progress in society as a whole. Not a few authors, painters and sculptors were coming to share the fraternalism and the dreams of a better social order which they found in the writings and speeches of their contemporaries. The sculptor David d'Angers, who was born a year before the fall of the Bastille, was the elder statesman of this left wing of Romanticism when he observed that art need not absorb all of a man's energies and that, before being an artist, one should be a citizen. In his work was to be seen the struggle between a smooth classicism inspired by his years in the Rome of Canova and the livelier naturalism of his statue of Condé, dressed not in the toga of convention but in the dress of his own time and place. Baudelaire dismissed him as a "carib of the wrinkle and the wart"; but his figure of *Liberty* stood on a shelf in the back room of a dairy shop where young rebels met to discuss their problems. Here, as Jules Champfleury recalled, "Art and republicanism were the order of the day."

These socially-minded artists found a few champions among the critics at a time when Gustave Planche of the *Revue des Deux Mondes* was becoming their most influential opponent. Planche in 1831 had called the *Liberty* of Delacroix a work of genius, the finest painting in the Salon, a parallel to the revolution of the previous year in its gesture of regeneration and renewal; but the writer had lost all enthusiasm for revolution when, in the late years of the decade, he charted a middle course between the stale formulas of painting and what he called eccentric novelty and caprice. The cool perfection of Ingres, his elevation of style, now claimed the allegiance of Planche, whose bitter campaign against "vulgar" realism was to make him the nemesis of Courbet.

Readers of *Le National* and *La Réforme* found judgments of a very different kind. Maurice-Alexandre Decamps, an ardent champion of Delacroix, saw Ingres moving toward a dead end; and Charles Blanc wrote that the arts would flourish only in a France where wealth and opportunity had been equalized and the entire community had become patrons of art. Equally democratic but far more sensitive was Théophile Thoré, for a time an inmate of the prison which Daumier had also known and an exile after 1848 for his share in the June uprising. The

Salon reviews of Thoré reveal his struggle to shape a philosophy which should reconcile the artist's need for expressive freedom with society's need for the artist. He could admire the obstinate integrity which gave character to the work of Ingres, though he called him the leader of the "resurrectionists" whose notion of an absolute beauty was a chimera; he could lament the proud isolation of Delacroix while pronouncing him the only colorist in the French school, a masterly composer of forms and details in the revelation of a thought, and a draftsman whose broken and tentative lines held the movement of life.

It was perhaps his conversations with Delacroix and his close friendship with the landscape painter Théodore Rousseau which made Thoré less doctrinaire as time passed. He could reproach the latter for a detachment from everything that was not art, the feelings which moved the rest of mankind, "this excessive isolation, this suicide of half your faculties"; yet he came to believe that the moral, the human effect of a painting was necessarily indirect and depended on a powerful plastic embodiment of an idea, a feeling or a perception rather than an obvious subject literally described. Thoré could thereupon dismiss the stilted and carefully itemized landscapes of the time and discover the new gifts of Rousseau, Huet and Diaz, in whose scenes he "heard the wind mutter and the sea roar," and whose visions of nature renewed sensibilities which city life had blunted and "gave the illusion of the miracles of light."

Fourteen years younger than Thoré was Charles Baudelaire, the most brilliant of all critics in the declining years of the July Monarchy, who wrote his first salon in 1845. By the breadth of his conception of art and the range and depth of his perception the poet managed to rise above the quarrels of the schools, the clash of doctrines, the debates between Classicism and Romanticism, between the champions of line and the partisans of color. He had tried more than once, he said, to lock himself up within a system in order to preach there at his ease, only to discover that in art there was always a new and unexpected element which eternally evaded rules. "The best criticism," he concluded, "is that which is both amusing and poetic." Since a fine picture is nature reflected by an artist, "the criticism which I approve will be that picture reflected by an intelligent and sensitive mind." True to his belief that the beautiful is always strange and that every age has its own conception of beauty, truth and ethics, Baudelaire challenged artists to look the present in the face, ignoring the canons of the past and the evasions of the academies:

> . . . the true painter for whom we are looking will be he who can snatch its epic quality from the life of today and can make us see and understand with brush or with pencil how great and poetic we are in our cravats and our patent-leather boots.

The artist interprets an age to itself. The dominant theme of his time was for Baudelaire the struggle of noble and sensitive individuals against the spiritual and moral decadence of the world in which they lived. There was a kind of stubborn heroism in Ingres, an "immolation on the altar of false gods," a sacrifice of imagination and of temperament to an out-moded Raphaelesque notion of beauty. But the painter who best recorded the heroisms of modern life, who best translated into the language of forms and colors the passions, the fears, the affirmations and the frustrations of the time, was Delacroix. When Baudelaire spoke of the latter as the Romantic artist par excellence, that bothersome term no longer connoted one or another choice of subject, no degree of truthful-ness or untruth in representation, but a mode of feeling, an imperious drive toward the transformation of reality. In this mood both Baudelaire and Champfleury could admire the lowly art of caricature for its inter-pretation of man and his condition. While the official world of art—the established critics, the Salon juries, the academies and museums—re-fused to acknowledge that a humorous sketch in a cheap newspaper could be a work of art, these writers found in its ludicrous deformations, its intense and direct expression of compassionate sympathy and bitter scorn, an effective ally in their war against the deadly average, the un-changeable rules of drawing, the hard-and-fast distinction between the beautiful and ugly, between the noble and the commonplace.

When Thoré and Baudelaire wrote their critiques in the mid-forties, Daumier had begun to paint. Since every artist, however independent, owes something to the imagery of others, one asks how much guidance this young lithographer, already a master of the crayon, derived from his friendship with painters and sculptors, from rambles among the old masters and the new ones in the Louvre, when he took up the brush. This quiet man could have few acquaintances among that Romantic coterie whose eccentricities of dress and behavior proclaimed their loathing for conventions, nor would Gautier's proclamation of the glorious useless-ness of art appeal to one whose pencil was enlisted in the most practical of causes. Between those involuntary figureheads, the impassively cool Ingres and the intense Delacroix, he could learn more from the latter. One would like to have overheard what the man from *Charivari* and the master of *Scio* said to one another on the few occasions of their meeting. Temperamentally, the former had little in common with this frail and elegant creature with troubled eyes under heavy brows, his olive skin stretched tight over gaunt features and stubborn jaws, who reminded Gautier of a maharajah. Yet Delacroix once wrote to Daumier that there was no man whom he more respected and admired, and a plate from the inimitable *Bathers* was pinned to the wall of his studio. And Daumier, struggling to put his experience into a strange and difficult medium, could not fail to see that this imperious painter had accomplished a revolution in restoring to art the pictorial gusto, the rich and compelling orchestration of forms and spaces which were to be seen in the Venetians and in Rubens.

It would be many years before the caricaturist-turned-painter achieved that bold and sweeping brushstroke. As a master of black and white he could suggest color in his lithographs but never as a painter become a colorist in the sense of Delacroix, whose strange reds and livid greens were for Baudelaire "a lake of blood haunted by fallen angels." Yet the intensity, the expressive unity of the younger man's best work owed much to the spirit if not to the letter of this innovator. The fever of execution which Delacroix worshipped in Michelangelo was to give Daumier's late lithographs and drawings their sting and bite—this and the broken tentative line which was Delacroix's alternative to the calculated linear finalities of Ingres as a means of suggesting form and movement. The dynamics of human effort, the muscularity and strain, the significant gesture, the impelling drive which the more accomplished painter did not always succeed in giving to his Hamlet, Constantine and Sardanapalus were in Daumier's unambitious studies of smaller heroisms—men straining to carry water, women plodding under the weight of laundry, riders lurching with the pull of drayhorses, refugees driven by panic. The Liberty Goddess of Delacroix in 1830 was a figure of allegory whom the painter dared to place among men in modern frock coats and trousers; Daumier's version of that figure confronted the politicians in a lithograph of 1848 and lost none of her imperious power for looking at the same time like a robust matron of the rue Saint-Denis. And the rhythm of the former's *Jacob Wrestling with the Angel* is relaxed and nerveless compared to the taut, thudding bodies of the latter's two rascals fighting in a gutter.

More congenial to Daumier than was Delacroix, and therefore more intimately his friends, were a few painters and sculptors of his own age whose common bond was their republican zeal and their war against the official juries which ignored or rejected their work. When these artists met to draw up a petition for a Salon without a jury, or to organize societies for mutual aid, Daumier was likely to be among them. In the drawing class at the Académie Suisse he rubbed shoulders with Paul Huet, Louis Cabat and Narcisse-Virgile Diaz, all of whom were to break down the old formulas of landscape painting with a fresher and more evocative study of outdoor light. The militant Philippe-Auguste Jeanron was also his friend, who fought in the revolution of 1830, made lithographs of its episodes and managed at the Salon of the next year to show his painting of children on the barricades.

A more gifted associate was a fellow caricaturist who turned to paint-

1. *The Horsemen*, oil
Museum of Fine Arts, Boston

III. *Visitors in an Artist's Studio*, water color
Walters Art Gallery, Baltimore

II. *The Miller, His Son and the Ass*, oil
Glasgow Art Gallery, Glasgow

IV. *The Washerwoman,* oil
Albright-Knox Art Gallery, Buffalo

v. *The Print Collector*, oil
Philadelphia Museum of Art, Wilstach Collection. Photo by A. J. Wyatt

VI. *Mountebanks Changing Place,* water color
Wadsworth Atheneum, Hartford

VII. [appears on following page]

VIII. *The Fugitives,* oil
The Minneapolis Institute of Arts, Minneapolis

VII. *Don Quixote and Sancho Panza*, oil
Courtauld Institute Galleries, London

ing and whose popularity derived from the intimacy and charm of small oils and water colors with a wide range of subjects—hunting scenes, episodes from the Orient, children at play, and monkeys behaving like people. Alexandre-Gabriel Decamps in the early 1830s was a frustrated history painter whose large *Defeat of the Cimbri* was snubbed by the critics of the Salon and by a public which seemed to prefer the picturesque authenticity of his Turkish soldiers and the mockery of his *Monkey-Painter*. Decamps was a master of close harmonies with his earth-reds, golden ochre and dull green-blues, and his exquisite technique was the outcome of patient experiments with glazing, rubbing and a rich impasto; the Goncourts would admire him as a "great silhouettist" for his figures darkly massed against walls which told their life story of rain and sun, his varied textures and his luminous shadows, as Thoré had earlier praised his water color of Don Quixote as a small masterpiece whose figures moved in a valley scorched by the sun and ridged with arid rocks.

In the small circle of Daumier's friends there were more sculptors than painters, a fact significant for his own development. Adolphe-Victor Geoffroy-Dechaume, who had worked with David d'Angers, was to play a major role in Daumier's later life. Jean-Jacques Feuchère lithographed a likeness of the young caricaturist and modeled portrait busts with competence; both Antoine-Louis Barye and Auguste Préault were men of greater originality and force whose work was first accepted and then systematically excluded year after year by the Salon juries. The beasts whose physiology Barye so thoroughly studied during these years of exclusion were not merely faithfully reproduced in his bronzes but became creatures of proud contour, of balanced thrust and counterthrust, of swelling tensions. Before these sleek images of bestial power, Gautier once said that all the poor marble lions with boneless bodies and wigs à la Louis Fourteenth which flanked public buildings, with one foot resting on a ball, would curl tail between legs and cringe in shame. The rapidly modeled and sketchlike reliefs of Préault, a gloomy and bitterly sarcastic man obsessed with death and disaster and soured by professional failure, were too savagely improvised for the Salon, which admitted his relief, *Famine*, in 1833 and two years later *The Massacre*, but had no place for *The Pariahs*, a lithographed version of which hung in Daumier's workroom.

When one attempts to trace the influence of these friends and contemporaries on the canvases and panels of Daumier, one can find no evidence of imitation and only a few echoes of their subjects and their technical procedure. There was in his case no master-pupil relation through which technical skills passed from the older to the young as they passed from Regnault to Guérin, for example, and from Guérin to

Géricault and Delacroix. His interest in the varied rhythms of expressive human action and his growing power to suggest them may owe something to the example of Delacroix, but derived more surely from his own powers of observation, his ability to feel in himself the action he wished to represent. The palette of Decamps with its low-keyed harmonies of creamy whites and warm browns must have commended itself to him, and the term silhouettist described him as well as it did his friend, although the technical cleverness of Decamps was far beyond his grasp. One can surmise but not know that the latter's painting of children pouring from a Turkish school, shown in 1842, was in his mind when he made a similar subject, and that the Don Quixote water color suggested the theme and general composition of one of his earlier studies of Cervantes' pair. The Goncourts remembered Decamps' *Defeat of the Cimbri* when they wrote of "panic driving the shaken and routed into a ravine, the milling of men, horses and cattle, sweeping along on the flood of their terror the despair of women"; and Daumier may have remembered the work also, for these words apply as well to his emigrants and his refugees. And Daumier's intercourse with sculptors doubtless confirmed his tendency to rely on modulation of light and shade rather than on color to define his forms. The same vehemence and roughly accented planes to be seen in the work of his friend Préault gave an amazing vitality to the small clay heads of Daumier. The jaunty twisted posture of his statuette of *Ratapoil* may owe something to the *Slaves* of Michelangelo which he had seen in the Louvre.

There is visible proof that, in the latter collection, Daumier had studied Rubens' *Family of Lot,* and there exists a photograph of a lost painting which purported to be his copy of that master's explosive bacchanal, *The Kermesse.* More suggestive and more profitable in the long run, however, were the subtleties of light and the mysteries of gloom in Rembrandt's *Saint Matthew, The Philosopher in Meditation* and *The Pilgrims of Emmaus.*

His vision of the world thus to some degree formed on pictures and sculptures seen, the young caricaturist taught himself and was taught by independent observation, and the pages of *Charivari* record the mutations of his style. In the beginning the single head or figure is fully realized in form, texture and "color," the thing-in-itself sculpturally presented in isolation on the sheet in a vacuum of undefined space. When a more complete composition is attempted, the results are uneven. He progresses in the 1830s from cluttered design and somewhat labored execution to greater freedom and assurance; and in the four extra-large lithographs of 1834 all the resources of his medium are used, if rather self-consciously.

In the social satires which follow he is less concerned with the spicy fragment than with whole situations where a variety of actions must be related to the environment—the bedrooms, the parlors, the gardens or meadows in which the bourgeois comedy is played. Here inventiveness keeps pace with necessity. There is less obvious exaggeration of face and figure, a quieter and more indulgent humor in scenes where men cope with the small problems of life. Daumier explores bourgeois anatomy and experiments with effects of candlelight; in his lithos of the 1840s he finds means for suggesting the slant of rain, the falling snow, the impact of wind, the glimmer of moonlight. The diffused sunshine of open fields in his *Pastorals* shows that he is already familiar with the countryside beyond Paris. In the best works of these years the carefully built-up tones give place to simple modeling, and line alone often characterizes people and suggests the texture and movement of their clothes. His handwriting in *A Souvenir of Youth* is as powerful as it is wholly his own, and the windblown skirts of his lady socialists are crisply drawn with a few swift strokes. Returning to the theme of *Wood is Dear,* he again presents two painters who are dancing to keep warm, but with greater economy and a firmer grasp of space-relations.

"At thirty," Claude Roger-Marx has written, "the lithographer of *Charivari* is in complete possession not only of his inspiration but of his craft." At thirty-seven he must have been heartened and somewhat surprised when Baudelaire placed him alongside his two most famous contemporaries, "something calculated to astound both friends and enemies . . . of each one of them." Reviewing the Salon of 1845, Baudelaire wrote:

> We know of only two men in Paris who draw as well as M. Delacroix
> . . . the first is M. Daumier the caricaturist; the second M. Ingres.
> . . . anyone who examines the matter slowly and carefully will see
> that these three kinds of drawing have this in common, that they
> . . . say just what they mean to say. Daumier draws better, perhaps
> than Delacroix, if you would prefer healthy, robust qualities to the
> weird and amazing powers of a great genius sick with genius. . . .

Neither here nor in a later essay is any reference made to Daumier's paintings, although it was Baudelaire who told Delacroix that the caricaturist found it difficult to complete his oils. Clearly, the fingers which could work wonders with the stubs of lithographic crayons found the brush clumsy and the new medium intractable. One does not know when these experiments began; some biographers say in the 1840s and others more reasonably in the previous decade. As early as 1832 he registered at the prison of Sainte-Pélagie as "artist-painter." The dating of Daumier's paintings has proven to be the most baffling problem connected with his life and work: he did not date his oils, often left them unfinished and sometimes reworked them at a later period. Few of them

30. *The Towman,* oil. Private collection, Germany. Photo Vizzavona

were sent to the Salon, the time of which could provide a terminal point, and helpful references in the letters and reminiscences of his contemporaries are discouragingly rare. Moreover, the parallel of subject matter with the lithographs, whose date of publication is known, is suggestive but misleading in the case of a man whose prodigious memory held a store of images to be drawn upon whenever he wished. Further to complicate the problem, many of the works have been "completed" by other hands than his, and the alleged Daumiers include a considerable number of outright fakes. No wonder that one finds more questions than answers, and that any chronological scheme must rely heavily on the evidence provided by the works themselves.

Among these, *The Etcher,* with its suggestion of Rembrandt's *Philosopher in Meditation,* must be among the earliest, if indeed it was done by Daumier. *The Nocturnal Strollers,* a dry and clumsy study of two riverside figures under an unconvincing moon, was still in his possession when he died, and the small panel *Workmen in a Street* never progressed beyond the rough blocking out of its figures and a suggestion of bridge

31. *The Water Carrier,* oil

and housefronts. The blurred silhouette of *The Towman* (Fig. 30)
strains at his rope against a murky sky, an action more succinctly
described in a lithograph of 1843. It has been suggested that Daumier
borrowed the subject of his *Oedipus and the Shepherd* from a painting of
the same subject by Millet in the Salon of 1847, but one thinks of the
former work as of an earlier date; moreover, its rugged simplicity, heavy
masses and stark contrasts have little in common with Millet's elab-
orately planned and rather Baroque forms and rhythms.

With *Two Men Drinking* and *The Water Carrier* a more coherent and
dynamic ordering of themes has been attempted. In the manner of
Decamps the sombre figures of the drinkers are massed against a yellow-
ish wall; the focusing of contrast in the center and the over-arching tree
are in the mode of the vignette. The water carrier (Fig. 31) is superbly
placed in space, his weight pressing the earth, his lower body half lost
in darkness and his twisted and muscular shoulders defined against a
sunlit wall; the downward pull of one arm is repeated in a vertical
shadow and the other arm, outflung for balance, is paralleled by the
sloping roof. Here Daumier's power as a sculptor of tense action breaks
through his limitations—the even and rather thick impasto, the narrow
range of opaque browns and ivories. The same muscularity is in several
studies of broad-flanked horses and their riders. In the largest of these,
the *Horsemen* of the Boston Museum of Fine Arts (Color plate I),
Daumier has struck in with black pigment the main shapes of two
plunging animals and has begun to model one of them with a thick
yellowish-white. The black horse has been scraped as though in preparation for more indications of form; a large area in the foreground is the
untouched dark brown ground of the canvas; behind and above the
horsemen is a scumble of greenish-brown. The painting is a technically
unfinished but astonishingly complete statement.

The painter of the *Water Carrier* and the *Horsemen* is still cautious
with color and heavy-handed with pigment, but his men and animals
move freely in their spaces and he is beginning to suggest the air and
light of outdoors with the brush, as he had already learned to do with
crayon. Among works which would seem to be of this early period are
several studies of bathers and children, some of which he never completed, while others show signs of retouching by other hands. The
problem of relating a number of figures in a spacious outdoor setting
was a new one for the painter: the chalky pink flesh tones and the pale
greenish-blue of the water and sky in *Young Girls Bathing* suggest his
search for a livelier palette, but each of its figures seems unrelated to
the others; and there is a lumpy modeling in the horizontal composition,
The First Bathe, and a huddled stringing together of its people along the
river bank. Some of these bathing scenes must have been observed in

the open country; in others, a glimpse of housefronts and the shadowed arch of a bridge place them alongside his own quay in Paris. There are other paintings in this group where skies have been made too brightly blue and where raw accents of red, green and yellow suggest an "improving" hand. If *The Good Samaritan* is a retouched original, (Alexandre referred to it in 1888 as a "large unfinished sketch") its thickly applied shadows, over-accented foliage and flat, squarish brushstrokes have obscured whatever of Daumier may once have been there.

One turns with relief to the one example of Daumier's "first period" as a painter which can be securely dated, a sketch for *The Republic* made with some diffidence for a competition organized by his friend Jeanron to celebrate the February Revolution of 1848. The contest opened in March of that year, and a jury of which Delacroix was a member selected twenty-four compositions from among several hundred for showing at the École des Beaux-Arts toward the end of April. Daumier, doubtless to his surprise, found his sketch among the chosen.

His task was to be allegorical without being tiresome and the figure he chose was not of his invention, the goddess Liberty whose image the Romans had multiplied in bust or full length with a laurel crown, a jeweled coronet or a freeman's bonnet on her head. In the first days of the Revolution hundreds of French artists designed Liberties for prints, popular song sheets, posters and state documents. Whether seated, standing or flying through the clouds, whether framed in cornucopias, oak branches or symbolic beasts, all the versions of the emblematic female, as Jules Renouvier said, were sisters. The grandsons of those who had followed her effigy through the streets in processions designed by David undertook to revive her in forms more appropriate to their own revolutions; Delacroix's *Liberty* of 1830, young, vigorous and shapely, with breasts bared and feet planted firmly on the barricades, was part deity and part woman of the people, and matched the verses of Barbier:

> A woman sturdy and of puissant breasts,
> Hard-beautiful and raucous-voiced,
> Brown-skinned, with eyes of fire,
> Moving with swift long strides. . . .

Daumier's goddess (Fig. 32) is more quietly imperious, and her seated figure, with children nursing at her breast, is in the classic posture of Charity, a posture made traditional by generations of artists from Andrea del Sarto to Prud'hon. She resembles a figure in the background of one of the lithographed *Philanthropists of the Day* and reappears in one of his drawings; perhaps the opulent young woman of Diaz in the Salon of 1847, with cupids at her knee, reinforced this image in his mind. In the background of a water color, *The Two Print*

32. *The Republic,* oil. Louvre. Photo Bulloz

Collectors, stands a small statuette so similar in pose and action as to suggest that he may have modeled his Republic before painting her. With a clay group before him, the artist could more surely have noted the shapes of light and shadow under the impact of light falling from directly above; the canvas in the Louvre indeed gives the impression of a sculpture in its massive and compact unity. Daumier first outlined the four bodies in reddish pigment on a neutral ground, then gave them their volumes by the simplest means, with one thickly brushed tone for the principal lights and a thinner one for shadows warmed by reflections. The folds of Liberty's white robe are brushed with a bold assurance, and the tempered harmony of the whole is enlivened by the rich red and blue of her flag. This decisiveness, rare among these early paintings, may be the young artist's response to what was for him a very special occasion.

When the competitive sketches were shown, Champfleury was there to survey a melancholy assortment of Republics, of which he wrote:

> There were red ones, pink ones, green and yellow ones; marble ones, stone ones, ivory ones; some were a baker's brown, some mellowed like a pipe, some scratched and some scraped; Republics in flowered dresses, in National Guard uniforms, in silk skirts and in dressing-gowns, Republics dressed in chains, dressed in symbolic trappings, dressed in nothing at all. . . . In the midst of all this, lost in a clutter of mediocrity, one could have noticed one canvas that was simple, serious and unpretentious. A seated woman supports two children at her breasts; at her feet two children read. The Republic nourishes her children and instructs them. . . . There were in Paris a few men who kept on saying that Daumier was a great artist. These fifteen people were taken for freaks. . . . It required this strong and sober sketch by the caricaturist to prove to the scoffers that Daumier can stand beside Delacroix, Ingres and Corot, the solitary masters of French art in our time. . . . On that day I cried, *Long Live the Republic!* for the Republic had made a painter: DAUMIER.

VIGNETTE: FAMILY MAN

Two years before the end of the July Monarchy Daumier conformed to the middle-class pattern by marrying a dressmaker fourteen years younger than himself whose father lived and mended windowpanes in the section behind the Hôtel de Ville. Marie-Alexandrine Dassy would seem to have been one of those simple and work-hardened creatures whom Balzac considered the admirable product of the lesser bourgeoisie. She would need to be thrifty; a few years before, her husband had struggled without success to repay a debt, had been hounded by a sheriff and forced to sell some of his furniture; the payment for his stones varied from forty to fifty francs apiece (about seven to nine dollars.)

The impecunious pair set up housekeeping on the quiet, tree-shaded Île Saint-Louis, that fragment of Paris edged on both sides by the river and lined with the venerable façades of once noble mansions which were now rented out to small businessmen and impecunious artists. The Island, as Zola described it in the opening pages of *The Quarry,* "communed sleepily with itself in a quarter seldom troubled by the noise of carriages. . . . You would think yourself a thousand miles away from that modern Paris alive and swarming with every form of self-gratification, loud with the roars of millions" (Fig. 33).

At number nine on the quai d'Anjou near the tip of the Island the couple followed for some seventeen years the same homely domestic routine which Daumier set forth in *Conjugal Mores.* Among the few scraps of his own writing that have survived are half a dozen brief and sentimental notes which could have been penned by any one of the contented spouses of his lithographs. They were addressed to "Dear Didine" when she had gone to the seashore of Normandy in the summer of 1849:

> I'm sorry, my poor Didine, that I didn't write you Tuesday as I promised, but I couldn't help it. Instead of delivering my stones on Monday as I'd hoped, I didn't get them done until Thursday. . . .

and a few days later:

> When I got here yesterday I went to see your mother. I gave her all the details about how you were settling in and how well you are, although you get tired. She's delighted and sends you a thousand hugs and kisses,—and Bibi does too,
> > Good-bye, old girl
> > > H. Daumier.

A few doors from his own lived Daubigny and Geoffrey-Dechaume. At number seventeen, which had been the magnificent Hotel Lauzun, the Baron Pichon rented rooms to a group of artists which at one time included Charles Baudelaire. The daily grind of the interminable stones for *Charivari* was relieved by an occasional evening of Mozart and Beethoven in the salon of the Baron, where Daumier shook hands with

33. The quai d'Anjou. Photo Yvon, Paris

Delacroix, by excursions with his artist friends to the countryside, by evenings of Molière at the Théâtre-Français and with hours in the small bistros of the Island where he drank cheap wine with the riverboatmen and solemnly addressed them as "mon Capitaine."

In the attic above his apartment he made himself a workroom not unlike those which formed the backgrounds of his drawings of life among the artists: bare walls with one or two prints after Delacroix and Préault and a few medallions by David d'Angers, an easel with an unfinished painting, other canvases stacked in corners, a white-hot iron stove, and on a table the clutter of lithographic tools. To this garret came Bonvin and Courbet to persuade the modest Honoré to submit a competitive sketch of the *Republic;* here Baudelaire was impressed by the radiant good sense of the man's conversation. Here Champfleury observed that the semi-recluse found it difficult to express himself in words but that his small questioning eyes saw everything; to this future author of a history of caricature Daumier confessed that the essay in which Baudelaire had compared him with Delacroix and Ingres was for him a bizarre and embarrassing tribute. When Théodore de Banville came in search of a vignette he found his host humming the air of a popular operetta, "O happy dwellers in the vales of sweet Helvetia," while his hands moved over the stone with the broken stubs of old crayons which "lent themselves to the feverish caprice of his deft fingers":

I admired his face glowing with strength and good nature, his small piercing eyes, his nose uptilted as though by a breeze, his gracious mouth, his fine artist's head so much like those of the bourgeois in his pictures, but warmed and tempered by the flames of intelligence and wit.

From his high window Daumier looked down on a branch of the Seine as lazily smooth as a country stream, its broad embankment shaded by arching trees. Small boats moved upon it, massive workhorses came dripping from their bath and fishermen stood motionless; children with bare legs played under the eyes of their elders, and washerwomen climbed the stone steps with heavy bundles. Beyond were the ragged profiles and oddly spaced windows of houses on the quai des Célestins; directly beneath were moored the floating bathhouses whose naked occupants could be spied upon by the caricaturist, as they were by the Renée of Zola.

From the quai d'Anjou Daumier strolled in search of a subject for tomorrow's lithograph, to the office of *Charivari* where he would drop a few mild but shrewd sentences, or to some gathering where his fellow artists were planning their campaign for a Salon without a jury. A lithograph by Benjamin (Fig. 34) presents him with hands in pocket, a portfolio under his arm, an ordinary citizen in a top hat who once remarked to a companion, "What do I need? Two fried eggs in the morning and at night a cutlet or a herring. Add a glass of Beaujolais and tobacco to fill my pipe. Anything more would be too much." A flâneur through the narrow byways of the Island or along the quays would never have known that the squat, snub-nosed, chin-whiskered man whom he jostled in passing had made a King sweat with anger and dozens of politicians chew their fingernails, or guess that he would one day have an important share in the toppling of an Empire. He looked too much like any good citizen out for an airing to put one on guard against an eye which raked the passer-by from skin to skeleton and a memory whose images convulsed the sidewalks and back parlors of Paris for some forty years. Returning from a musical evening on the Island, perhaps a little unsteady with wine, he was overheard to murmur, "How I've aged! Once upon a time the streets were too narrow to hold me, and I scraped the walls on both sides. Nowadays I'm lucky to dislodge a windowblind."

34. Portrait of Daumier by Benjamin, lithograph. Photo Alison Spence

4: THE REPUBLICAN HONEYMOON

For thirteen years since 1835 the government had spiked the guns of Philipon's small army, and we can only imagine what Daumier's daily comments would have been if the press laws had not stayed his pencil. We may be sure that he would have shown us a revolution in the making. He would have celebrated the election of Opposition deputies in 1842 and exposed to scorn the vote-buying, the jockeying and the wangling which followed. He would have contrasted the stockjobbery and the shortsighted protectionism of the conservative régime with the mounting distress of men whose harvests had been disastrously poor for years and whose fields had been destroyed by floods. On the eve of February in 1848 his drawings would have rallied the strangely assorted forces of rebellion—the desperate workers of the slums, the socialist clubs, the radical journalists, the violent young men of the Latin Quarter whose favorite teachers had been persecuted, the lesser bourgeoisie who grubbed in offices, sold groceries, bore arms in the National Guard but could not vote, the democratic idealists among the professional class.

These were the combined forces which in three February days dethroned a decrepit King and improvised a republic. Between Daumier's home and the office of *Charivari* crowds pressed against the boards to read the proclamations of the Opposition leaders, the order mobilizing the National Guard and the appeals to beware of reckless actions which would give the authorities an excuse for bloodshed. Daumier could hear men shout, "Long Live Reform!" and "Down with Guizot!" and watch the students marching with their petition to the Chamber, while older men who had left their offices and factories to mass in the Champs-Élysées were driven back by the police into their own districts, where they collected old chairs, paving stones and stray lumber for barricades. On the twenty-third, drums sounded the assembly for the National Guard which, instead of routing the insurgents, hobnobbed with the crowd. By afternoon of that day Guizot had announced the end of his ministry and the good citizens took their usual constitutional, stepping over the débris. By six o'clock in the morning of the twenty-fourth the rattle of gunfire began again. A military guard from the Foreign Office had mowed down more than a hundred demonstrators in front of the office of the *National*. The street cries changed to "Long Live the Republic" as insurgents seized the Palais-Royal and the Hôtel de Ville and flowed from all directions to storm the Tuileries.

At lunch time on that day Jules de Goncourt ventured as far as his own balcony. Across the street a boilermaker's sign read COPPER-SMITH TO THE KING, and on a ladder its proprietor was hastily beating out the last three words with his hammer. After lunch the brothers strolled in the gardens of the Tuileries, making mental notes for their diary: the head of a marble stag had fallen among the flower beds, and a stone Spartacus held blossoms in his hand and wore a Liberty cap on his head. On the balcony of the royal palace from which the King had now fled they saw a rioter who had filched the monarch's dressing gown and was entertaining the mob with a parody of Louis-Philippe's famous peroration, "It is with ever grateful pleasure that once again I . . ." a scene which reminded the Goncourts of a caricature by Daumier.

While some writers and painters fought in the streets, others recoiled from the brutal realities of February. The Goncourts saw in 1848 the fearful reappearance of 1793, "this homicidal dictatorship . . . of the porter's lodge, the servants' pantry, the informer, of all the jealousy and spite of the lower orders." And Delacroix, whose *Richelieu* had gone up in flames at the Palais-Royal, wrote that Paris had just witnessed a terrible catastrophe: "I've buried the man of yesterday with his hopes and his dreams of the future . . . we're all going to grovel like swine before the altar of the fatherland." Baudelaire on the other hand was seen prowling with a rifle in his hand, Champfleury made speeches at street corners, and many a young painter wore on his hat a placard, REPUBLICAN ARTIST.

Daumier himself did not at once make full use of the new freedoms. In February, his *Tenants and Landlords* and his series *Tragedy* continued in *Charivari;* in the spring and summer there were more of his *Papas, Good Bourgeois* and *Divorcing Women.* But two of his drawings celebrated the victorious moment. A swift sketch whose lines crackled like gunfire had the throne room of the deposed King for its setting; in *The Gamin of Paris in the Tuileries,* an urchin in a pilfered uniform kicks up his heels from the soft cushions of the royal chair and cries, "Jees! How you sink into it!" This lithograph was based on an incident which several witnesses have described; *The Final Council of the Ex-ministers* was an allegory published five days after the privilege of voting had officially been granted to all Frenchmen. The same goddess of the Republic who was taking shape on Daumier's canvas here steps into a darkened room to confront the men of the old order, her steady figure a counterpoint to their stumbling confusion. With a minimum of gesture and no heroics she takes possession of her own house (Fig. 35).

These opening weeks of the Second Republic have been described by the historian Émile Bourgeois as a debauch of idealism when even the Church and the most staunch reactionaries proclaimed their love for the

35. *Final Council of the Ex-Ministers*, lithograph
Museum of Fine Arts, Boston, Mass.

democratic masses who now forced unheard-of reforms. Capital punishment for political offenses was abolished, the organization of working-
men was legalized and universal male suffrage established; the new
government guaranteed the Right to Work, and thousands of the unem-
ployed, including artists, bank clerks and musicians could be seen
taking up and replanting trees on the boulevards under the eyes of
puzzled bystanders.

Republicans, however, had little time to exult over these achievements, since in the first days of the Provisional Government they split
into quarreling factions. While the leaders sought means of carrying
forward what they believed to be a social revolution, the moderates
split constitutional hairs and showed more concern to protect the
republic against mass disorder than to organize a new society. By April
thirty thousand workmen, ominously crowded into the eastern districts
of Paris, barely missed a battle with the troops in a pre-election demonstration. When the votes were counted they knew that country people
had used the ballots to defend themselves against the fire-eating
"radicals" of the capital, assuring victory to the moderates of law and
order. In May the new assembly met to the sound of rioting. In a scene
which cried for Daumier's pencil, Barbès threw proclamations from a
window at one end of the Hôtel de Ville declaring the Assembly super-
seded, while from another window the Mayor of Paris dropped leaflets
denying its dissolution. On the twenty-third of June the people of the

rue Saint-Denis made fortresses of overturned omnibuses, and near the Théâtre de la Porte Saint-Martin stood women with halberds they had plundered from its property room. By noon of Saturday barricades divided west from east in Paris, and a frightened Assembly handed over all power to General Eugène Cavaignac while planning its own flight from the city. On the "bloody Sabbath" of the twenty-fifth a half-starved people rose against the leaders who had betrayed them and were mowed down by the columns of Cavaignac, four to five hundred during the battle and another three thousand after it was over. Under a state of siege the more dangerous clubs were closed, the more militant newspapers seized; the government purged itself of its democratic and socialist elements while the middle class was still racked with terror of the "Reds."

Daumier was immune to the Red menace. During the public panic from April to June he published a series of seven caricatures, *Alarmists and Alarmed,* rebuking the solid citizen and his madame who started from their beds with the cry of "fire" when a match was lighted in the street below, trembled with every movement of the stock market, mistook the postman for an officer in search of concealed weapons, and were terrified into nightmares by the wooden swords of children playing soldier. In spite of such warnings as these, it was the fear of anarchy, exploited by demagogues, which would bring down the fragile Republic some three years later under the weight of its own contradictions.

One seems to find contradictions of another sort when Daumier turns from politics to painting. In the former he knows his direction and his method; in the latter he tries to reconcile the claims of sculptural form, which he had learned to see in modulations of white, black and intermediate greys, with those of color. He is an artist in quest of his own style, and external events now fortify his self-confidence. His close friends are up to their necks if not over their heads in the political whirlpool. Decamps as President of the Section of Painting in the newly formed Artists' Association summons him to meetings; Charles Blanc is Director of Fine Arts; Jeanron from his desk in the Hôtel de Ville issues orders for the protection of treasures in the National museums and plans a Salon without a jury to open in March of 1848. Almost as free was the show of 1849 for which the artists themselves picked a jury, and in 1850–51 the policy was still liberal, even though Jeanron had been replaced by a conservative. The sculptor Préault, ignored for more than a decade, now got commissions; Barye, after years of systematic rejection, made a victorious reappearance with *Centaur and Lapith* at the Salon of 1850–51, which also saw Corot's *Dance of the Nymphs* and Courbet's *Funeral at Ornans.* Even Daumier was encouraged by two commissions from the Ministry of the Interior: a letter of

September 19, 1848, addressed to "Citizen Daumier, painter," stipulated a payment of one thousand francs (one hundred and eighty dollars) for a painting to be based on a subject and a preliminary sketch approved by the administration; on February tenth of the next year a similar note came to him through Charles Blanc, this time for a work to receive fifteen hundred francs.

Thus heartened, the artist not only roughed out a *Magdalen in the Desert,* the agreed theme of his official commission, but decided to submit to the Salon jury two other works which he hoped would be acceptable in content and in degree of finish. Whether executed at this moment or somewhat earlier, these two paintings are like nothing else that he did. A hand and an eye long accustomed to the size of a page in *Charivari* had to meet the demands of fourteen square feet of space, with one exception the largest he ever attempted. Both *The Miller, His Son and the Ass,* shown in 1849, and *Two Nymphs Pursued by Satyrs,* hung in the show of 1850–51, confess an indebtedness to Rubens in the liveliness of their movement, the ruddy warmth of their flesh tones and the brilliant red-oranges and green-blues of their flying drapery. In the former (Color plate II) he uses one of his favorite compositional schemes, a group of large foreground figures in contrast with a smaller and more distant one. Out of Rubens' *Family of Lot Departing from Sodom* or Jordaens' *Christ Driving the Money Changers from the Temple,* both in the Louvre, comes the girl who balances a basket of fruit on her head, against a sun-warmed wall. Daumier has painstakingly modeled the luminous flesh of his three country girls with cool lights and warm reflections; their brightly colored garments bring them forward in space, and the figures of the miller and his son exist in the same mellow and pervasive light. The opulence and the bravura of the Flemish master are beyond the plodding Frenchman, but Champfleury in his Salon review of 1849 compliments Daumier for the verve and courage with which he has brought to life these healthy village girls. In the second canvas the plump, half-naked bodies of the two flying nymphs are brilliantly contrasted with the fresh greens of a sunlit meadow. Strong colors are here more successfully related and the sculpturing of full breasts and sturdy legs more artfully managed (Fig. 36).

Another of Daumier's rare ventures into classical myth was a small drawing in chalk and charcoal heightened in gouache, *The Procession of Silenus* (Fig. 37). This too went to the Salon of 1850–51, where the Goncourts admired its "bestial Olympian corpulence." Its general scheme, its flying scarf, its faun and its donkey were no doubt borrowed, as Maison and others have suggested, from an engraving of Rubens' *Triumph of Silenus,* and in its background appears again the girl with a basket of fruit on her head, and at the side a faun rather like the crea-

37. *The Procession of Silenus,* chalk with gouache
Musée des Beaux-Arts, Calais

ture painted by Jordaens in *Jupiter Nursed by the Goat Amalthea.*
Daumier contributed to the same show a work which has not been
surely identified, representing Don Quixote and Sancho Panza on their
way to the wedding feast.

These excursions into fable and myth so carefully executed with one
eye on the public of the Salons had less of the essential Daumier than
two paintings whose turbulence derives from the days of '48 and whose
range of tones is far less brilliant than that of his two Salon pictures.
Neither of them was completed or exhibited during his lifetime, and
one can only place them within this general period on the assumption that the sights and sounds of that spring and summer were still
fresh in his mind when he painted them. *The Uprising* of the Duncan Phillips collection (Fig. 38), which Arsène Alexandre rediscovered in 1924, is a horizontal canvas two feet by nearly four in which a

36. *Nymphs Pursued by Satyrs,* oil. Museum of Fine Arts, Montreal

38. *The Uprising,* oil. Phillips Collection, Washington, D.C.

blond insurgent in shirtsleeves with his right arm and clenched fist flung upward draws the crowd into the forward thrust of his own stride. Daumier had no more relish than Gautier for what the latter called the "bloody archaisms," the terrible savagery of revolutions; what he gives us here is the strength of good men made desperate. The dust and murk of a troubled street are in his muted colors, the heads of the crowd still have the outlines with which he first defined them with no loss of unity in the whole, and the sun of late afternoon strikes down on the fine sensitive head with eyes which see the future and a mouth which could well be chanting, "Bread or Bullets!" In spite of somewhat awkward later touches on head and shoulders which are possibly by another brush, the irresistible force and the compelling emotion of Daumier's vision are all there. In a work of the same title which Daubigny once owned, Daumier made a vertical composition with a similar central figure.

Again in *A Family on the Barricade,* a painting twenty-nine inches

39. Study, *Head of a Man*, oil. National Museum of Wales, Cardiff

wide and three feet high which was first exhibited in 1901 and is now in
the National Gallery of Prague, one noble head dominates the rest with
its bald pate and spare white locks, its deeply lined and workworn face.
Here one must take the intention for the deed, since wiry and insensitive
lines have destroyed the sculptured forms, while Daumier's colors have
been falsely intensified. His intention can better be seen in two versions
of the magnificent central head, one in black chalk and the other in oil;
and K. E. Maison has wisely suggested that the artist planned to rework
or repeat the unfinished Prague canvas and later made the oil study in
preparation for that task (Fig. 39). A small but sensitive oil sketch of
a boy's head is likewise related to a figure in the larger work.

Not revolution but its tragic aftermath was the subject of two bas-
reliefs and several paintings variously entitled *Fugitives* and *Emigrants*
whose dating has perplexed the experts because of marked stylistic differences and because the phenomenon of people uprooted from their
homes was a recurrent one in Daumier's time (Fig. 40). It has been sug-

40. *The Refugees*, bronze relief, National Gallery of Art, Washington, D

gested that the reliefs were modeled in the early 1830s when the Polish
revolution drove many families from Warsaw into Russia and France;
a more likely source of inspiration was the deportation to the French
colonies in 1848 of thousands who were accused of supporting the insur-
rections of May and June and who were permitted by the Government
to take their wives and children with them to Guiana, Lambessa or
Algeria. The tragic defeat of the Hungarians, who had been encouraged
by the February revolution to rise against Austria, was also in his mind,
as he wrote in 1849 to his wife.

Daumier roughly shaped in the clay the nude figures of his defeated
stragglers, perhaps with some help from the plaster casts of details from
Trajan's Column which a visitor once saw in his studio, perhaps also
remembering the frieze-like groups in Decamps' picture of the routed
Cimbri. An impression of huddled misery dominates both sculptures,
some of whose figures stand out boldly while others are merely sug-

gested. The imagery of flight into exile continued to haunt the mind of the artist, and the several paintings on this theme differ too much in conception and execution to be placed within one period. A small study in the Petit-Palais may well be the earliest of the series, his response to the human displacements of 1848 or the still more violent ones which were soon to come (Fig. 41).

That spring and summer of revolution and reaction had seen fewer caricatures by Daumier than the previous years, but in the fall he became a full-time commentator whose lithographs for the next three years were almost wholly political. From November his series of individual portraits, *The Representatives Represented,* appeared at intervals for nearly a year, to be prolonged by a second series in 1850, a parade of ineptitude and skullduggery drawn without malice and without illusions in which he relied on the old and banal device of the big head on a little body. October of 1848 saw the start of another series, *Physiog-*

41. *The Emigrants,* oil. Musée du Petit Palais, Paris. Photo Bulloz

nomy of the Assembly, and a year later came *Parliamentary Idyls,* a sequence of small, slight satires which transformed well-known public figures into sly fauns and fat-bottomed cupids within rococo frames. The caricaturist was far from his best in these routine and tiresome assignments; his crayon required specific situations and urgent issues.

We see him responding to the latter in the four precarious years of the Second Republic with eloquent and incisive images. The aim of the first republican campaign in *Charivari* had been to tear down a régime; the task now was to defend and strengthen a new one. Burlesque exaggeration and graphic horseplay are not congenial to a Daumier just turned forty, and his victims come to the page as diminished and shady creatures whose moral scale is dwarfed by the majestic figure of the Republic who moves in these drawings. Picture and text become more affirmative and more thoughtful, more astute in distinguishing between friend and enemy, more quietly sure of the eventual triumph of a cause. The draftsman must tread lightly at a time when laws are multiplied in order to silence the republican press; now one must post huge sums as security, now "insults" to members of the Assembly are made illegal; now all papers of less than ten pages must bear an official stamp. In this "motley jumble of crying contradictions," as young Karl Marx called it, Daumier works to resolve jumbles and explain contradictions.

At this moment his shrewd foresight and his ability to distinguish the genuine foes of the Republic from artfully contrived bogeys stand in sharp contrast to the political fumbling of his great contemporary

Victor Hugo. The poet's father had been one of Napoleon's generals, his mother a fervent royalist of the Bourbon stripe. While Daumier as a child ran errands in the slums, Hugo knew only the walled garden of the Paris home which had once been a convent. At twenty-two the caricaturist launched his first barbs against the Monarchy and Hugo wrote a poem in praise of Charles the Tenth, followed three years later by an *Ode to the Column* which recalled the glories of Napoleon. Militant republicans looked askance at this enormously gifted, bumptious and egotistical young man whose humanitarian sympathies were vague and whose sense of political realities was by no means clear, who had been made a peer in 1845 and three years later was elected to the Assembly at a moment when the rightist "Party of Order" in that body was intriguing to undo the progress that had been made since February. Because such men as Louis Blanc and Ledru-Rollin stood in his mind for the Republic of Terror, Hugo supported the partisans of order, his dream a generous and peaceful partnership between the extremes of rich and poor. In the crisis of June he spoke of the "misled workingmen," but deplored the bloody reprisals against their leaders; in August he was one of the founders of the newspaper *L'Événement* under the slogan, "Vigorous hatred of anarchy; profound and tender love for the people."

The Second Republic had now acquired a constitution, and the question which tormented both Hugo and Daumier was, who would become its first President? There were bloodstained Cavaignac and the democrat Ledru-Rollin; there was also the possibility of a dark horse. Eight years before a nephew of the great Napoleon with a small clique of fanatics had tried to seize the government of France, a venture which had earned him a cell in the prison of Ham. His followers had moved among the rioting crowds of June, then dropped from sight, and in July *Charivari* wondered what had become of the men who every night had shouted "Poleon!" September saw Louis-Napoleon elected to a seat in the legislature, where he sat in watchful silence while his friends quietly sounded out this or that politician, priest or socialist, reminding the radicals that he had once written sympathetically about the evils of poverty, ignorance and exploitation, and at the same time nursing among liberals the illusion of a reign of liberty guaranteed by a powerful leader. In an interview with Hugo, Prince Louis promised to be another George Washington rather than a repetition of his uncle, and *L'Événement* threw its support to the adventurer:

> France has need of a man who will save her and, not finding him amid the somber tempest of events, clings with a supreme effort to the rock of Saint Helena. A dangerous reef? Or a calm haven?

Daumier's sarcastic comment on this blowsy endorsement was a litho-

42. *Victor Hugo and Émile de Girardin,* lithograph
Museum of Fine Arts, Boston, Mass.

graph in which Hugo and his coeditor Émile de Girardin seek to elevate
Prince Louis, the former averting his face as though doubting his own
wisdom (Fig. 42). In another drawing, *The Napoleonic Steamboat,* the
Prince tries to reach shore in an inverted Napoleonic bonnet towed by
a wet and bedraggled eagle; still another caricature presents the pro-
Napoleonic press as an ugly and decrepit cabal. On the tenth of
December Ledru-Rollin polled half a million votes, Cavaignac a million
and a half, but Louis-Napoleon was elected by five and one half millions.
The steamboat had made port.

   The next three years were for Hugo an intensive and painful education
in those realities of political life which Daumier had understood from

43. *Motto for the Year 1850* (Montalembert), lithograph
Museum of Fine Arts, Boston, Mass.

the beginning. Hopeful that the new executive would build a government of moderation, Hugo saw the royalist Odilon Barrot made chief minister in a coalition of clericals, monarchists, Bonapartists and sheer opportunists which included the ultrareligious Falloux and the banker Faucher. He watched the old standbys of reaction crawl back into the arena. Between a majority united by their hatred of republicanism, a group derisively nicknamed after his own play "the Burgraves," and the minority whose leader was Ledru-Rollin, the poet-turned-statesman stood uncertainly in the middle.

Between the Party of Order and the Party of the Mountain, Daumier never hesitated. The Chamber whose members he paraded in his drawings with and without their clothes was in his mind the last refuge of republicanism, and he lashed the Burgraves day after day, exposing their intrigues and attacking the Catholic extremists whose front they represented in caricatures whose titles indicate their purpose—*Three Little Saints, Re-entry of the Capuchins into Their Dear City of Paris.* He sketched the Comte de Falloux "in his capacity as a friar of the Ignorantine Order," and his many satires of the Comte de Montalembert, the most eloquent orator of the Church party, showed the face and costume which the Goncourts described:

> long, limp gray hair, a full face, the features of an old child, a sleepy smile, deep listless eyes . . . a feminine softness in handclasp, and a clerical dressing gown (Fig. 43).

It was through steady pressure by such men that the Church won her two great victories under the Republic, the Expedition to Rome and the passage of restrictive laws against education, suffrage and the press. Louis-Napoleon by his electoral bargain with the Ultracatholics had made himself their debtor. The time for collecting arrived when late in 1848 a revolution in Rome forced the Pope to take refuge at Gaeta. In February of 1849 a Roman republic was proclaimed and the French ministry decided to rescue Pius the Ninth from his own subjects under the pretext of saving the Italians from domination by the Austrian forces. With some misgivings Hugo and his newspaper persuaded themselves to support the venture, and when Daumier got around to the poet in his series of legislative portraits the troops of Oudinot were besieging Rome. The poet in the lithograph, with his beetling forehead and his look of godlike meditation, "has been asked a grave question and gives himself up to somber reflection." A similar mild scorn is in several plates which show him presiding over a World Peace Conference in Paris during the summer, a wreath of laurel on his head. But when debates on the Roman question resumed in the fall, the true shape of the expedition became clear even to Hugo; the Pope issued a *motu proprio* which proved that he had no intention of yielding any of his temporal powers, and the poet displeased the President by a vigorous speech against the Pontiff and his friends in the Assembly, a tirade which the leftwing press saluted as "magnificent in its verve, its strength and its incisiveness."

After the Expedition to Rome came the Expedition from Rome to the Interior, as the facetious Montalembert called the efforts of himself and his ultraclerical friends to subject French education to their control and to "save" society by drastic restrictions on the spoken and written word. One instrument was the School Bill which the Comte de Falloux had introduced in June, 1849, authorizing the Church to set up denominational colleges beside those of the government, and in effect giving priests control of primary education. In the debate which followed, the oratory of Hugo matched the blistering caricatures of Daumier. Declaring that he wanted religious instruction, but wanted it inside and not outside the churches, Hugo turned on Montalembert and his colleagues:

> I do not want to see everything done by our fathers undone by you. . . . Ah! We know the clerical party. 'Tis she who forbids science and genius to challenge the prayerbook, who builds out of dogma a cloister for human intelligence. Every step toward knowledge that Europe has taken was taken without her and in spite of her. . . . And you ask to be the masters of education! I refuse your law . . . as a disgrace and humiliation to my country.

It was for this or a similar occasion that Daumier made *One Glory Quenches the Other,* which showed Hugo extinguishing Montalembert with a candlesnuffer.

In spite of the poet's eloquence the Falloux Law was passed and the twelve Burgraves moved to build further defenses against "socialism." The one hope of the democrats was in the fact that Frenchmen could still vote, although Daumier's drawing of May twentieth was a warning: the Lilliputians of reaction have bound the huge Gulliver of Universal Suffrage and crawl over his body. When three radicals were elected to the Assembly on March tenth, Hugo's newspaper remarked that this was the blackball which Paris had cast against the Falloux Law, and Daumier published *The Feast of Belshazzar-Véron,* in which the editor of the *Constitutionnel* and his friends recoil in horror from these three names. But the handwriting on the wall was duly heeded by the Burgraves, among them the wily Thiers, who had no use for the "vile multitude." On the last day of May in 1850, a law was passed by which three million men, nearly one third of the electorate, lost their franchise.

In a caricature of June the political moths are shown fluttering around the candle of February, their faces recognizably those of Berryer, Montalembert, Thiers and Molé, their cheeks distended in the effort to blow out the flame. Once more the crayon of Daumier was prophetic, for within a month the Chamber was debating laws whose intent was to destroy the opposition press. Attacked by Hugo in a thunderous oration and by Daumier in a litho which charged Louis-Napoleon and his parricidal accomplice Thiers with responsibility for them, the Press Laws were enacted. Hugo's period of self-deception was over, and there was no place for him to go except to the Mountain: "Open your ranks, I am one of you." While his erstwhile hero went to the country campaigning for a second term which the Constitution forbade and assuring provincial audiences that he would always respect their sovereign will, *L'Événement* flatly announced its complete and final rupture with the President.

Henceforth the sonorous phrases of Hugo would parallel the incisive lines of Daumier. When Michelet was driven from his classroom at the Collège de France in March of 1851, the former congratulated him rather pompously for having been persecuted "for the sacred cause of the French Revolution and of human intelligence." In Daumier's version of that incident a repulsive priest is lecturing to a classroom empty of all auditors except for two sleeping porters. It was rumored that men close to the President were pressing him to seize power by illegal means, but that half-shrewd and half-mystical man was not yet ready, not sure of the provinces, of his ministers, or of an army commanded by Changarnier. His first step was to dismiss the General, his next the formation of a ministry more sympathetic to his plans and more willing to fight his battle in the recalcitrant Assembly. During the spring and summer both Hugo and Daumier concentrated their fire on the right wingers of Catholicism who were now promoting the adventurer's cause. In *Alliance of the Bonapartists and the Capuchins* the one embraces the other with only half-concealed repugnance. On another page, Montalembert with Berryer, Thiers and Molé swear allegiance to reaction in a parody of David's *Horatii*.

The cause of Louis-Napoleon found one of its most militant supporters in the scurrilous editor of *L'Univers Religieux*, who wrote that freedom was a word devoid of meaning in a Christian land and that the common people were a perpetual minor to be governed. Louis Veuillot, who raged against the reading of Ovid, Tacitus, Cicero and Horace in the schools, was described by one of his contemporaries as an ugly small creature with thick and sensual lips and a nose as red as a beet cut by a knife; and thus the pockmarked crusader appeared in Daumier's lithos. The crusade against classic writers was the theme of *Auto-de-fé*, where Montalembert applied a bellows to the pyre of Sophocles and Molière. Another fanatic, Auguste Romieu (Fig. 44), found himself under the caricaturist's pencil when he wrote *The Red Spectre of 1852*, a tract which looked forward to the presidential election:

> The year 1852 is close at hand . . . the masses want blood, wine and pillage . . . there is no woman brought to bed in our day who was not brought to bed by a socialist. . . . When the crisis comes in a few months a great man will establish an absolute dictatorship. . . . After a short and bloody struggle, a strong power will open the new authoritarian era. . . .

To the realization of this prophecy there remained one chief obstacle, a Constitution which made a second term as President illegal. On the fourteenth of July in 1851 the Assembly celebrated a national holiday by opening its debate on the revision of that inconvenient document. Hugo, whose paper had been suppressed and whose brothers had been sent to prison, cried:

44. *Two Future High Dignitaries* (Romieu and Véron), lithograph
Museum of Fine Arts, Boston, Mass.

We have an intrigue to unmask. France must not find herself one
morning in possession of an Emperor without knowing why it happened.

And then he lashed the intriguer himself in a famous antithesis, reminding his listeners of the great Charlemagne and of Napoleon who had
done colossal things and at last dropped his sceptre and his sword:

Now you come along to pick them up and grasp in your small fist the
sceptre of Titans, the sword of giants. And for what purpose? What,
after Augustus, but Augustulus? What now! Because we have had
Napoleon the Great, we must now have Napoleon the Little!

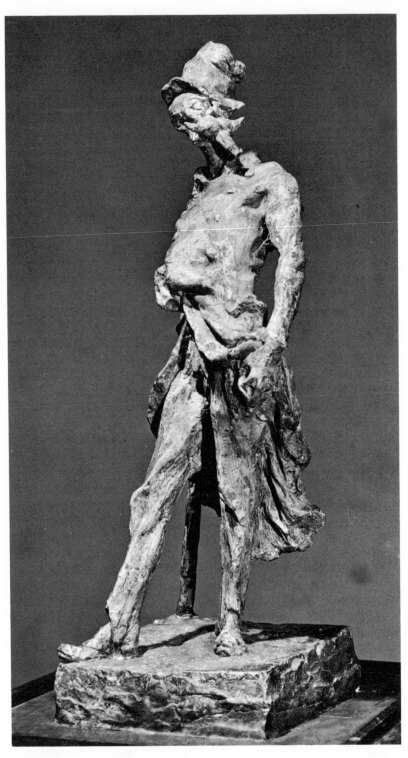

45. Plaster cast of Ratapoil. Albright-Knox Art Gallery, Buffalo, N.Y.

When the vote was counted, the President found that less than the required majority favored re-election. There remained no lawful means to prolong his power, and when the Assembly adjourned for the summer his plans for the seizure of that power went forward.

The Prince could count on Montalembert and on the shrill warnings of Veuillot, but an even more effective instrument for his propaganda among city and country people was the Society of the Tenth of December, a vaguely "benevolent" association recruited among the shiftless and the desperate of Paris, the broken-down remnants of old armies, the ruffians for hire. Out of these elements Daumier created his *Ratapoil*. As he had done twenty years before, he modeled his subject in clay before using the eighteen-inch statuette as a source for lithographs (Fig. 45).

The man's ramshackle body swings insolently on the pivot of a burly club which supports one hip, the movement of the figure both nonchalant and sinister. From boot tips aggressively turned up, through knee-bagged and drooping pantaloons to a shapeless frock coat straining at one button, to his mean eyes, broken nose and bristling moustache and goatee, and the battered top hat aslant his bony, birdlike skull, Ratapoil writhes with evil intention and is falsely debonair. The artist has made him the storm trooper, the vigilante, the bribed thug, the stool pigeon of all time, with a beaked profile to suggest his present meaning by his resemblance to his employer.

This is the creature sent ahead when Louis-Napoleon traveled, to cheer him at railway stations, dispatched to the farms where peasants needed to be convinced, and sent into alleys to club unlucky republicans. Daumier shows him doing all of these things and many others in about forty lithographs. Club in hand, he collects money for the Prince from door to door. To a dullwitted farmer he whispers, "If you love your wife, your fields and your heifer, sign up; you haven't a moment to lose." (Fig. 46). On the parade ground he leads a drunken claque in "Long Live the Emperor!" In a drawing of September, 1851, he offers his arm to the Republic, who spurns it with the remark, "Your affection is too sudden to be convincing."

Her rejoinder needed no explanation, for at that moment the adventurer, always a blend of ruthlessness and caution, made one more gesture toward legality by urging the Assembly to prolong his term of office by changing the Constitution, and to restore universal suffrage. The gesture failed and on the morning of December second, the anniversary of Austerlitz, he wrote RUBICON on the cover of a portfolio which held the blueprint for the coup d'état. Handbills composed in the night by typesetters with a gendarme on either side announced that the Assembly was dissolved and that the people of France, their suffrage restored, would be asked to vote on a new constitution. Members of Parliament were rudely bundled into cabs, Thiers arrested in his nightgown on a conspiracy charge and hustled off to jail; every strategic post, newspaper office and public building was occupied by troops, while Hugo and his friends, hounded by the police from one refuge to another, made and unmade plans behind drawn shutters, their sentries posted at streetcorners. On the third, a day of dodging and of divided counsels, one could hear an occasional cry, "To Arms!" and "Long Live the Republic!" Resistance began on the grey and drizzling fourth when around the Porte Saint-Denis barricades were made from carriages, boulevard settees and iron sidewalk railings; but it had been decreed that all public gatherings would be dispersed by force and without warning. Out of nowhere Napoleon's troops took up positions facing the crowd, and Colonel Rochefort's lancers sabered their way among café chairs and tables, while volleys from the infantry made the gutters of the most fashionable boulevard in Paris run with blood.

On the night of December second the harassed Hugo met the man he had once called a wretched shyster, the philosopher Proudhon. The latter had managed to get himself temporarily released from prison to join his cronies, declaring, "I belong to the Revolution"; but his difficulty was that of the poet—an inability to find the revolution. Leaning on the parapet of a canal so near the place de la Bastille that they could see the flash of bayonets, they argued for the last time. Proudhon had come to warn Hugo:

> You're fooling yourself, the people won't budge. This idiotic restoration of universal suffrage has tricked the simple-minded. Bonaparte will succeed and you will fail. On his side he has force, guns, the delusion of the people and the stupidities of the legislature. . . . You are honest, and he has the advantage of being a rascal. . . . Stop your resistance, believe me. . . . We must wait. . . . What do you hope to accomplish?
> Nothing.
> And what are you planning to do?
> Everything.

There was nothing more to be said. The prisoner went back to his cell and the poet prepared to escape across the frontier in the disguise of a laborer.

Both men told the story of December Second in pages written after the event. Proudhon's long essay, *The Social Revolution as Demonstrated by the Coup d'État,* composed during the last weeks of his prison term, was no more calculated to please the republicans than was his previous expression of contempt for all collective action. The masses, he now wrote, were incapable of understanding social and political questions and were thus impelled to support a one-man power; meanwhile

46. *Ratapoil Making Propaganda,* lithograph
Museum of Fine Arts, Boston, Mass.

the politicians spent their strength in reforms, rivalries and compromises, dropping apart one after another until victory could be seized by the biggest scoundrel, a man without virtue and without shame. For Proudhon the only true revolution was economic and social, a transformation of society which he believed to be inevitable and irresistible. Louis-Napoleon had been chosen by history for this task and would either accomplish or deny his fated mission; "either anarchy or Caesarism." Not without some twinges of conscience this dealer in paradoxes urged his friends among the republicans to support Napoleon and thus force him to become the instrument of their program.

While Proudhon was thus conferring a kind of historical legitimacy

on the seizure of power and summoning the people of France to expiate
their follies, Hugo sat down in Brussels to sketch the chapters of his
History of a Crime and *Napoleon the Little,* the latter nearly completed in sixteen days. He too had learned how easily people could be
seduced into betraying their own cause, but his chief purpose was to
crucify Louis-Napoleon and his accomplices—the lackey Rouher, the
valet Troplong, the eunuch Baroche. On the second of December, he
wrote,

> This man grasped by the throat the Constitution, the Republic, the
> Law, and France; he stabbed the future in the back and trampled
> under his feet justice, intelligence, rights, reason and liberty. . . .
> Treason lifted her shameless skirt and one saw the nakedness of a
> soiled and sick spirit.

This bastard of Machiavelli lies as other men breathe, and his crime is
"a closed and silent shroud with streams of blood seeping from it"; but
he is still Napoleon the Little, the dimensions of whose crime have not
changed his own stature. He may hold France, hence the whole world,
but now,

> one man who wanders, a despoiled and ruined exile, rises to attack
> him. Two powers stand beside the vagabond without a passport,—
> Right which is invincible, and Truth which is immortal. . . . Ah,
> Frenchmen! Regard this slime-covered pig as he wallows in a lion's
> skin!

In four years of graphic effort Daumier had exposed the crime while
it was in the making. He never believed, as did the jailed anarchist, that
Louis-Napoleon could be the evil tool of a good purpose; and while
Proudhon reviled a corruptible electorate, the artist aimed his attack
at those who would corrupt it. If he read a smuggled copy of *Napoleon
the Little,* he must have sympathized with the honest wrath of an outraged humanitarian; but he could also have observed that the very
extravagance of the exiled poet's abuse magnified its object, and he
might have suspected that injured vanity was somewhere between the
lines, and some of their heat generated by hero-worship in reverse. For
Daumier the man of December Second was neither a puppet of fate nor
a colossal villain. It was the intrigue and not the intriguer for whom he
had found a symbol in the shoddy Ratapoil. Just as important to him
were the makers of the coming Empire who set the stage, whispered his
lines to the principal performer, and soon would split the financial,
political, social and religious profits of a drama which would run for
nearly twenty years.

For most of those years Daumier would be forced by censorship to be
a silent spectator, a terrible test of endurance for him, as his editor

recalled. Across the desert which the Emperor called peace, the heartening voice of Michelet came to him a few months after the coup d'état. The historian had seen the clay Ratapoil in a corner of his friend's studio and had cried, "Behold the Napoleonic idea forever pilloried!" Now he asked,

> When shall we see each other again through the rubbish and ruins of this hovel that has been thrown together under the very nose of France? . . . What consolation for us both to believe that my country is unconquerable . . . even when the spirit of the people seems morally eclipsed! Be sure you keep this marvellous youthfulness, this lively humor which proves your strength. For both of us, those are the promise and token of resurrection. Every time I see your drawings, no matter how gloomy I may be, I find myself humming the old song, "Poland Is Not Yet Dead."

5: THE HUMAN COMEDY, ACT TWO

Two weeks after the coup d'état the Presidency of Louis-Napoleon was endorsed by seven and a half million voters, and Hugo taunted the victorious gambler: "You have counted too many ballots and too few corpses." For the ambitious bourgeois this new régime would offer spectacular opportunities for self-enrichment in the building of railways, roads and harbors, the multiplication of banks and credit, the expansion of transatlantic shipping and of the postal and telegraphic systems; for the lower orders there were assurances of employment, of the arbitration of disputes and sometimes of mutual assistance. At Bordeaux in September, 1852, Napoleon promised his audience that "the Empire means peace"; after a performance of *Cinna* at the Théâtre-Français in October the great Rachel appeared as the Muse of History in a star-spangled peplum with a corsage of olive branches, to declaim flattering verses in the mode of Pindar. "The eagle has resumed his flight," she intoned, and next morning received a ten-thousand franc bracelet from the Man of Peace. Shortly after this flamboyant curtain raiser the Senate obligingly decreed the Empire and eight million voters confirmed it.

Even in these months of transition Daumier and his friends saw their country becoming a political desert swept bare of all effective opposition. Presidential decrees dissolved the workmen's association and the National Guard, packed the courts with sympathetic judges and made the University a hireling of the government, while the police rounded up some twenty-six thousand democrats and republicans to be tried by special commissions or hounded into exile. After a few days in jail Thiers resumed his private life to complete a history of the Consulate and the first Empire while he waited in the wings for his cue to rejoin the cast. The decrees of February, 1852, assured the conformity of the press for years to come by requiring advance permission for the printing of any text or picture and by inventing a new device, the *avertissement*, a warning issued by the Ministry as a prelude to the suppression of a newspaper without resort to the courts.

Thus silenced, the Left could only watch the makers of an Empire raise the "hovel" of which Michelet had spoken. Louis-Napoleon's half-brother the Duc de Morny, an elegant roué, served for a time as Minister of the Interior and was replaced by Persigny, an honest servitor whose devotion to the House of Bonaparte was absolute; Saint-Arnaud became the Minister of War and Maupas Superintendent of Police, both of them duly rewarded for their part in the Second of December;

Baroche, whom his employer called a lawyer without convictions, presided over the Council of State; the banker Fould was made Minister of Finance; Comte de Nieuwerkerke, who loathed Millet and Courbet, was head of the Department of Fine Arts. The edifice was halfheartedly supported by the royalist factions while they nursed their dreams of a restoration. Even the followers of Saint-Simon were sympathetic, and Père Enfantin cried, "Where gunpowder once roared, let naught be heard but the ring of hammer on anvil!" Among the Catholic leaders loyalty ranged from lukewarm to fervent: on the eve of the plebiscite Montalembert warned that a vote against Louis-Napoleon was a vote for the socialist revolution, but his tone was sarcastic when he observed the President's effort to please the military with banquets, new uniforms, parades and decorations, and concluded that the régime needed the support of "the guardroom and the sacristy." More enthusiastic, at least for the moment, were Romieu and Veuillot: the former became Inspector General of the Royal Libraries, perhaps as a reward for his *Red Spectre,* and the latter annoyed even his coreligionists by a virulence which earned him the title, John the Baptist of the Gutter.

Every society has its Samuel Pepys, and this one had the dyspeptic monarchist Comte Horace de Viel-Castel to collect its scandals and venalities for his diary. The Count detested the bourgeois, compared the revolutionists of 1848 to Huns and Vandals, and sneered at the "new peerage" of the press, bought by the Emperor to endorse his leadership. In Renan the diarist he saw a crusader against the immortality of the soul, in Béranger a singer of sedition; when Rachel died, he noted "a great talent, but the most arrant whore on earth."

Less rancorous comments of the time reveal the artists and the writers uncomfortable in this heady but stifling atmosphere. In a soirée at the house of Prince Jerome, Delacroix recoils from the mixed company of royalists and republicans, "the whole lot of them squeezing in together and rubbing shoulders." The poet Alfred de Vigny is seen at Compiègne, swelling with pride that he has been invited. The fastidious Goncourt brothers move with their usual delicacy along the fringes of the new society, while the colleagues of Sainte-Beuve, noting his friendship with the Princess Mathilde, set him down as an imperial lackey. The powers have forgiven Gautier for the immorality of his *Maupin* in order to attach his star to their constellation. He must now turn out reviews and articles, but confides to his friends that this patronage has its price; a certain person of importance hopes, for example, that the critic will write favorably about the debut of Mademoiselle X, since otherwise his pension will be dropped. And when Banville publishes his *Funambulesque Odes* in 1857 he defends their extravagant style and explains that they are verbal caricatures no more to be resented than Daumier's

exaggerated versions of Thiers and Montalembert. Many a prop of the
Empire could recognize himself in the odes, but the government reluc-
tantly allowed them to achieve a second edition.

In this climate *Charivari* quickly learned that it must adapt or perish.
After a brief suppression it appeared in a larger format and under a
changed management, with more space given to reviews of plays, literary
satire and gossip of the town. The audacious Philipon had departed to
start other ventures, and among the editors were the writer of barbed
essays, Clément Caraguel, and Arnould Frémy, a specialist in abuse-by-
implication. Several of the draftsmen who had fought the first republican
battle had died or gone elsewhere, to be replaced by younger men, of
whom the most promising was Cham.

One must tread more cautiously now and attack by indirection. The
anticlerical Daumier was allowed only two occasions during the first
years of the new order for comment of this kind. When the Bishop of
Paris briefly suppressed *L'Univers Religieux* in 1852 a drawing represented its abusive editor Veuillot being slapped by the official ferule; in
The Triumph of Paganism this foe of the classic authors is being taunted
by his victims in a nightmare. Milder in tone were the few references
by Daumier to the military ventures which soon gave the lie to the
word "peace" in the Bordeaux oration. In the spring of 1853 Greece
and Turkey were contending for the control of the Holy Places and the
French Emperor struck up an alliance with England whose aim was
variously explained as a gesture to sustain French honor, a means of
preserving the balance of powers, and a move against the growing
strength of the "Colossus of the North," as Napoleon called the land of
Czar Nicholas. When the Russians were finally defeated in the fall of
1855 the Emperor could congratulate himself on the prestige he had
gained among the quarreling nations of Europe, while his subjects could
mourn their twenty thousand compatriots killed in battle. Early in the
affair *Charivari* submitted a Daumier drawing in which the National
Assembly is blowing up a balloon-colossus to scare the people of Paris,
but its publication was forbidden. During the siege of Sebastopol, which
lasted nearly a year, the government needed to work up anti-Russian
feeling at home, and an album, *Cossacks to Laugh At,* was issued, to
which Daumier contributed nineteen caricatures in which comic-opera
moujiks ate candles and were driven into battle under the whips of their
commanders. A second album also contained work by Daumier. In
1855 the censors passed a few satires against the King of Naples, and
four years later the Emperor welcomed a pictorial attack on the Aus-
trians at a moment when he was posing as the champion of the Italian
Republic.

With these exceptions the more than nine hundred lithographs which

Daumier made for *Charivari* in the decade of the 1850s are a satire of society, a sequel to those of the July Monarchy. They are the second act of his Human Comedy, played in a changed setting by a new cast of characters. One must think of him now as both draftsman and painter. The unfinished canvases are stacked against his studio walls, and no painting is sent to the Salon in these years by a man who must still give most of his hours to the stones which are the source of his small income. In the best of these he can suggest the quickened, nervous tempo of life in the Second Empire, its showier dress and manners. One of his problems is to adapt himself to the thin and unresponsive paper on which his work is reproduced and the hasty printing which sometimes turns the richness of his tones into leprous greys and sooty blacks. The originals are sometimes drawn on thin paper and thence transferred to the stone, and in 1851 a method is patented by Firmin Gillot by which the sketch is applied to a sheet of zinc to be engraved in relief, a process during which the finesse of the artist tends to be lost.

Under these circumstances Daumier can sometimes achieve the richness of his former manner, as he does in a superb study of three old women gossiping by candlelight, but he can also suggest a powerful light which blots out details by brilliant simplifications and an adroit use of the untouched paper in his drawings of amateur dramatics or in the figure of a lightly pirouetting ballerina glimpsed from the wings. His pictorial shorthand is thus an adaptation to technical change but at the same time the expression of his maturing power to say more with less.

While Daumier in his lithographs opened wider spaces to the play of light and air, a like transformation was taking place around him. When the Emperor called Baron Haussmann to the Prefecture of the Seine in 1853 he had already drawn red lines across a map of the city to devise a master plan for a new Paris. In the ancient city too many quarters were picturesque but unhealthy, too many twisting streets were an invitation to barricades. Great expositions, flashing parades, gala performances and the flood of tourists and titled visitors pouring from railway station to luxurious hotel, demanded freedom of circulation. The reconstruction which Napoleon had in mind would give the glitter and pomp of his régime an appropriate setting and invite the upper classes to a banquet of speculation, the lower to the rewards of pick and shovel.

When the Baron took command of the operation Zola remarked that old Paris was having her veins gashed to nourish a hundred thousand demolishers and masons, as the implacably straight new boulevards cut across the network of ancient thoroughfares in a clatter of steel hammers, a rumble of falling walls, a parade of moving vans and a scurrying for new shelters which lasted for fifteen years. Two mighty channels divided the town into four quarters; in the old heart of Paris, Notre

Dame was cleared of its medieval incrustations; bridges were rebuilt to follow the new axis and old squares were broadened to become the meeting place of many radiating avenues which bore the names of Imperial victories. From the place de la Concorde the capital leapt toward Passy to provide a home for Second Empire society in the Champs-Élysées; fifteen hundred mines were exploded at the same moment to celebrate the birthday of the Prince Imperial and to level the Hill of Chaillot. The parks of England had pleased Napoleon, and his Prefect provided them at the four points of the compass, complete with artificial cascades, riding and carriage paths, outdoor restaurants, zoos and botanical gardens. When Guizot remarked that the Emperor tore down like Genghis Khan and built like Aladdin, he must have been thinking of the endless uniform façades of vaguely Renaissance aspect whose rooms were brilliant with red velvet, white marble stairways, immense mirrors, and gaslit globes upheld by nymphs of gilt bronze; or of the new Opéra which was like the coloratura of Patti fixed in stone; of huge stores upholstered in straw-colored satin and the more venture-some fabrics of iron and glass which housed the markets and railway terminals.

Parisians counted the cost of this transformation in cash and in senti-ment. The miles of new streets and sewers, the vastly increased supply of water, the levelling of nearly thirty thousand dwellings to be replaced by over one hundred thousand new ones, swelled Haussmann's accounts to scandalous proportions. Hugo condemned the vandalism which con-jured away the ancient setting of his *Notre Dame of Paris* and the Gon-courts felt like strangers on boulevards which drove straight toward the horizon without a redeeming hump or hill. In a lighter vein Banville assured the readers of *Charivari* that it was his destiny to eat plaster as he walked in the midst of destruction, and calculated that he would soon have digested a block of five-story houses. As Champfleury strolled through these clouds of dust a wall suddenly fell and he saw the imita-tion marble fireplace and the pink flowered wallpaper of a room where he and his girl had once kept house. The grimy streaks where smoke had once gone up chimneys were not so dismal, he wrote, as the streaks of disillusioned memory in his heart.

In a similar mood Daumier represented an old couple gazing at a house which no longer had façade or floors: "Behold our nuptial cham-ber, Adelaide." (Fig. 47). The artist knew that there was strategy be-hind the substitution of macadam for the paving stones which so often had been the weapons of insurrection, but confined himself to showing the Parisians mired in the sticky surface. He knew, as Zola demonstrated in *The Quarry,* that men with advance information of Haussmann's plan could buy up properties which they then sold to the State for fantastic

47. *Behold Our Nuptial Chamber,* lithograph
Museum of Fine Arts, Boston, Mass.

prices, but there was no hint of this in the thirty or forty drawings by
Daumier on the Haussmannization of Paris. Instead, a householder joyously discovers that he has acquired a view and a few rays of sunshine
on his flowerpots; a citizen returns from his vacation to find an empty
lot where his home once stood; dislodged people sleep in barrels, in
kiosques, in doghouses and in the trees of the Champs-Élysées, while
landlords reject children either born or about to be born; a terrified
couple start from their beds when a workman looms outside their window with the grim warning that their turn has come. When the city
breaks down its old customs barriers to swallow the small suburban
villages a farmer exults, "To think that we're Parisians now!" A pom-

48. *Dr. Véron at Auteuil*, lithograph
Museum of Fine Arts, Boston, Mass.

pous father explains to his small boy that the walls of prejudice have
gone down before philosophy and reason, and the child asks, "Why are
they building them up again a little farther beyond?"

Within this transformed environment the society whose human mutations had been so richly set forth by Balzac was acquiring new types,
new fashions, new modes of behavior to be probed and dissected by
Zola with a scientific thoroughness which reminded one of his readers
that the novelist's father had been an engineer. The author of the
Human Comedy had died two years before the coming of the Second
Empire, and as the Rougon-Macquart series of Zola grew to twenty
volumes its creator claimed that in the history of a single family would

be revealed the comprehensive portrait of the Empire in four neatly listed categories—high society, the world of business, the life of the bourgeois, and that of the laboring classes. Balzac's Crevel had built an unstable fortune on a fake cure for bronchitis; the Aristide Rougon of Zola develops the plot by spectacular gambling in real estate and raises an Aladdin palace in the Parc Monceau. The shop owner of the *Reine des Roses* would not have recognized *Le Bonheur des Dames,* where everything is sold. The priests of Balzac reappear, but they are more deviously dishonest, more deeply mired in politics; the Abbé Fanjas is Tartuffe by gaslight. The bourgeois is no longer a contented mediocrity but a man with a mania for speculation who, if he succeeds, will become His Excellency Eugène Rougon, will tighten his grip on politics and set the style in clothes, houses and extravagant recreation, as he sets the flimsy moral standards of his time. At the very base of society the miners and peasants, the railwaymen, metal workers and dressmakers take a place in Zola's novels proportionate to their growing importance in the scheme of things. In contrast to the urban workman who now challenges the basic principles of society and learns the power of collective action stand the peasants of Zola, stubbornly defending their acres from "progress" as defined by factory owners and jugglers in real estate; they are creatures of savage independence whom one observer likened to the ground-fish who live at the bottom of the sea and are seldom aware of its storms.

Less painstakingly comprehensive and more tolerantly humorous was Daumier's picture of the Second Empire. Zola, writing after the event in a period when authors were relatively free, could document his study of rascality down to the last detail; in the 1850s the caricaturist could seldom touch this theme, and then only in the fictional personage of Robert-Macaire. Once in 1850 and again four years later he placed that scoundrel and his companion Bertrand as statues on the pedestals of the Bourse in a drawing which may have provided Hugo with an image for his *Chastisements:*

Here is a new god mounting to the pediment of the temple . . .
There shines resplendent, motionless in the eternal sky,
On you, O pantheons, on you, O propylaea,
Robert Macaire with his down-at-heel boots.

Another embodiment of shameless ambition, this one a living person, could still be used as a symbol during the short years of the Republic. Louis Véron had already been lampooned as the profiteer in a quack remedy when Daumier returned to him in 1848. The gross doctor, his face half hidden between the wings of his cravat, had long since become the butt of the boulevard wits, who recounted his purchase of Rachel, christened him the proconsul of the Opéra, and described the banquets where his liveried servants bore in a naked ballerina on a silver platter garnished with watercress and parsley. Now he owned the *Constitutionnel* and would use its columns to support Louis-Napoleon, provoking a flood of pictorial abuse from *Charivari*. In the first of thirty-three caricatures by Daumier he was Saint Anthony, cowering in a monk's robe in the wilds of Montmartre as the temptations plague him—gourmandizing cherubs bearing champagne, compliant actresses, and Thiers with a devil's tail. In subsequent transformations his terrier's snout and protuberant belly were always recognizable: Véron as Saint Sebastian, as Clytemnestra, as Crispin, Almaviva, Oedipus and Hercules; Véron retiring into his cravat when his political fortunes decline; Véron as an Arcadian shepherd in the glades of Auteuil, serenading a puppy with his clarinet, an allusion to the editor's campaign against mad dogs (Fig. 48); Véron as a disconsolate and horribly naked Silenus. In his memoirs the Doctor boasted that he was the first to laugh at the lithos showered upon him at this time: "I even hung the drawings, which were sometimes witty, on the wall of my salon." The fact remains that, when he got himself elected as deputy in 1852, the shower stopped.

When Daumier turned to the more general field of social satire it was evident that the giddy world in which the Rougon family moved would not have interested him even if he had known it firsthand, a world where landaus rolled over the sleek new boulevards, arches of triumph sprang up overnight to greet visiting royalty, open-air balls exploded in fireworks and the waltz contended with the frenetic cancan. He could not have relished the feminization of Paris, from the sculptured nymphs of Carpeaux on the Louvre to the ones that Baudry painted on the ceiling of the Opéra. Like Frederick Thomas Graindorge, a fictional pork merchant from Cincinnati invented by Taine, he would have been dazzled but also shocked by the five hundred lights in the chandelier at the Théâtre des Italiens, the provocative half-nudity of the ballet and the soiled insolence of the overdressed boxholders who paid no attention to the performance. From the opposite end of the social scale came the sturdy folk, the burdened washerwomen and the tired passengers in the third class carriages, with whom he most deeply sympathized; but these were more often subjects for his drawings and paintings than for his lithographs. Once more, as in the days of Louis-Philippe, he devoted himself mainly to the bourgeois comedy of manners, to the individual and group behavior of the class he most intimately knew.

Daumier's last lithograph of Véron was published on the third of August, 1853; less than four weeks later the artist was provided with a safer model in the fictional person of Joseph Prudhomme. That worthy citizen had been created by Henry Monnier, a draftsman who could also

49. *Henry Monnier in the Role of Prudhomme,* lithograph
Museum of Fine Arts, Boston, Mass.

act and write. Monnier had eaten more ill-cooked dinners and listened
to more deadly conversation in the soirées of the Chaussée-d'Antin than
he cared to remember, and Prudhomme was his revenge, a character
pieced together bit by bit in the monologues and drawings with which
he amused his friends. When he wrote and performed the farce *The
Improvised Family,* Prudhomme became a national figure of bourgeois
self-inflation with his awkward swagger, his bulging spectacled eyes, a

50. *I Want to Leave a Monument*, lithograph
Museum of Fine Arts, Boston, Mass.

Punchlike profile which reminded some people of Thiers, a collar with
gigantic wings, and a few hairs bristling from the summit of the edifice,
as Gautier said, like brambles or parasitic plants. A second comedy of
1852, *Grandeur and Decadence of Monsieur Prudhomme*, drew this comment from the poet-critic:

> Is he happy! Is he radiant, as he lets fall from his thick lips these
> cast-iron aphorisms! . . . What a magnificent imbecile. . . . Never
> before has human stupidity so richly burst into flower. . . .

Prudhomme was henceforth common property and his extravagantly
mixed metaphors were quoted everywhere: "Gentlemen, this sword is
the fairest day of my life! . . . The horizon darkens and the chariot
of State navigates above a volcano." Champfleury invented a dialogue
in which Joseph at the Salon refuses to buy a catalogue, since Roman

history, Greek history and mythology have no secrets from him. Among all the young painters, he observes, the greater number will not survive another year: "Painting undermines the health, you know; it's the smell of the varnish; the stomach quickly falls to pieces." Less than a month after the première of the second play Daumier presents him in full declamatory flight over the footlights of the Odéon in the first of some fifty caricatures which will keep him alive in *Charivari* for the next eighteen years (Fig. 49).

The Prudhomme of these lithographs is less hilariously funny than Monnier's embodiment. The pressures of the time are working on him— the cult of money, the veneration for official honors, the need to be seen in the best drawing rooms of the new bourgeois aristocracy, the pursuit of cultural sophistication—but some of the older virtues persist in him too—the solid complacency, the uxorial benevolence, the National Guard's patriotism, the self-protecting prudery. He is a creature of contradiction as he struts from the July Monarchy into the giddier atmosphere of the Empire, never quite comfortable in this new world but never without a sententious comment (Fig. 50). In one drawing he promenades his paunch in a hideously striped bathing suit while he avers that it is dignity alone that distinguishes man from the animals. At the Exposition he goggles at a twenty-nine-horsepower turnspit; he solemnly inspects a vapid moonlight scene on the easel of an artist, pronouncing it a picture which one could show to the ladies. In 1856 he ruefully compares his bulk with that of a prize hog at an animal fair; in 1857 he carries a lantern in the daytime because the newspapers have predicted an eclipse of the sun. From the hillside above Paris a few years later he points out to his son the Temple of Peace, only to be reminded by the youngster that the Military School stands beside it. Before the pyramids of Egypt the tourist Prudhomme ("improving" on Napoleon) declaims to his Madame, "From thence, forty centuries and three-quarters look down upon us!" Daumier is sharply satirical when Prudhomme teaches his child to pray before the gods of money; but for the most part the tone of these drawings is mildly humorous—Joseph caught in a turnstile at the Exposition, or refreshing his sun-parched vegetables with sprays of Seltzer water.

That light touch is in the series of *Aquatic Sketches, Summertime Sketches,* and *Emotions of the Hunt,* where a masterly draftsman resumes topics which he had developed many years before, sometimes in a more incisive manner and sometimes with a hint of bored exhaustion. Most of his bathers disport themselves in the public bathhouse, but their ignoble anatomies are more brilliantly summarized than in the 1830s; in other scenes he moves them from the banks of the Seine to the seashore, perhaps recalling his own trip to the watering places of Nor-

51. *Ladies of the Demi-Monde,* lithograph
Museum of Fine Arts, Boston, Mass.

mandy. The timorous creatures of his earlier hunting scenes now proceed to fall into swamps, shoot their companions and get treed by pigs. His sun-blistered couples wander among dusty clumps of trees where once dense forests had been. In *Drinking Paris* he runs the gamut of thirst from absinthe to the plain horse trough. The townsman of the 1850s has more leisure than his counterpart of the 30s, and Daumier shows him in search of fresh diversions, recording his efforts as an amateur actor in one series, while in another he and his neighbors play excruciating quartets and his six-year-old prodigy torments his guests with a sonata. Each year the Empire saw Frenchmen in the grip of a new fad, a fresh sensation, and Daumier's crayon noted them all: the crusade of Véron against the mad dogs of Paris; the mania for summoning up the spirits of the dead to tip tables; the "potichomania" of the collectors of old chinaware; the suddenly fashionable crinoline skirts which, on the caricaturist's page, sweep pedestrians from the sidewalks, mow down the flowering borders of gardens and choke omnibuses. Sometimes these airy structures behave disastrously as balloons. Under these hoops the naïve pullet lays eggs, and on their domed surfaces pile snowdrifts (Fig. 51).

The talk in 1856 is of the photographer Nadar and his journey over the capital in a balloon. This many-sided friend of Daumier whose real name was Félix Tournachon was the first to make views of the city from above, and one of the best lithos of the period shows Nadar "elevating photography to the height of art." (Fig. 52). On one of these flights the host provided his thirteen passengers with a stock of food but no means

52. *Nadar Elevating Photography,* lithograph
Museum of Fine Arts, Boston, Mass.

of cooking it, and the messages addressed in seven languages proved useless when he came down twenty-seven miles from his point of departure. In 1857 everyone was waiting for a comet which never appeared and for which, in a Daumier series, Prudhomme and his wife prepared themselves by sitting neck-deep in the Seine to avoid being electrocuted.

These enthusiasms were of short duration. What more deeply interested Daumier were situations which brought people together—an audience at a play or a huddled row of railway passengers. Here was a challenge to his powers of composition and his skill in suggesting both collective states of mind and the variations of individual character within them. No situation more consistently appealed to him, for example, than people looking at pictures, a theme to which he returned year after year not only in his lithographs but in drawings, water colors and oils, as though he found its possibilities inexhaustible. In his caricatures the patrons of art are the unlettered Philistines plodding among the forests of paintings and guiding their children away from sculptured nudities; in his more seriously considered works the print, the canvas or the statue becomes the focus of contemplation for true connoisseurs.

In satires of the late 1840s Daumier had revealed his knowledge of artists at work, his sympathy with their ambitions and disappointments; a decade later he may have been thinking of his own commission when he sketched a painter whose *Resurrection* had been refused by a jury. For the most part, however, it was the tribulations of the gallery goer, not of the artist, which he celebrated in *The Public at the Salon* in 1852, and subsequently in scenes of the Exposition of 1855 and the Salons of 1857 and 1859 (Fig. 53).

The page of *Charivari* seems too small to contain these jostled, sweating and footsore visitors who are driven by the sight of so much naked marble to take refuge in the beer gardens outside, who thrust and shove to get closer to a Meissonier and leave empty space before a Courbet. Here one artist examines the work of a rival with his nose; here one sententious citizen murmurs that the color is a little *flon* while his companion ventures that the drawing is perhaps a little *flic-flac*. When Baudelaire reviewed the show of 1859 he called it a triumph of mediocrity—"so many successfully completed platitudes, so much carefully labored drivel." And Daumier made clear that, as between pictures and people, the mediocrity was mutual. One seems to see Joseph Prudhomme striking a pose of critical infallibility, and hear his comment on a painting of hills and forests, "Without the art of perspective, no landscape," or his declaration that no art was possible without the nude model, "It's a necessary evil." Daumier represents Joseph contemplating his own portrait bust in which the sculptor has turned him into a

53. *Even So, It Is Flattering,* lithograph
Museum of Fine Arts, Boston, Mass.

noble Roman but, to the disappointment of the sitter, has failed to include his spectacles and the high wings of his collar.

Another theme on which the artist played endless variations was the
railway. In the 1840s when this mode of travel was still a rather terrifying novelty, he had found material for a whole series of misadventures
of its patrons; now some fifty more drawings in *Charivari* and in *Le
Journal Amusant* explored every droll and extravagant aspect of the
subject. The urbanite is drenched by showers on the open top of an
excursion train or is carried stiff as a log from his freezing compartment;
all the gradations of discomfort from the soft upholstery of first class
to the wooden benches·of third are amusingly set forth (Fig. 54). But

54. *The Charms of Railway Travel*, lithograph
Museum of Fine Arts, Boston, Mass.

these small figures with enlarged heads are the staple device of conventional caricature in this labored catalogue of the thousand and one torments of travel-for-pleasure, and one senses that Daumier is here exploring the fringes of a subject to be set forth in his oils and water colors with more power and penetration. One of his lithographs represents a crowded omnibus, a pictorial scheme which is similar to that of a water color done some ten years later and reproduced as a woodcut; and a litho of 1855 shows a row of people facing the spectator from the depths of a railway carriage, a situation which will be the essential theme of some of his finest paintings.

Although much of Daumier's space was occupied by the salon-crawler and the harassed excursionist, nothing more fascinated him now as in previous years than the world of plays, actors and audiences. His lithographs and wood engravings between 1851 and 1864 reveal an intimate knowledge of this world—another series of *Tragical Physiognomies,* three sequences with the title of *Dramatic Sketches*, and many single drawings. He knew that, as the tone and tempo of society changed with the coming of the Empire, the playhouse and its audiences changed. At a time when Persigny as Minister of the Interior could dictate what was to be performed or not performed on the stages of Paris, ambitious playwrights had to develop a humor which was both impertinent and cynical, but always light on its feet. Persigny's letter to the Director of the Théâtre-Français was a warning to avoid controversial drama: for a long time, he wrote, the theater had shown the rich and poor in plays designed to prove that the latter had all the virtues and that the former was capable of every crime; "the stage should improve morals by showing what is beautiful, and not demoralize people by dramatising discord." As for the critics, the more astute ones kept their jobs by praising the mistresses of important politicians, and Gautier writhed under the necessity of inventing compliments for "old sluts and strumpets." As the middle class grew more prosperous the presentation of its character in the theater became more brittle and its dominant themes were money and women.

In this atmosphere the measured tirades of Racine and Corneille at the Théâtre-Français lost their appeal to the younger generation, and the patrons who appear in Daumier's drawings are elderly and old-fashioned citizens. One such person stands at the rear of the theater with arms folded and listens with a kind of ferocious concentration to an actor in classical dress, "a Parisian who has stayed faithful to the cult of tragedy"; in another litho a stout housewife prods her sleeping husband with "Wake up. Let's go, Oedipus is finished." The Director of this playhouse recalled that he had often seen Daumier there. Perhaps the caricaturist was refreshing his memory for the ten lithographs in which he once more exposed the heroes and heroines of *Andromaque* and *Athalie* to the merciless glare of footlights. Looking about him at the empty house he once observed that this vacancy was due to a vacancy on the stage, the absence of Frédérick-Lemaître; and he called attention in two drawings to the fact that after Rachel's death there was a dearth of tragedy queens. In one of these a noble Roman who has obviously stepped from the boards of the Théâtre-Français strides in search of a partner among the small playhouses of the Boulevard of Crime.

In 1852 the Comédie made one more effort to revive the ancients with a new three-act tragedy by Ponsard. The success of his *Lucretia* had earned its author the flattery of the upper-class salons, a knighthood in the Legion of Honor and the possibility of an election to the Academy. *Ulysses,* a thin sequence of episodes in dry, pretentious verse with choruses set to music by Gounod and conducted by Jacques Offenbach, had only twenty-six performances; *Charivari,* which had no liking for this self-proclaimed republican who accepted official positions in the Empire and a few years later would write charades for Napoleon's parties, issued a parody by Louis Huart, *Ulysses, or The Pigs Avenged,* with ten vignettes on wood by Daumier, published nine days after the opening. Among these small and rather crude illustrations was a lanky Telemachus who seems to have strayed from the *Ancient History* series, a chorus of obnoxious swineherds and an "apotheosis" with three delightfully drawn pigs dancing before the vision of Minerva.

Equally unwelcome, so far as the new public was concerned, were the efforts to revive a type of quasi-historical tragedy which only Hugo or the elder Dumas could bring to life in the theater. Ten years before, the debacle of the *Burgraves* had seemingly ended the short vogue of Romantic drama, and when Victor Séjour presented his *Richard III* at the Porte Saint-Martin in 1852 the critics made short work of its false history and its pretentious style, and Daumier made thirteen drawings for *Charivari* on wood, *Souvenir of Richard III*, to show the claque which had been hired to applaud it and to ridicule the "rather badly constructed fellow" who was its central character (Fig. 55). In one vignette Shakespeare leans grinning out of a box, amused to find in this piece a tomb scene which he had written for *Romeo and Juliet.*

If Daumier's beloved Frédérick was not to be seen in the rue Richelieu, he knew where to find him. The creator of Macaire was playing on the boulevard du Temple in a series of hilarious farces which had the topical banter of a modern revue. There were no empty seats at the Théâtre des Funambules where, in this year 1852, Paul Legrand and Charles Deburau were rival Pierrots and drama was not confined to the stage. Many a famous actor had received his baptism of vegetables in this ramshackle house where the hiccoughs of a drunken player were echoed by the mocking gallery gods. On one occasion a rash playgoer at the Funambules greeted the mime Deburau with a donkey's bray and was tossed from hand to hand and booted into the street. A wood engraving by Daumier in 1836 had described just such an incident; nearly thirty years later he made a brawling balcony the scene of a superb lithograph.

In this fabulous street the pantomime and the vaudeville shared customers with the gory melodramas for which it had been named, pieces which seemed to the Goncourts to stimulate the lowest appetites. "A woman with a well-shaped bottom," they wrote, "and legs that are not too knockkneed, saving the French flag—that is sublime! That is glory!" In the year 1862 a Daumier wood engraving showed a gloomy crowd issuing from a drama on the Boulevard of Crime as another group comes laughing from a vaudeville. Within a few months of its publication one of Haussmann's great avenues pierced the quarter and left only one playhouse standing where there had been a dozen, dislodging the side-show barkers, the trained fleas, the strolling acrobats, the strong

55. Wood engraving from *Souvenirs of Richard III*
Photo Alison Spence

men and the human skeletons, that swarm of weary entertainers who gained a second life in the water colors and oils of Daumier.

Although Joseph Prudhomme and his kind might sleep through Corneille and give perfunctory applause to the pseudoromantic intrigues of characters drawn from remote history, their heartiest pleasure was to see themselves reflected in the new comedies of manners. Only the intervention of Morny made it possible for *The Lady of the Camellias* by the younger Dumas to be performed in 1862, a piece which Viel-Castel considered "a shameful insult to public morality"; but in the following year Ponsard achieved a major success with his more "wholesome" piece, *Honor and Money*, whose hero is financially ruined to save the reputation of his family and who loses his fiancée only to marry her more faithful sister at the end and recoup his fortune. Daumier salutes the opening night, three years later, of Ponsard's *The Bourse*. All Paris, from the Emperor down, praised this sermon on the corrupting force of speculation, although Gautier thought its message more cynical than moral: "If you have won three hundred thousand francs on the Exchange you will do well to marry the girl you love and go live in the country." Now Émile Augier would spice his "pot-roast lyricism" with bits of shrewd observation and an adroit appeal to sentiment in *The Son-in-law of M. Poirier*, while the shallow skill of the younger Dumas in *The Demimonde, The Natural Son* and *Claude's Wife* paraded the plain virtues of the bourgeois, tapped the top layer of his emotions and not too painfully exposed his vices.

While the patrons of Augier, Scribe and Sardou watched themselves being rewarded for their solid virtues and punished for their sins, Daumier now and then portrayed the more affluent clientele of the great musical theaters of Paris. At the Opéra, where the stage spectacle matched the extravagance of Rossini and Meyerbeer, he observed its starchily dressed men and its languid, powder-whitened women; in a pen drawing lightly touched with water color, *A Box at the Opera*, these pampered ladies seem to be listening to the terrible drama of *Trovatore*, as some one said, with the serene smile of one who melts a meringue on one's tongue. In the lithographs a connoisseur in the dress circle ogles a ballerina through his opera glasses or watches Venus being hoisted skyward on a cloud. At the Théâtre des Italiens, most lavish of all playhouses with its huge chandelier and four tiers of balconies, where Patti made her debut in Bellini's operas, he shows us somnolent dark figures in a box, with a glimpse beyond of the brilliant stage. Perhaps from the Opéra-Comique come the two singers in a lithograph who are tearing to shreds a melody of Auber or Donizetti.

Only one pictorial reference was made by Daumier to a form of entertainment which was created during the Empire, the opera bouffe, where

56. *Recalled with Enthusiasm,* lithograph
Museum of Fine Arts, Boston, Mass.

the malicious wit of the boulevards found its perfect expression in the librettos of Meilhac and Halévy and the light-fingered tunes of Offenbach. In *Orpheus in the Underworld* their chorus was a Public Opinion manipulated by a King of the Gods who could easily be identified with an Emperor of the French. The critic Janin protested this insult to antiquity, but Daumier would have agreed with the comment of the Goncourts that the wit of Athenian Lucian was born again in this ironic banter—"An echo of his laughter is still to be heard from our boards, rising against the gods in their sky." He may also have wondered whether his own *Ancient History* had not served to suggest this modernization of antique legends, as it would shortly find a close parallel in *Fair Helen.*

When the vogue for amateur theatricals swept society in the late 1850s some of the most delightfully crisp drawings the artist ever made were in his series of sixteen on this theme (Fig. 56). As a means of showing off, appeasing boredom and competing with one's social rivals these private performances had enlivened soirées in the eighteenth century and during the reign of Louis-Philippe; now scarcely an evening was without its one-act farce or its operetta, from the Court spectacles with indecorous tableaux vivants which gave ambitious beauties a chance to compete for applause and for more tangible rewards, to the modest drawing room entertainments. Daumier depicts the latter with a superb economy: on one side of the improvised footlights sit the indulgent

57. *A Queen Preparing for a Grand Tirade,* lithograph
Museum of Fine Arts, Boston, Mass.

guests, and on the other an elderly professor of declamation recites, and
pupils from the Conservatoire attempt *Phèdre* or *Athalie* with one eye
on the influential auditors. The host and hostess perform while their
servants criticize their efforts through a keyhole, and one guest makes
love to his neighbor's wife with an ardor beyond the needs of the occasion.

Frequently in his theater drawings of this period the artist imagines
himself backstage where he can see both actors and audience from the
wings. Here it is the comic antithesis that beguiles him—the rosy cloud
launched into the sky by a rope, a pulley and a stagehand in shirtsleeves,
or the fireman on duty who offers a pinch of snuff to the star. What "the
most intelligent public in the world" accepts as an ocean is a sheet of
canvas billowed into waves from beneath by dusty and sweating workmen. A queen of tragedy prepares herself for her tirade by blowing her
nose (Fig. 57) and a mother performs the same service for a repulsive
child who will shortly appear as Cupid. Through several of these lithos
stalks that bizarre type which Ludovic Halévy liked to describe. "I
must confess," the writer said, "that I adore the mothers of dancers,"
aging creatures who sold fruit during the day and at night guarded their
offspring from the young dandies who "debauch our daughters without
our permission." One such matron, who had once worn tights and who
now bemoans the decadence of the modern ballerina, could have stepped
into Halévy's tales from one of Daumier's lithographs in which the

58. *A Box at the Théâtre Ventadour,* lithograph
Museum of Fine Arts, Boston, Mass.

mother of a debutante dissolves in happy tears as bouquets fly through
the air, forgetting they were ordered by herself.

When one looks back over more than a decade of these theater studies
one concludes that the audiences rather than the players appealed to
this analyst of behavior. Their varying responses are so wisely delineated
that one can almost name the piece and the playhouse. As time went on,
two pictorial schemes recur most often, and always with significant
variations. In one, the shapes of people in the half-darkened auditorium
are silhouetted against a brightly illuminated stage which is framed
from above by the ceiling of a box or the under edge of a balcony (Fig.
58). In that glimpse across the footlights Daumier manages to suggest
with a few lines what makes the patrons tense with excitement or simply
bored—a toga-clad tragedian in the climax of his tirade, two bellowing
Italians whose legs only are visible, a desperate juvenile who turns from

59. *They Say the Parisians Are Hard to Please,* lithograph
Museum of Fine Arts, Boston, Mass.

the body of his slain rival to cry, "He was your lover, Madame!" The second image records the impact of plays on patrons without describing its causes, in lithos where one sees only the rows of spectators, the nearest of them clearly revealed in light reflected from the stage, the distant ones half-lost in the gloom of the house. The theme is given endless variations—the quick and sudden laughter of vaudeville and farce, the dutiful solemnity which greets a classic, the intelligent smile evoked by Molière, the self-conscious appraisal of a ballerina's leg. This sea of faces is sometimes chopped with the cross-movements of conflicting reponse; at other times he swings it into the smooth rhythm of complete enjoyment or steeps it in collective torpor (Fig. 59). There are Daumier audiences in which one man's delight is indefinitely multiplied and others whose vacuous ovals build a wall of indifference. One of his finest lithos presents a turbulent "literary discussion" in the second balcony of a popular playhouse (Fig. 60). The best of these caricatures were published in 1864 and 1865 and have their counterpart in the superb water colors on this theme which were made at the same period.

In years to come, this knowing playgoer was to prove that he could use the playhouse not only as literal subject but as metaphor. At one critical moment of his country's life his restless audience would demand that the curtain be raised on the next act of the tragedy of real-life politics; at another, he would place the owlish head of Thiers in the prompter's box of history.

60. *A Literary Discussion in the Second Balcony,* lithograph
Museum of Fine Arts, Boston, Mass.

6: CITIZEN-PAINTER

"**J**anuary 14, 1852. Baudelaire takes me to Daumier's place on the quai d'Anjou . . . the simple workroom of an artist who doesn't have to plan for public visitors." The publisher Poulet-Malassis thus begins a page of recollections as useful as it is rare in its reference to specific works by his host. Daumier, he notes, is pressed for time, preparing a lithograph for *Charivari;* and well he might have been, since nearly one hundred and fifty stones were made during this year. To the visitor's question whether the caricaturist will have a painting in the coming Salon the latter replies that he has no idea and does not count on it. "On an easel there is a sketch for a martyrdom. . . . He is also doing some sculpture; I see a kind of bacchanal in wax on the wall of the studio. Several unfinished studies, a *Magdalen,* a *Washerwoman* pulling a small girl along the quay in a high wind. A sketch of so sombre a feeling that one would think the enormous bundle of laundry under her arm is on the way to the pawnshop. There are a good many canvases turned against the wall—for another time."

These are tantalizing notes; and both Jean Adhémar, who published them, and Maurice Gobin have tried to identify the works mentioned. The former suggests that the "martyrdom" on the easel may have been *We Want Barabbas!*, the large grisaille of a taunted Christ which never went beyond a brush-drawn indication and a few broad and muted tones, the curious crowd below the walled platform and the tense figure above whose finger of scorn points to the calm prisoner. This canvas, put aside by an artist who was perhaps defeated by its sheer size, already had achieved a majestic unity and a controlled dramatic power; one recalls the words of Jean Gigoux, that "even when the canvas was scarcely covered, it had always something unexpected, something which revealed his mind and his heart."

The *Magdalen* seen by the visitor was obviously the never-completed oil commissioned by the government some three years earlier. This rough study of the half-nude figure in hot brownish tones, long owned by the descendants of the functionary to whom it had been sent for approval, was first seen by the public in 1930. More puzzling is the "bacchanal in wax." Was this a lost relief by Daumier or a work by Préault? Gobin's speculations seem rather tenuous. If Poulet-Malassis mistook clay for wax, a medium never used by Daumier, is it not possible that he saw too hastily the two bas-reliefs of the *Emigrants* or *Fugitives,* either in the original clay or in the tinted plaster casts which were made from them? As for the *Washerwoman,* the reference has been taken to designate the terra cotta figurine now in the Walters Art Gallery, whereas a careful reading of the visitor's description with its reference to the quay would rather suggest one of the painted versions of this theme which were doubtless made with the help of the sculpture and are called *The Heavy Burden.*

When one considers the "good many canvases turned to the wall," frail conjecture becomes pure guesswork. Three paintings returned from the Salon may well have been among them, the *Don Quixote,* the *Miller* and the *Nymphs.* One might add to these without hope of confirmation works which seem to be of the 1840s and early 50s: a canvas where Sancho Panza sits crouched under a spreading tree; *A Waiting Room,* whose principal figure was never fully defined; a superb *Washerwomen on the Steps of the Quay* whose delicately harmonized reddish browns and cool blue-greens at least declare the artist's intention; *On a Bridge at Night,* with the laundress and her child hastening through a magically invoked darkness; a version of *The Emigrants* to whose closely huddled forms the artist has given a sombre unity and a slow, forward moving rhythm.

Some of the stacked oils would come down to us as they were at this time, while others would show signs of having been worked upon afterward. Not the least significant phrase in the notes of Poulet-Malassis is Daumier's remark, "I begin everything over again twenty-five times." The same point was made by Jean Gigoux who once wrote, "When a picture 'did not come,' he put it aside." And when Arsène Alexandre saw the *Nymphs* in later years, he found it "peculiarly messed up with hasty retouches" by the artist himself. These comments serve as a triple warning to those who would easily assign a single date to a painting by Daumier.

A further complication for the Daumierist arises from the man's tendency to attempt more than one version of the same scheme. K. E. Maison, for example, has listed several replicas of *The Heavy Burden.* Each has some significant variation and all of them try to capture in paint the complex movement of the terra cotta figurine, a little less than fourteen inches high—the woman's forward-thrusting leg, the torso twisted backward by the weight of the bundle, the head turned sharply to counter the pull of her burden, the parallel stance of the clinging child. One sees in the clay the mark of Daumier's swift fingers as he nudged the skirt into windblown folds and used a knife blade or the end of a brush handle to define the clasped arms and the wrinkles of cloth over the breast. In oil he could only approximate this small masterpiece,

61. *The Heavy Burden,* terra cotta figurine Walters Art Gallery, Baltimore, Md.

62. *The Heavy Burden,* oil. Burrell Collection
Art Gallery and Museum, Glasgow

most successfully in two canvases which were once owned by Arsène
Alexandre (Figs. 61, 62).

Daumier told his guest that he did not count on having a painting in
the Salon, and for a decade after 1851 there would be none. The hopeful moment which followed the February revolution had ended, and
there would be no encouragement in the new order for artists whose
thought or whose themes reminded the Empire of its less privileged
subjects. Delacroix and Ingres, the former in his late fifties and the

latter in his seventies, now received honors and commissions which were probably more advantageous to the donors than to them, and both were generously represented in the Exposition of 1855. The rival merits of the two masters were still subjects of dispute, and one could choose between the review of Gustave Planche and that of Baudelaire. The one preferred Ingres' *Apotheosis of Napoleon* to the *Apollo* ceiling of Delacroix, and his opinions on these and other artists would bolster the reactionary standards of the government, the Institute, the Salon juries and the schools of art for years to come; the other compared the eloquence of the great Romantic with the "heroic immolation" of Ingres, a man "quite devoid of that energy of temperament which constitutes the fatality of genius." The horses, the chariot and the Emperor of Ingres' *Apotheosis,* he observed, were falling earthward "like a fully ballasted balloon without gas."

Baudelaire noted at the same time that a young man of unabashed indelicacy had recently made his debut "with all the violence of an armed revolt." When the *Bathers* of Courbet was shown in 1853 Gautier found it proof positive of a great talent gone wrong and Delacroix recoiled before the commonness of its forms and of its thought. Two years later the showing of forty Courbet canvases was the signal for a critical campaign against the self-styled socialist painter in which he was accused of depicting the life of ordinary people in all its most vulgar aspects in a revolt against the established order in art and in politics.

For those artists of the period who, like Daumier, had neither the established reputation of Ingres and Delacroix nor the thick hide of Courbet, the struggle to become known, exhibited and purchased was discouraging and dismal. How does one sell six or seven miles of painting from the Salon? asked Taine. A number of young men who would have made good clerks, he noted, were buying gaiters, growing beards, and trying to be artists; many of them were reduced to painting shop signs or the backdrops of photographers, while others took to the provinces in search of patrons whose taste in portraits was not too exacting. Still others dressed up and moved in social circles where they might attract the attention of influential critics and so impress the bourgeoisie that it would be ashamed not to pay well for their pictures.

When one reads Taine's word of praise for the honesty and idealism of these hopeful men, their freshness of vision and the boisterous high spirits of their gatherings in the taverns of Fontainebleau, one thinks of Daubigny, Diaz, Rousseau and Millet, all in their late thirties or early forties, stubbornly working in the face of official indifference. Thoré congratulated them for leaving the city where human sensibilities are blunted, to seek the regenerating influence of nature in the country; and Baudelaire coupled his admiration for Rousseau with regret that the

63. *Yes, Madame Fribochon,* lithograph
Museum of Fine Arts, Boston, Mass.

underhand plotting of the authorities had long kept his work from exhibition. As for Millet, whose *Sower* was seen at the Salon of 1851, Count Nieuwerkerke dismissed him as one of those painter-democrats "who don't change their linen and want to impose themselves on polite society." When Daumier spent some time at Valmondois in 1853 he renewed his earlier friendship with these innovators, a relationship which was to grow more intimate in the next years.

One would look in vain for direct influences of these Barbizon artists in the paintings of Daumier at this time. It is possible that they made him more sharply aware of how light behaves in the open air and of more

64. *Three Gossiping Women,* water color
Photo courtesy Wildenstein and Co., New York

65. Study for *The Thieves*, charcoal
Collection Claude Roger-Marx, Paris

delicate and subtle tone-relations for its presentation. He could admire
their technical skill and he was morally supported by their admiration,
but his exploration of his painterly problem was his own. He would not
long be satisfied with the stark simplifications of *The Drinkers* and *The
Towman,* but sought a richer variety and a more resonant orchestration of his forms. After the *Miller* and the *Nymphs* he seems to have
decided that the effort to combine powerful contrasts of light and shade
with equally strong contrasts of color was not for him; a touch of warm
red or blue-green would now suffice for an enlivening accent as he
worked to create a pervasive atmosphere—the dim warmth inside a playhouse, the failing daylight along the Seine, the musty interior of a
railway carriage, the chiaroscuro of narrow streets whose people emerge
from shade into broad sun or stop to peer at prints on the half-shadowed
walls of shops, the filtering of daylight through the trees of a tavern
garden.

66. *The Thieves and the Ass,* oil. Louvre. Photo Bulloz

Drawing itself plays a more active part in the painting of what one might call his middle period. Daumier is now a master draftsman who can suggest character, mood, movement and three-dimensional form by line alone when he wishes to do so. The best lithographs of the 1850s brilliantly prove this gift: Nadar in a balloon with a wonderfully indicated Paris below him, or *A Light Breeze,* where three people are caught in a gale of wind, or the *Demimondaines* with its crisp indication of billowing hoopskirts. In four lithographs of lawyers in 1851 his drawing is more free and more economical than in earlier satires of the law. These and some of the railway scenes are a kind of rehearsal for water colors and oils in which similar characters and postures will be found.

Nothing is more typical of Daumier than these reappearances in more than one medium of themes and situations which had lodged in his mind. In 1852, for example, he drew three ancient housewives gossiping by candlelight on a landing, in a lithograph which made the most of the odd effect of a single flame on their faces (Fig. 63). A drawing of their heads in pencil, black chalk and charcoal, and a similar one in pen and ink over charcoal, served as preliminary sketches for a rather finished water color (Fig. 64). Five years after the first lithograph, the artist restated the same theme with variations in one of his series, *The Comet of 1857.*

Again, it would seem that a caricature in *Charivari* was the germ of a subsequent oil. In 1845 a furious street fight had provided a subject for a lithograph. In two drawings of the same figures Daumier now strips them of their clothes and powerfully defines their interlocked bodies and their contracted muscles, making their mutual impact more brutal than in the caricature (Fig. 65). Behind them in one of these sketches a few lines suggest the mule of La Fontaine's fable and indicate that these were preliminary studies for the painting in the Louvre (Fig. 66), whose figures have been clothed again, their heads personalized and the gesture of the underdog changed for a more effective tonal contrast. The general scheme of a large foreground group in diagonal relation to a small distant one was not new for Daumier and the outflung arms and legs are done in somewhat the same manner as in the *Miller;* but Daumier's range of color here is narrowed to variations on dull browns and greens which give a russet half-daylight to this patch of forest, and his forms are more subtly built up on their linear foundation. On this occasion the various elements in a developing style have found a splendid synthesis.

In 1862 the artist made a lithographed version of this painting, the only instance of such a procedure in his lifetime, and five years later Gustave Doré borrowed its compositional scheme for one of his illustrations of the fables.

When Poulet-Malassis visited Daumier's studio he must have seen, although he did not mention them, the portfolios which grew fatter every year with drawings, hundreds of which have survived. Many of them were done swiftly with crayon, pencil or pen on small scraps of paper—the head of a rapacious lawyer, the whirling figure of a dancing girl. To a few evocative lines Daumier frequently added one or two

67. *Centaur and Woman,* pen and wash
Collection Claude Roger-Marx, Paris

simple washes of India ink or sepia to clinch the forms, as he did in the
superb *Child Running* and in a pen drawing of *Centaur and Woman*
which was snapped into three dimensions by a single washed tone (Fig.
67). Such notations seem to have been done for the pleasure of the
doing, while other drawings have the essentials of a complete composition, among them several studies of connoisseurs in an art gallery and
of women and children at a market. *Man Reading in a Garden* was first
sketched in pencil, then reinforced with pen and ink and with water color,
and a similar feeling for the flickering patterns of light and shade is in
Politics in a Beer Garden (Fig. 68). Many a stark Quixote in line and
wash kept the theme alive in Daumier's mind. Still another group of
drawings, published and discussed by Maison, our surest guide in this
area, was clearly done as part of a careful and systematic preparation for
more finished water colors and oils, a practice which the artist seems to
have followed consistently in the middle years.

These years, and especially the period from 1860 to 1864, the respite
from *Charivari* which left him relatively free to paint, mark the culmina-

68. *Politics in a Beer Garden,* pen and wash
Collection Albert Ch. Nussbaumer, Lugano

tion of his effort toward the rich and full embodiment of descriptive images. From this time can surely be dated the majority of his most finished water colors, many of which were made for sale. It is now that one finds the closest parallel between works in different media. The same pretty woman whom he lithographed in 1864 smirks beside her pleading lawyer in a water color; the same weary passengers travel in the railway carriages of his drawings, water colors, and oils as in his caricatures.

Not merely to please the customer but to satisfy himself, and because he was now less pressed for time, Daumier took infinite pains with these water colors. They vary in their size, ranging from about six to ten

69. *The Side Show*, water color
Philadelphia Museum of Art

inches in their shorter dimension to about eight to twelve in their longer
one; and K. E. Maison has shown how a preliminary drawing was usually made, then transferred to the paper on which the work was to be
done. Sometimes the drawing was reversed as though the artist wished
to see whether this would improve its effect; sometimes by tracing
Daumier made a nearly identical replica. One can follow the evolution
of his ideas for *The Side Show* through several drawings, one of which
looks like a tracing and another seems a fairly complete rehearsal in
which the lighting effect is indicated by washes over black chalk and
pencil. This study was dedicated by the artist to his friend Jules Dupré,
in whose studio it was seen by Jules Clarétie—"an old mountebank,

toothless and wrinkled, beating the drum in front of a tent at a fair to which the crowd does not come; it has the smell of death in it." (Fig. 69).

Why was Daumier in more sure command of water color than of oils at this moment? In the former one works from light to dark, making the most of the luminosity of the original surface, a procedure not unlike that which for years he had followed on the stone. Three-dimensional forms, moreover, could be cautiously and gradually constructed with successive washes of the transparent pigment. There was less risk of losing detail in dark shadow, and nothing is more remarkable in these papers than the way in which the half-mysterious prints and paintings on the walls of a studio or shop keep their place behind the connoisseurs, or a row of spectators achieves a kind of secondary existence at the back of a courtroom. The method is fairly complex, with a line drawing in crayon or charcoal which receives washes of color in varying degrees of transparency, then reinforcing accents in pencil or pen, sometimes with a hatching of certain areas with lines to give them depth and atmosphere, sometimes with passages made more solid with touches of opaque paint. On one or two occasions Daumier attempts a larger format. *Visitors in an Artist's Studio* in the Walters Art Gallery, with its wonderful suggestion of pictures on a far wall, is somewhat more than twelve by twelve inches (Color plate III); the work with the same title in the Montreal Museum of Fine Arts is even larger. Either of them, or the *Connoisseur* of the Metropolitan Museum, would suffice to put Daumier beside Rowlandson and the other supreme masters of this medium.

That this mastery was achieved in the years of his freedom from the routine of caricature is made evident not only by the stylistic character of the works themselves but also by a few references to them by his contemporaries. Among these are the notes, published by Adhémar, in which Philippe Burty recorded a visit to the studio of Daumier's close friend Geoffroy-Dechaume. The year was 1862, and Burty saw there a dozen of the water colors which had been made to sell for fifty francs: the interior of a booking-office, perhaps *The Waiting Room;* some people playing dominoes, probably the version once owned by Geoffroy-Dechaume himself; some half-lengths of men flying in terror; a courtroom scene in which "a thin and bilious prosecutor rages against a prisoner with bowed head" as he does in the pen-and-wash called *The Speech for the Prosecution;* another where "a long-winded old buffoon . . . points an unconvincing finger to Heaven"; and three old women sewing by the light of a candle and "listening with expressions of varying degrees of terror, incredulity and idiotic belief to the tale told by one of them," words which come close to describing *The Three Gossips.*

Two years after Burty's notation George A. Lucas, an engineer from

70. *Lawyer with a Woman Client,* water color
National Museum of Wales, Cardiff

Baltimore who made purchases in Paris for himself and for other
Americans, wrote in his diary that he had paid one hundred francs each
(about nineteen dollars) for two water colors of first and second class
carriages. These and an omnibus scene were done to his order. With
other works in the same medium now in the Walters Gallery, they represent, as Agnes Mongan has shown, a Daumier at the very summit of his
powers.

On the fifteenth of March, 1865, the Goncourts recorded that they
had seen a group of Daumier's water colors at a shop in the rue Tait-
bout, "a panathenaic festival of the judiciary, of lawyers meeting, of
judges parading against somber walls and through dank corridors."
These men, washed in with a sinister ink and funereal blacks, had for
them the ugliness of antique masks: "there is something faunlike in
these macabre advocates." If one wished to illustrate this passage one
would face an embarrassment of choice among the numerous drawings
in which Daumier now fully exposed his legal types in all their variety

of pride, complacent cruelty, hypocrisy and smooth lechery. In *After the Trial* they smugly congratulate one another; in *The Stairway of the Palais de Justice* one of them sweeps proudly down the long flight of steps; in *Lawyer with a Woman Client* (Fig. 70) there is palpably false reassurance; in *A Famous Case,* a water color for which Daumier made a preliminary wash drawing and several pen sketches, there is a visual antiphony between the quiet watchfulness of the lawyer on one side of the courtroom and the frenzied oratory of his opponent on the other.

It may have been drawings like these which inspired the Goncourts, in search of an opening scene for a novel, to attempt a word-picture of a trial which they saw in 1869 in the new room at the Court of Assize, with a large Crucifixion on the wall above the aged and toothless presiding judge, who reads a love letter to the jury, stressing each word with a malign and sinister enjoyment. Between two gendarmes at the bench stands a frightful old woman. The accused man has the eyes of a terrified animal in a face which seems to grow thinner and to crumble as the interrogation proceeds. On a later occasion the authors describe the kitchen knife with which a woman was killed, and the lawyer for the defense, "that licensed acquitter of assassins . . . a bad actor in a vulgar melodrama, with a false emotion, a gesticulating and ambulatory declamation—nothing but a demoniac brawler." All this, from the smirking judge to the frenzied advocate, even the Crucifixion behind the bench and the telltale knife on the table, is in these water colors of Daumier.

Although the infinite mutations of the legal species, the tired travelers by train, the amateurs of art and the clowns and acrobats of city streets and country fairs are the favored subjects in these small masterpieces, they are not the only ones. *The Drinking Song* celebrates the rough congeniality of the tavern; *A Butcher at Work* conveys the mighty effort to move a side of beef by a man who has distant relatives in some lithographs of the late 1850s; two reserved playgoers are contrasted with their smiling neighbors in *The Critics in the Theater.*

Already a master of two media, Daumier pursues in this same period of the late 1850s and early 1860s his struggle with the less tractable method of painting in oils. On canvas or on panels his command of line enables him first to define his figures with a small brush, but he is too sculpturally minded to depend on these outlines for more than a framework which will gradually be assimilated as his modeling proceeds. We are indebted to David Rosen and Henri Marceau for the suggestion that a kind of cross-fertilization takes place at this time between two media, as the rather even and heavy impasto of earlier work gives place to a more complicated way of building up the forms with successive washes of semitransparent pigment, handling oil as though it were water color, a method which contrasts with that of his contemporaries who achieved their effects with a single direct application of a well-loaded brush. The head of *The Reader,* for example, provides us with a close view of a form whose main features have been given outlines around and over which the brush has moved in sculptural fashion as though the artist were modeling his volumes in clay rather than on a flat surface with pigment.

This sculpturing with paint was noted by Rosen and Marceau when they examined the Louvre version of *The Washerwoman* by means of infrared photography which penetrated its top layer to show how Daumier's brush had followed the swellings and concavities of the woman's head. The scheme of this painting is a simple one and shows the artist still fond of making his points by means of a silhouetted mass, in this case the toiling laundress and her child, in richly dark tones of brown-red and olive against the sunny yellow of distant housefronts, with only a glimpse of luminous green water between the near foreground and the opposite quay. One version of this work was shown at the Salon of 1861, where the critic Thoré admired its originality, its simple grandeur and its vigorous color harmonies (Color plate IV).

No work of this period so clearly reveals Daumier's procedure as *The Third Class Carriage,* a study of contrasting character among the weary passengers who face the observer on their hard bench, behind them the backs of fellow voyagers. A letter written by the artist Arthur Stevens from Brussels in 1864 asks Daumier to send him the painting which Baudelaire saw in the studio "some time ago"; the writer imagines what it must be like because he has already seen the admirable water color of the same subject—no doubt the one which Lucas bought. When Daumier began his version in oils he had made preparatory drawings, from one of which he enlarged his composition by squares on the canvas. These squares are still clearly visible on the unfinished oil in the Metropolitan Museum (Fig. 71). Visible also are some of the bold brush-drawn lines which define the sharply angular and deeply ridged face of the old woman and the rounded cheeks and breasts of her young companion. Over these outlines the artist has begun to lay his sculptural washes of pigment, differentiating the yellowish-brown cloak of the central figure from the pinkish-red of the girl's dress, using a rather intense green-blue for other passages, and bringing his figures into sharp relief against the prevailing reddish brown of the compartment. What he would next have done is illustrated by a more complete version of the same theme, of almost exactly the same size, in the National Gallery at Ottawa, where the preliminary outlines have been resolved into a smoother modeling and the harsh contrasts of colors have disappeared in a quieter harmony (Fig. 72). To compare these two oils is to find both gain and loss; the

71. *The Third Class Carriage,* oil. Metropolitan Museum of Art
Bequest of Mrs. H. O. Havemeyer, 1929

atmosphere of a dim place has been achieved in the Ottawa work, but the rugged features of the old lady, the folds of her cloak and the full-breasted body of the young mother are less salient and less eloquent of character than in the New York canvas.

Another work of the period, the *Crispin and Scapin* of the Louvre, depends for its vitality on brush-drawn lines which have been largely incorporated into the modeling of one head but in the other have been left much as they were first set down. Its theme is a stage whisper, the two faces brilliantly exposed by the upward glancing footlights. When it left his hands the painter may well have felt, as modern critics do, that a more meticulous fusing of its forms would only have lessened its mischievous intensity (Fig. 73).

The Drama demonstrates the fitness of the term "draftsman-painter" which Rosen and Marceau have applied to Daumier. It was inevitable that the theme of a brightly lighted stage seen from a dark auditorium, exploited more than once in the lithographs, would also be attempted on

72. *The Third Class Carriage*, oil. National Gallery of Canada, Ottawa

canvas. In a print of 1856 the Italian players were thus seen from a box and in 1864 appeared a litho which has been inaccurately described as a reproduction of the painting. The same elements compose both canvas and print—an audience whose eager faces catch a glow from the stage, the actors melodramatically posturing, and the framing edge of the underside of a balcony which gently curves in the painting but is straight in the lithograph, to the detriment of the latter.

Towards 1860 it would appear that Daumier often shifted his attention from a physical action to a psychological situation, as he did with his groups of amateurs whose attention was focused on a painting or a print. In the lithographs this was the occasion for good-natured satire; in oil the artist more delicately set forth a state of delighted concentration which subtly varied among the participants. Such were the *Print Collectors* of the Clark Collection, their heads drawn together in common appreciation, and *The Connoisseurs* of the Boymans Museum, a simpler study in which the same men appear. A similar activity is

73. *Crispin and Scapin,* oil. Louvre. Photo Giraudon

represented out of doors before shops in several paintings of the period, and the artist allowed himself a relatively bright palette in *The Curious Ones,* where the stabilizing motive is a man in a dark coat and top hat lost in contemplation of prints whose character, under a protective awning, is merely hinted, while the attitudes of other strollers are effectively related to his own.

Daumier had other ways of presenting this situation. In a canvas which now belongs to the Burrell Collection a single collector stands rather stiffly, hands in pockets, in front of a print-laden wall; the figure is only a little less wooden in a very similar picture at the Art Institute of Chicago, although Daumier has better organized the various elements. Far superior to these are two works in which the amateur bends to examine a half-opened portfolio, a gesture which gives focus and meaning to the whole composition. No longer, as in *The Washerwoman,* does the artist rely for his effect on a uniformly dark silhouetted figure; in the *Print Collector* of the Petit-Palais the man is defined on one side by lighter accents against a shadowed wall and on the other by a bright patch of light which throws into relief his head and arm. There is no element here which does not play its part in the whole, and Daumier has made sparing but excellent use of color accents: a drawing in red chalk is suggested on the wall, its warm tone an echo of the man's face and hands, and on the right these notes are balanced by their complementary color in a greenish blue portfolio. The Philadelphia Museum owns a somewhat smaller painting whose basic plan is the same but whose forms have been more lightly done, giving the effect of a moment quickly seized (Color plate V). Both of these works have a solid unity and an assurance of execution which the struggling painter could not have attained before 1860 or shortly thereafter.

Even at this time there are puzzling variations of style in the oils of Daumier, some of which depend for their incisive strength on the persistence of the linear structure; in others, like *The Singing Couple,* no linear element appears and the movement of light over the forms is softly blurred. There are also a few paintings seemingly of this period in which we see the artist moving from a quasi-water color method to one which more fully uses the properties peculiar to oil, the direct application of thickened pigment to bring into more powerful relief the forms of heads and hands. This bolder touch is in the *Head of a Buffoon;* the bearded player in *A Game of Draughts* gains a lean strength from the way in which his collar, his forehead and the tip of his nose have been made to catch the light by being touched with a heavily loaded brush. In *Three Lawyers* the white neckcloths, the documents, the pudgy features of one barrister and a patch of sunlit wall were accented in this fashion, perhaps when the picture was first done, perhaps on a subsequent occasion.

A painting once owned by Corot and now in the National Gallery in Washington suggests as well as any other Daumier's conquest of a painterly style more than twenty years after his first fumbling encounters with the medium. In *Advice to a Young Artist* (Fig. 74) two figures are superbly placed in a space defined by a studio wall and in a well-planned harmony of colors the grey-browns steadily support the luminous whites of the young man's drawings and are relieved by touches of the familiar red and blue in the far couch and the near portfolio. Thin washes have established the space itself, and a more solid touch has sculptured the two absorbed heads without losing the strength and expressiveness of the way in which they were first drawn.

If Daumier continued to haunt the Louvre now as he had earlier done, he could have found analogies between himself and others. The dignity and strength of a blacksmith at his flaming forge had impressed Louis Le Nain before him. His *Scapin* was in the spirit of the *Gilles* of Watteau. His preoccupation with the strange effects of candlelight paralleled that of Georges de La Tour; and the women who carry their laden baskets home from market in his water colors are descended from those of Chardin. The caricaturist had become in the early 1860s a master in the

fine tradition of French genre painting, a fact more evident to us than it probably was to him.

Nor can he have fully known how his art looked forward, at a moment when the great reputations were those of Gérôme, Cabanel, Bouguereau, Baudry and Meissonier. By an ordinance of August fourteenth, 1863, the State took over the direction of public exhibitions which the Academy had long exercised; two years later the first medal of the Salon went to Cabanel for his iron-hard portrait of the Emperor and Gérôme was made a Professor of the École des Beaux-Arts. Baudelaire was one of the few critics who refused to admire these "spoiled children" of art, these toymakers whose exclusive concern with technique, he wrote, had brought about the degradation of the artist; the *Ave Caesar!* of Gérôme "substituted the amusement of a page of erudition for the joys of pure painting." And Thoré, returning from exile to write a few Salon reviews in the 60s, recalled the battles of 1830–1848 when a few critics fought against the Gods of Olympus and the Romans of the Academy. Now, he said, the critics do not lead but are content to follow. Thoré finds the resuscitated Greeks and Romans of Gérôme as ridiculous as had Baudelaire; the painter of *Phryne* has turned ancient senators into smirking, lecherous Frenchmen. At the Salon of 1861 Thoré pronounced the *Sheep Shearer* of Millet and Courbet's *Combat of Stags* strong medicine for a sick art and had nothing but scorn for the boneless, bloodless Venuses of Cabanel and Baudry. When Rousseau was accused of lacking "finish," the critic reminded his readers that some works are more expressively complete before the artist proceeds to minute detail.

This prescience of what was to come enabled Thoré to see a true artist under the seeming eccentricities of Manet as early as 1863, at a time when the painter of *Olympia* was the butt of writers and caricaturists, with the exception of Daumier, whose only reference to that scandalous picture was a litho in which a bourgeois family stands perplexed before it at the Salon of 1865. One year later, Thoré mentioned a Barbizon landscape by Monet as the work of a promising new man and prophesied the oblivion of those who practised "grand art," the perpetuators of old forms which no longer had any relation to life, in a constipated style which could not have survived if this pagan and Catholic mythology had not been necessary to a policed state. Equally perceptive was Émile Zola when he compared the *Luncheon* of Manet with the rice-powder nudes of Cabanel, the plaster Cleopatras of Gérôme, and other bonbons of the modish confectioners of art. After this river of milk, he observed, Manet seems bitter.

74. *Advice to a Young Artist,* oil
National Gallery of Art, Washington, D.C., Gift of Duncan Phillips

Both writers knew that an art was in the making which promised a new relation between a painting and its beholder. Increasingly, as Ernst Gombrich has recently pointed out, the observer would be challenged to transform the painter's suggestions into an image through the exercise of his own imagination. The literal-minded layman who cannot thus participate in the making of the work of art will always prefer the lazier pleasures of mere recognition. In the 1860s he preferred Meissonier to Daumier. As for the former, both Baudelaire and Thoré acknowledged his technical prowess, his kinship with the little Dutch and Flemish masters of genre; but Baudelaire pointed out that when Delacroix could scarcely find a buyer at one hundred francs the "practically invisible" figures of Meissonier were fetching ten or twenty times as much.

In *A Painter Showing His Drawings*, Meissonier described the same situation that one finds in Daumier's *Advice to a Young Artist*. In both, two figures stand beside opened portfolios in a studio with pictures on its walls. The Meissonier is faultlessly correct in every eighteenth-century detail, while Daumier's figures are of his own time. One reads the former like a book—the picturesque costume, the shine of a polished slipper, the highlights on a vase, the reflections in a mirror, the adroit suggestion of textural variations, the canvases on the wall; and its unity is a unity of cleverness, of delicate touch, of agreeable enumeration. In the Daumier the figures are much larger in relation to the whole and no accessory detail competes with the interaction of their minds, the grave intensity of their concentration. The reality of the scene exists not in the assembled details on the canvas but in the mind of the observer who himself fills out the few broad and simple suggestions. One does not know what counsel the young artist hears. Perhaps it is the advice which Zola proffered to the painters of his time:

Be makers of men and not artificers of shadows.

VIGNETTE: TIME OF CRISIS

"Think of Daumier!" wrote Baudelaire to his publisher in April, 1860, "of Daumier free, kicked out of the doors of *Charivari* in the midst of the month and with only a half-month's pay . . . and with no other occupation than painting." Since the close of 1859 his friend had indeed lost contact with the journal he had helped to launch nearly thirty years before and with it a steady if meager monthly income. We may never know the precise circumstances of this break and must content ourselves with the conflicting comments of his friends. In *Le Journal Amusant* in 1861 Charles Philipon observed that Daumier and his public had wearied of each other and that the former, by lazily repeating his own themes, "assisted at his own funeral," abdicating his throne as Daumier the First in order to have time for painting. A year later Philippe Burty described the artist in a "cruel state of privation . . . having no longer either lithographs or woodcuts to do. The newspapers won't have anything from him any longer. *Charivari* didn't renew his contract. *Le Monde Illustré* won't accept his series; his wood engravings, I hear from Champfleury, make subscribers drop off."

Burty exaggerated, since during the four-year respite from his old position Daumier made ten or a dozen lithographs for Carjat's *Le Boulevard,* among them some of his finest, and a few of his wood engravings appeared in *Le Temps* and *Le Monde Illustré*. To what extent was his new freedom of his own making, to what degree forced upon him? He may well have been bored by the more obvious aspects of the life around him and impatient with the routine of caricature as he developed his mature power in oil and water color. *Charivari* was now in competition with other satiric journals. The readers of *La Vie Parisienne,* for example, found its drawings more flippantly amusing than his robust and solid satires; and in *Charivari* itself he had a formidable rival in Cham, eleven years his senior, a superficial and clever draftsman whose real name was Amédée Vicomte de Noé and who had been a pupil of Delaroche and Charlet. For what it may be worth one notes that the older man's break with the journal came at a time when its editorial staff was shifting in the search for new ideas; as Taxile Delord and Louis Huart dropped out their places were taken by Pierre Véron and the militant Henri Rochefort.

The rupture, whether or not mutually satisfactory, certainly made a heavy task for the family man on the quai d'Anjou to "drag his cart," as he put it. In May of 1862 he borrowed fifteen hundred francs from Rousseau, giving him a painting at the same time; a year later when Tavernier asked him to come up to Paris he enclosed a postal order for railway fare "in case lack of money should prevent your coming." When he received five hundred francs at this time from two of his old comrades it was because they had come to his aid by making themselves salesmen for a group of his drawings.

Although poor in pocket he was richer now in friendly support and appreciation than he had ever been. At the Divan, a café with a small garden where one drank, played dominoes or prodded Couture and Courbet into violent debate, the journalist Audebrand saw and described Daumier as a republican of the heroic school of 1830 who quietly observed, "The democratic truth will see the light some day; let's learn how to wait." When he left the calm backwaters of the quai d'Anjou in 1863 for the noisier Bohemia of Montmartre, where his shifts of lodging suggest a series of impatient landlords, he joined the writers and illustrators of the Café de Madrid, whose company included the makers of old revolutions and the young firebrands who dreamed of new ones. Félix Pyat was there, and that veteran of many jails, Delescluze, returned from exile to keep republican fervor at white heat. There Gustave Mathieu improvised anti-Napoleonic songs for an audience some of whom would end a few years later before the firing squad. One of the group recalled that in these meetings Daumier was "the master without equal," a stubby thickset man with blunt and strongly sculptured features whose chin beard and long hair turned white as he approached sixty.

The stature of this man among his artistic colleagues in the 1860s is reflected by the number and variety of portraits they made of him. A medallion modeled by Michel Pascal was engraved to illustrate Champfleury's history of modern caricature, with accompanying verses by Baudelaire. For the first issue of his *Boulevard* in 1861 Carjat drew a lithographic *portrait-charge* which made much of his snub nose and sharply observant eyes, presenting him as a painter with brushes, palette and maul-

Et. CARJAT.

75. Caricature-portrait of Daumier by Étienne Carjat
Baltimore Museum of Art, Joseph Katz Collection

76. Daumier's House at Valmondois. Photo Josse-Lalance, Paris

stick in his hands (Fig. 75). The photographic studio of Nadar in the mid-fifties was a place where one could meet Dumas and Berlioz, Doré, Corot and George Sand, and where likenesses were made which best preserve for us the face of Daumier. In the studio of Carjat, who also practised photography, the Goncourt brothers compared him to a fat and mischievous lawyer and waspishly noted that he was the "crayon-God of the establishment."

Timid with strangers and ill at ease in formal company, this man could be his genial self only in the small circle of painters and sculptors who lived and worked at Barbizon and at Valmondois. Taine once described the carefree life of artists who ate and drank in the country taverns there or carried their easels into the forest to paint all day or to sleep away an afternoon in the shade of that leafy canopy. As early as 1853 Daumier had spent his summers at Valmondois, a small village twenty-three miles from Paris in the valley of the Oise. There Millet, Rousseau and the latter's wife came to dine with the Daumiers, while at Barbizon Rousseau gathered his friends on Saturday nights around a long table in his barn, among them Diaz, Barye, Millet, Corot, Daubigny and Daumier. On one such occasion the host remarked that Daumier was racy and Rabelaisian. In a more serious vein the company planned an Independent Society of Artists to fight the vulgarity and cheap sensationalism which now pervaded the world of official art, a project which ended with the evening's talk. Another scheme devised but never executed was an edition of La Fontaine to be illustrated by several members of the group.

Daumier could now once more count on a steady income from *Charivari,* whose staff changed again in 1865 with the death of Huart, the departure of Rochefort to *Figaro* and Caraguel's transfer of his loyalty to a monarchist paper. The chief editor now was Pierre Véron, a man with republican principles as firmly rooted as his own and a profound affection for an artist whom he considered far too selfless for his own good. Some of the best lithographs of the 1860s were made to illustrate captions devised by the resourceful wit of Véron. In October of 1865 Daumier was in sufficient funds to sign a nine-year lease for a cottage at Valmondois, where Corot and Daubigny had lived for a time, and long before them La Fontaine had written the fable of the miller, his son and the ass; Daumier's old comrade Geoffrey-Dechaume had bought a nearby piece of land some years before him (Fig. 76). Geudé, the owner of the property, agreed to build a studio in the garden beside the cottage, a modest structure some twenty-four feet wide and thirty-one in length. Daumier kept his rooms in the boulevard de Clichy until the last year of his life, but only for brief visits to Paris. At fifty-seven, when he drew *Country Pleasures,* he was no longer one of those urban bourgeois whose forays into the countryside he had so often satirized, but a villager with a decade of quiet work before him. These years at Valmondois would yield a ripe autumnal harvest.

7: THE REPUBLIC VICTORIOUS

If Daumier's friends expected that his resumption of work for *Charivari* in 1864 would be the signal for a renewed attack on the régime, they were disappointed. The time was not yet ripe and the prudent Pierre Véron, as he later remembered, sometimes paid the artist for a drawing which he dared not publish. The lithographs of the years 1864 and 1865, some two hundred in all, which appeared in *Charivari* and in *Le Journal Amusant* were a continuation, sometimes perfunctory, of his satire of the social scene—another series of railway and of hunting scenes, several drawings of the public at the Salon, more of his familiar *Bathers*, and other work which ranged from the banal cliché of the big head and little body to the pictorial richness of his superb series of 1864, *Sketches Made at the Theater*. The six *Country Pleasures*, as many of his drawings at this time, were printed by the Gillot method from etched metal plates, a process in which some of his original verve was lost. Artists were now using paper for drawings which could then be transferred to the stone, and Daumier's editor once asked whether he wished to receive stones or paper for a given commission. Many caricatures of the late 1860s suggest that he had used the latter.

During the months when Daumier refrained from comment on political matters he could watch the régime becoming more vulnerable with every passing day. As Émile Bourgeois has said:

> No government has ever come under the analysis of the historian, whose actions both at home and abroad have been so lacking in coherence, whose language has been more uncertain, whose purposes have been so obscure, whose efforts to reconcile the irreconcilable have been so sterile.

Ever since the Crimean venture Louis-Napoleon had thought of himself as the champion of nationalities and the arbiter of European rivalries, and every year recorded his fumbling performance in that role. In 1858 his troops helped the Italians to fight a restricted war against Austria in the Po valley with no significant gain for France. In 1859 he was blamed by the Ultracatholics at home for the effort of Italian patriots to seize Rome from the Pope; in 1860 he sponsored a ghost-written pamphlet which argued that the Pope should limit his temporal power to the Eternal City, and the ensuing wrath of the Church party forced him to seek help from liberals by making parliamentary reforms, a gesture which marked the end of his autocracy and the beginning of what was optimistically called the Liberal Empire.

The year 1861 found Napoleon still trying to reconcile the demands of Catholics with the pressures for a united Italy. In the next year Garibaldi's plan to attack Rome was thwarted with French help while the Bishops who met there demanded the restoration of the temporal power; in Poland, the Emperor's effort to intervene was balked; in Mexico in 1863 French armies crushed Juarez in preparation for the establishment of the Archduke Maximilian as ruler, a venture which would end disastrously four years later with the execution of the puppet Emperor. In 1864 Bismarck took his first step toward the domination of Germany by swallowing the Danish territory of Holstein, a success made possible by the benevolent neutrality of the Emperor of France, while Pius the Ninth issued a *Syllabus of Current Errors* and an Encyclical in which he denounced all freedom of thought, all notions of progress whether scientific, social or political.

The Imperial hovel, buffeted from without by the winds of competing powers and nationalities, was steadily being undermined from within. Among the critics of policy the most annoying but on the whole the least dangerous were those politicians whose effort was to reduce the ruler's absolute power, to rescue the national finances from his too lavish hand and to save France from the consequences of his tortuous and vacillating course in Europe. Some of these men were monarchists, others mild republicans, still others disaffected Catholic liberals. Their opportunity to heckle came with the Liberal Empire, a moment when, the suave Morny said, "the hand of the Emperor has opened . . . to restore to the country, in the midst of tranquillity and peace, a portion of the rights which she had wisely relinquished to him." Émile Ollivier, Jules Favre and others of "The Five" were busily making use of the new parliamentary freedoms, the former a republican of sorts who dreamed of an Empire willing to share its authority with ministers and parliament, a preacher of constitutionalism who urged Napoleon to be strong enough to grant liberty. In 1863 these revisionists were startled by the strength and unity of an Opposition which they had so feebly represented. The loyal Persigny tried to stem the tide and on the eve of the elections sent instructions to the prefects:

> The suffrage is free. But in order that the good faith of the people be not deceived by clever words or dubious professions of faith, clearly designate those candidates who inspire the greatest confidence in the government.

On May 31 and June first the provinces obeyed, but Paris and the larger cities rejected all the Imperial candidates for office. The Five became thirty-five and Ollivier was emboldened to form a Third Party. Wily Thiers, more owlish than ever with his topknot turned white, reappeared on the rostrum as a deputy from Paris with speeches intended not to subvert the Empire but to denounce the folly of the Mexican invasion and the risks of the Roman entanglement, and to warn his countrymen of the deadly power which a united Germany would hold.

To these critics of the régime could now be added the chief spokesmen of the Church. The Comte de Falloux, who had neither approved nor condemned the coup d'état, watched the collapse of an Empire in bitter silence; Montalembert concluded that a Church which began as an accomplice and a dupe of autocratic power would end as its victim, and was twice brought to trial for an article in which he contrasted the corrupt and stifling fog around him with the clean, free air of England; Veuillot in his newspaper poured scurrilous abuse on the man whose pamphlet against the Pope's temporal power he called the kiss of Judas.

More threatening still were those republicans who were also democrats and whose aim was not to reshape the government and thus to prolong its life but to destroy it. The amnesty of 1859 had freed many an old fighter from his exile. Hugo refused to quit his island, content for the moment to undermine Napoleon the Little by means of the copies of his pamphlet which were smuggled by the hundreds into France, and two dozen of which, it was said, were imported in a plaster bust of the Emperor. *Napoleon the Little* had been translated into several languages, and many a rebellious spirit could recite passages of it from memory. Sainte-Beuve remarked of Hugo, "Under the very nose of the government that exiled him he has snatched the greatest popularity of our time . . . everybody reads him. Editions go out of print between eight in the morning and twelve at noon." Among the proscripts who did return were the pure democrat Hippolyte Carnot, the unquenched firebrand Félix Pyat and the implacable Delescluze, to hobnob at the Café de Madrid with younger radicals who had grown up in the dictatorship. Lafargue spoke for the latter: "The Empire condemned us to silence and study; we now stand before it stout of heart and strong of brain."

This new generation sometimes complained that the "old beards" were more concerned with revolutionary theory than with action, more anxious to be right than to be effective; when you go down into the sewers, Gambetta remarked, you don't wear slippers. Pending the time for action, however, the published word was their best weapon. From time to time the Empire's iron grasp of the press was slightly relaxed, and every gesture of this kind was the signal for some new journal to appear, each with its staff of sappers and miners of the Imperial edifice —*L'Opinion Nationale, Le Temps, Journal des Débats, L'Avenir National, L'Électeur Libre* and so many others that Daumier drew a harassed citizen wading ankle deep in newspapers, *The High Tide of 1868*. In the *Courrier du Dimanche* the mischievous Eugène Assolant congratulated the government on its triumphs:

We have founded in Mexico an empire which shall be, one hopes, as solid and eternal as our own; we protect the Pope against himself, against his cardinals and against Italy . . . and if it is a glorious thing to meddle in the affairs of all one's neighbors, we are the most glorious of men. . . .

In the *Journal des Débats* Lucien Prévost-Paradol wittily evaded the censor by describing Soulouque, who had made himself the ruler of the Antilles and founded an ephemeral aristocracy in the Dukes of Lemonade and of Marmalade, "titles which will be preserved only in the history books." A provincial schoolteacher named Louis-Auguste Rogeard founded *La Rive Gauche* and wrote a series under the pseudonym of Labienus before quitting France to escape a five-year prison sentence. His description of Rome was his reply to Louis-Napoleon's *Life of Julius Caesar:*

Slowly rising through the mist of blood which crimsoned its dawning, the star of Julius climbed, and its soft light poured down on the silent forum. The curia was tongueless and the laws were mute. . . . Everywhere was the *pax Romana:* a single tribune, Augustus; a single army, the troops of Augustus; a single will, his own; . . . a single censor, a single praetor, always he . . . Livy put down his pen. Cicero's books were forbidden. Society had been saved.

The poisoned shaft of Henri de Rochefort, wrote Hugo, was in the Empire's flanks. This office clerk whose father had been a Marquis and whose lean and angry face someone described as a barricade in human form worked with Daumier on *Charivari* before issuing his own paper *La Lanterne* in 1868, in which he could sting his adversary even in a gossipy note on the death of the Emperor's pet dog:

Nero is dead. Last evening he simply fell asleep after dismissing his courtesans (for I must tell you that French courtesans are not proud; when they cannot approach the master, they lie down with the dog). . . . In the morning, the servants . . . beheld him stretched out on his rug, legs in air, as stiff as justice. . . . They say he has been buried in the private garden of the Tuileries. I myself would have preferred a tomb in Saint-Denis between Turenne and Philip-Augustus. One should never do things by halves. . . .

It was items of this sort which sent Rochefort into brief exile in Belgium. An even more violent sheet was *Le Réveil* which Delescluze established in 1868, one of whose projects was the collecting of funds for a monument to the deputy Baudin who had been shot during the coup d'état. When brought to trial for this venture the editor hired for his defense a swarthy Italian lawyer with a black beard and a sonorous voice, and Léon Michel Gambetta turned the case into a trial of the Empire in an oration which mingled shrewd logic with old but serviceable clichés. The Emperor has never dared, he cried, to declare the Second of December a national holiday.

> Very well! This anniversary shall be the Day of the Dead for the rest of us. . . . Each year without fail we shall commemorate it . . . until that day when the people shall again be master and shall impose on you its great national expiation in the name of Liberty, Equality and Fraternity!

Small wonder that the victim complained of a veritable conspiracy among writers against his government. Even the mild Théophile Gautier, when he reviewed the revival of Hugo's *Hernani* in 1867 for the *Moniteur,* summoned up the courage to send in his resignation as critic along with his piece and demanded that the ministry choose one or the other. Théodore de Banville's *Occidentales* of 1869 included the pro-republican and sharply anticlerical articles he had been contributing to *Charivari.* When the critic J. J. Weiss surveyed the shortcomings of current plays in 1866, he attributed their brittleness and their harsh and narrow view of man's life and destiny to the repressive atmosphere of French society. Our plays, he wrote, leave us with a bad taste in the mouth, a vague dissatisfaction, and our submission to them is part of our submission to political conformity.

A few years before, Offenbach and his librettists had found a way to stigmatize that conformity in *Orpheus* by calling their chorus Public Opinion and showing how Jupiter shaped it for his own purposes. The composer "turned the Iliad into a cancan" with *Fair Helen* in 1864, reducing the heroic legend to the dimensions of Napoleonic intrigue, debauchery and cynicism. When Helen was shipped off to the Island of Cytherea to sacrifice a hundred white heifers, her husband glibly informed the populace that they would pay for the animals. Other episodes must have seemed to the audience like a dramatization of Daumier's *Ancient History* series: he had drawn the baptism of Achilles and now that hero remarked, "She might have dipped me into the Styx one leg at a time," to which Orestes answered, "Yes, that's a thought which should have occurred to a mother." On more than one occasion the caricaturist had presented venal political henchmen as the high priests of antiquity; now Calchas, Chief Augur in the opera bouffe, complains:

> Paltry offerings, really . . . two pigeons, a jug of milk, three small cheeses. . . . Gone are the days of heads of cattle and sheep; the Gods are going! Hit the thunder sheet hard. One must strike the imagination of the people.

The actress Hortense Schneider, "a Rubens come down from its frame," was the exquisite and insinuatingly vulgar Helen of the occasion and three years later played the Grand Duchess of Gerolstein in a piece whose surface frivolity could not hide the sting of its attack on the militaristic mind, personified in this case by the extravagant stupidities of General Boum. Daumier paid his compliment to men who must have borrowed from him when he drew *History as Revised by Operetta,* a turbulent ballet of legendary kings and heroines which reminds one of Francisque Sarcey's tribute to Offenbach:

> At the first stroke of the bow which set the gods of Olympus and the underworld in motion, it seemed as though . . . the whole century, with its governments, institutions, customs and laws, were plunged into the whirl of a tremendous, all-embracing saraband.

Taking up his political crayon again in the year 1866, Daumier entered the final campaign for his beloved Republic with a series of lithos which were no less effective than the jeremiads of Thiers, the libels of Veuillot, the wicked sarcasm of Assolant and Rochefort, the rumbling of Gambetta's orations and the light-fingered malice of Offenbach's tuneful parodies. Henceforth with few exceptions the fate of the Empire will be his theme; but his presentation of the issues, his warnings and his affirmations, will take a different form from earlier ones. Partly in order to compensate for the pictorial losses which the new techniques involved in elaboration of detail, in richness of tonal contrasts and textures, in subtlety of spatial relations, the work of Daumier achieves in this last phase a terse eloquence and a stark simplicity through the intensity of line alone and the compression of his thought into a few blacks and whites.

During the July Monarchy and the Second Republic the vices and virtues of men and parties had often been embodied in exaggerated but unmistakable portraits of public figures. To publish such likenesses now was to risk punishment and suppression. Two drawings of Émile Ollivier in the early months of 1866 discreetly showed him with his back to the observer, but in spite of this caution the second one, in which he hesitated between the right and left parties, was not permitted to appear. Moreover, Daumier in his older and wiser years preferred to attack policies, not personalities. In his best drawings the *portrait-charge* gives place to the symbol: Peace is a buxom and benevolent female with an overflowing cornucopia and Diplomacy an emaciated hag in the dress of the eighteenth century. The god Mars and Father Time move in these lithographs, clerical intolerance is embodied by Basile, and Death is a horribly grinning skeleton.

Some of his sharpest arrows were aimed at the Ultramontaine press which in one drawing clutches the robe of Father Time to stay his forward motion. Since Veuillot was the most intransigent foe of progress, several caricatures were given to his crusade against pagan authors and

77. *I Wanted to Smear Him,* lithograph
Museum of Fine Arts, Boston, Mass.

the writers of the French Revolution. Armed with his conviction that
"the people is a mind meant to be governed," Veuillot backed the petition of his fellow churchmen for a law which would forbid the sale of
Voltaire, Rousseau, Michelet, Renan, Taine, George Sand, Flaubert,
Hugo and Sainte-Beuve in bookshops and ban from the curricula of
schools the "voluptuous naturalism" of Lucretius, Horace, Cicero, Ovid,
Seneca and Tacitus. In Daumier's *Dialogue of the Dead* an angry priest
complains that people on earth are concerning themselves with Galileo
and Voltaire. The editor of *L'Univers* was fulminating at this time over
the sculptured groups of Carpeaux at the portals of the new Opéra, who
were more than naked, he wrote, and were not dancing the minuet.
When someone threw ink upon them he reminded his readers that Renan
had been spattering ink in the face of Christ and that a well-paid band
of caricaturists was smearing human dignity. Daumier returned the

78. *The New Cinderella,* lithograph. Museum of Fine Arts, Boston, Mass.

compliment with a picture of a priest who had tried to throw ink on the statue of Voltaire but had only succeeded in besmirching himself (Fig. 77). Veuillot referred to the campaign in *Le Siècle* for funds for this statue as the most brutal insult to the Church since 1830, and a litho shows the lean and angry Basile trying to stay the sculptor's hand: "I don't want him to have his statue as long as I don't have mine!" In a "project to console the enemies of the statue" Daumier clothes the author of *Candide* in the black surplice and shovel hat of the priesthood.

More devastatingly specific is the plate which *Charivari* published at the time of the episode of Père Hyacinthe, a Carmelite who could not square his liberal convictions with Papal policy. At the Peace Congress in June, 1869, he observed that man was on the earth not to dream of salvation but to earn it by his labor, and based his indictment of war on three of the Ten Commandments. Veuillot at once condemned the speech as a dangerous and infantile performance. Ordered by his superiors to change his tune or to be silent, the priest quit his order and was excommunicated. In an article, *Father Hyacinthe Departs,* his Nemesis happily declared that henceforth, "stripped of the holy robe which he drops on the path of modern thinking, he will come to know the error of his vanity if not of his heart." Daumier's drawing took another view of the matter, and showed the defrocked preacher escaping the clutch of Veuillot and his colleagues, leaving behind him only a vestment with the letter H upon it. "The cloak stays in their hands, as in the story of Joseph."

Daumier knew that the French involvement in Italian affairs was largely due to the claims of men like Veuillot who demanded that the Emperor repay them for their earlier help in his rise to power. Perhaps to avoid censorship however, his caricatures of this time emphasize the quarrel between Prussia and Austria over the northern provinces rather than the fumbling interventions of France. Venetia as a noble and tragic figure watches that dispute with a mixture of grief and hope; in another drawing Austria has become a withered and repulsive Cinderella who leaves the boot of the Italian peninsula behind her (Fig. 78). In October, 1866, Daumier symbolizes the Italian people by a peasant driving a chariot while the reactionary press of France tries in vain to thrust a stick into its wheels. A year later Garibaldi has been crushed at Mentana and Daumier's cruelly indifferent Jesuit walking beside the reproachful skeletons of the victims is too terrible an indictment to be published. One of his last references to the subject in January of 1868 represents the Roman question as a huge knotted rope which endless memoranda, diplomatic notes and ultimatums have failed to untie.

With more latitude on the German problem the artist multiplies his images of the fat Prussian officer who strangles Germany in his "embrace" (Fig. 79), grapples with Austria over the prostrate body of Holstein, swells to the proportion of a Gulliver as he gathers in the small states, climbs on the wall which separates him from France to read the sign that there are wolf traps on this side, is awarded the first prize for "expansiveness" in 1867, and disguises himself as a dog to watch over the sheep of Hesse, Baden and other prospective victims. A monstrously swollen female with gigantic breasts, her belly labelled Prussia, proved to be unpublishable, but Daumier made the same point with more finesse in *The Human Pyramid,* where Bismarck's warrior stands on the weak shoulders of Holstein, Hanover and Nassau. Prussia had swallowed the North German territories when, in a drawing of December 26, 1868, she was metamorphosed into a torpid snake with a swollen belly over the caption: "The boa is digesting; no fear that it will move." But Daumier knew that it would move. The metaphor in a litho of June 4, 1867, is that of the French and German locomotives rushing toward each other

79. *Let Us Embrace,* lithograph. Museum of Fine Arts, Boston, Mass.

on a single track, a symbol which Daumier used for several caricatures of this time and one which may have inspired the prophetic words of Prévost-Paradol:

> Nobody wants this terrible collision; there are screams and hasty gestures; the engines are reversed; the brakes squeal and are shattered. The effort is futile because the momentum comes from too far away.

The issue of war and peace was for Daumier the crucial one and inspired a sequence of drawings whose bitter irony and controlled anger give them a special place in his work. For once this former enemy of Thiers found himself in agreement with the little man whom he now represents, with an olive branch in his hand, on a political seesaw out-

80. *The Lady of the Eggs,* lithograph
Museum of Fine Arts, Boston, Mass.

weighed by Mars. Man's ingenuity in creating means for his own destruction threatens to outrun his will and his capacity for constructive action. With a hideous smile the inventor of the needle-gun dreams of the field on which are strewn the corpses of its victims, a drawing of 1866 which finds an echo two years later in Banville's poem where Chassepot has devised the king of rifles and cries to it, "The future is yours!" In other lithos the bayonet is variously used; Father Time exchanges his scythe for this weapon, the ghost of Galileo finds the surface of the earth prickly with it, and the nations balance the globe of Europe on its points. When Daumier borrows from mythology France becomes a Hercules bent under the weight of the military budget or a Sisyphus endlessly straining to roll the burden uphill.

By way of contrast Daumier shows us the ineffectual crone Diplomacy rocking the cradle of a Mars who will not go to sleep, offering a rickety chair to the plump goddess of Peace, blandly cutting up the map of Europe with her shears, and perilously balancing herself on a ladder among the brittle eggs of Rome, the Orient and Germany (Fig. 80). Several times during the International Exposition of 1867, one of whose exhibits was a Temple of Peace, he reminds us that the shadow of war hangs over that celebration of human progress, and his project for a statue of Peace for the fair is a militant female who stands with sword and rifle beside a cannon. Some twenty years before, Daumier and his friends had ridiculed the windy idealism of the Peace Congress over which Hugo had presided in Paris; *La Réforme* had tartly reminded the delegates that world order was incompatible with monarchies, with permanent armies and with "all those special privileges by which some men try to fatten themselves on the blood and sweat of their fellows." By 1867 however, the peace movement had become more realistic and its social and political goals more immediate and concrete; its second crusade involved well-organized societies in America, England and France, who met in Geneva when Napoleon's government refused them hospitality in Paris in the year of the Exposition.

Daumier's contribution to this cause in 1867 and 1868 included drawings whose terse eloquence he never surpassed. All he needed was a bundle of crackling lines and a few stark indications of light and shade to balance a woman nervously on a smoking bomb in *European Equilibrium* (Fig. 81) or to mock the militarists who bow and smile but will not enter the council of disarmament in *After You!* (Fig. 82). The artist who once said that he disliked allegories now creates symbolic creatures which are like noble statues come to life. One of these is Autumn with her garlands of fruit, who has asked Father Time the password and to whom he whispers, "Fraternity and Artillery"; and there is Pax, the "laureate of 1868," bending to receive her crown of bayonets; in still another drawing, Europe on Christmas morning of that year finds her gifts of cannons and cannon balls on the hearth. When a new peace conference is held in Paris during the early weeks of 1869 Daumier publishes two rueful drawings which seem to say that its efforts come too late. One of his scrawny beldames tries to mend the wooden leg of a decrepit world whose crutches are guns; another wields an inadequate paintbrush in the effort to restore the crumbling Temple of Peace.

With the approach of the May elections in this year the caricaturist boldly turns from symbol to portraiture in order to contrast the true with the false friends of the republic. A law of March seventh has

81. *European Equilibrium,* lithograph
Museum of Fine Arts, Boston, Mass.

abolished some of the worst penalties on published opinion and in the next few days Émile Ollivier is shown trying to wash some of its original color back into the flag of France, posing beside an electoral urn, and falling between two saddles as he tries to ride the horses of progress and reaction in the political circus ring. Before the election Daumier drew diminutive candidates parading before the towering figure of France, who is "preparing to judge them by size"; in another litho they bow and scrape to a countryman in smock and sabots whose solid strength reminded Michelet that the people is sovereign and that statesmen are its subjects, not its masters. "Your poetry attracted a very great attention yesterday in the rue Rambuteau," he wrote Daumier, explaining that he had refrained from buying the only copy of this litho in a merchant's window lest it be taken from the sight of the crowd.

Daumier's peasant was once more deceived into supporting the Napoleonic candidates on May twenty-third, a day which was none the less a brilliant success for the republicans. The names of men elected in the cities, many of them uncompromising radicals and all of them sworn enemies of the régime, proved that they were no longer feared by the urban middle class—Pelletan, Simon, Picard, Raspail, Rochefort, Gambetta. Ollivier was defeated by Bancel, and Daumier celebrated the victory with a pictorial pun in which the latter uproots an olive tree, a joke which did not amuse the censor and was never published. *The Morning After the Battle,* printed two days after the election, showed the corpses of dead candidates strewn on the field, and a month later Liberty was singing at the piano while *Charivari* listened: "Her voice is certainly stronger."

There was no time for self-congratulation when the new Chamber met at the end of June to reshape the Constitution. Ollivier had got himself elected from the Var district and now led the efforts of the Third Party to reconcile a sovereign with his people by chipping away the former's power and presenting to the latter the mirage of a parliamentary government. Thiers was active among these compromisers, and Flaubert wrote, "I can't tell you how I want to vomit when I see this ancient diplomatic melon swelling his stupid sides on the bourgeois garbage pile. .. . . Like mediocrity, he seems to be eternal." Daumier's best drawings in July and August are warnings against pseudo progress: the Constitution lies on a slab beneath the scalpels of parliamentary doctors or takes the form of a balloon kept afloat by throwing out ballast; she pins up the robe of Liberty, who admonishes her, "Not too short, if you please"; as a hypnotist she puts Liberty into a deep slumber. Shortly after the Senate decree announced the new Constitution in September, Daumier implied the dissatisfaction

82. *After You!*, lithograph. Museum of Fine Arts, Boston, Mass.

of democrats with all this tinkering in a drawing of a French citizen watching the "progress" of a line of snails.

Lest Frenchmen preoccupied with constitutional questions forget other issues, the God of War was shown sharpening his sword in a lithograph of June, and in the autumn there began a series of bitter comments on the Ecumenical Council which was to meet in Saint Peter's in December to affirm the Pope's infallibility. In a *Rehearsal for the Council,* priests are trying to blow out the flame of free thought; in another plate Basile holds a scales in which the papal syllabus outweighs the Bible. Five days after the dogma of infallibility was voted, a puppetlike ecclesiastical figure is being hoisted into the clouds by ropes and pulleys while birdlike creatures with the heads of priests circle about, under the caption, *The New Assumption.*

The Emperor of the French, now sick and irresolute, could do nothing to prevent the Pontiff's action. One by one his dictatorial powers were being stripped from him with the bland ministerial assurance that every concession was an addition to his strength, while the agitators of the extreme left were planning a violent demonstration to protest his delay in reopening Parliament, a revolutionary action which was prevented by the cooler heads of Gambetta and others who knew that the moment of deliverance had not arrived. To those timid bourgeois still haunted by fear of a Red Republic Daumier offered a drawing of December ninth which seems an illustration of Hugo's lines in *Napoleon the Little:*

> Red chambers, red specters, red scarecrows, are all alike. Those who parade these fantasmagoria at the end of a stick before the frightened people know what they are doing, and laugh behind these fluttering rags and tatters. . . .

In Daumier's caricature a citizen on the road to liberty cowers before just such a scarecrow while his guide reminds him that it is only a stuffed dummy.

On the last day of this troubled year there was no false optimism in Daumier's drawing of a Father Time who whispers the password to the arriving 1870, "Reaction, Pardon me, Liberty." On January second in *Charivari* the old year hands over to the new a bundle of diminutive politicians—"Here are your toys, don't break them"; and in real life the fatuous Ollivier becomes the head of a new "ministry of good intentions." Under the heading, *The Parliamentary Arena,* we see Gambetta, Rochefort and Jules Favre flexing their muscles in preparation for the battle; on another page the decrepit cabal of their opponents makes its appearance with the cry, "Make room for the young!" Daumier gives us Thiers as Egeria, the nymph of mysterious silence, Thiers as an acrobat sustained by the rue de Poitiers, Thiers in the prompter's box, delighted to direct the play without being seen by the audience.

The last act of the Imperial melodrama has begun. On the day after Ollivier presented his plan for sharing the power of constitution-making between the Senate and the Legislative Body the ineptitude of the parliamentary majority and the futility of the ministers were summarized by Daumier in an image borrowed from the fables of Florian. A blind old lady carries on her back a paralytic with his crutch and his portfolio. "I shall walk for you," she says, "and you shall see for me," as they lurch toward the edge of a precipice.

One last device for avoiding disaster, in the minds of Napoleon's supporters, was a plebiscite which, ostensibly to ratify a new constitution, could be turned into a reaffirmation of his prestige. The trick had worked in 1852 and might again. In April the Senate and the Emperor summoned the country to such a vote and Daumier voiced the scornful opposition of the republicans with a litho in which the mayor of a village explains to two farmers that a "bibiscite" is a Latin word meaning Yes. The question to be decided on May eighth was cleverly worded:

The people approve the liberal reforms introduced into the constitution since 1860 by the Emperor.

Unable to approve Napoleon's concessions without at the same time endorsing his régime, nearly two million Frenchmen abstained. In sophisticated Paris the negative votes outnumbered the affirmative, but the country as a whole provided over seven million favorable votes to one and a half million of dissent. "I have my figure," said the Emperor.

We have no comment from Daumier on this victory, nor can we follow in his drawings the events of July which precipitated the final catastrophe: the decision of the Hohenzollern Prince Leopold to accept the vacant throne of Spain; the pressure of the war party on Napoleon to seek glory and renewed strength in a war; the vain efforts of the Emperor to acquire Italy and Austria as military allies and the vague and secret gentleman's agreement which was all he could secure and which was no secret to Bismarck; the bland announcement of Ollivier on June thirteenth that wherever one looked one saw no bothersome question, and at no period had the preservation of peace in Europe been more assured; Leopold's renunciation of his candidacy; the suicidal insistence by French officials that the King of Prussia guarantee that no such effort would be made in the future; the eloquent pleas of Thiers to prevent a conflict for which his country was ill prepared and his stubborn refusal to vote for it; the declaration of war by France on July fourteenth and the journey of the ailing Emperor to Metz a few days later to take command of an army inadequately mobilized and poorly equipped whose only hope was to defend the frontiers.

At the opera on the night of the nineteenth the aged composer Auber listened to the *Marseillaise* before a performance of one of his operettas. He had heard it as a child of ten in 1792 and now muttered, "That bodes no good, it's always the signal for bloodshed." A few days later the Prussians invaded Alsace and Daumier shortly published two drawings in which he contrasted the forced mobilization of the Germans at the point of bayonets with the surging French volunteers who hail the statue of their country as they pass with "Those who are about to die salute you." (Fig. 83).

They died in their thousands at Froeschwiller and Forbach, in the siege of Metz and the crushing of MacMahon's cornered army at Sedan, thanks on the one hand to a carefully planned Prussian campaign skill-

83. *Those Who Are About to Die* . . . , lithograph
Museum of Fine Arts, Boston, Mass.

fully executed and on the other to the panic and cross-purposes of
demoralized French forces led by incompetent generals. Daumier had
drawn the nightmare of Monsieur Bismarck, with a grinning skeleton
of Death who points to the corpse-strewn battle field; the nightmare of
France was just beginning when the people of Paris, now more warlike
than their own government or their military leaders, learned on September third that Napoleon had surrendered with his army at Sedan.
The next day saw climax and anticlimax: the people of Paris invading
the Assembly with cries of "Long live the Republic!" and the conflicting efforts of rival groups to improvise a government; Gambetta's
words from the tribune, "We declare that Louis-Napoleon Bonaparte
and his dynasty have forever ceased to reign in France," and his
announcement of a Government of National Defense, most of whose
ministers were less than passionate republicans and whose President
was General Trochu, a royalist convinced that more than a token
resistance to the invaders would be futile.

Daumier was among those who would not admit defeat, and his drawing of September twentieth, *The Republic Calls Us,* was a tribute to the National Guardsmen who now undertook to defend the city. Event followed event too swiftly to be noted by his crayon, as Thiers scuttled from London to Vienna and from Florence to Saint Petersburg for help and came back with none, while the Prussians cut the last railway line and isolated Paris from the rest of France except for carrier pigeons and the balloon of Nadar. The siege of the capital, one hundred and thirty-two days of mounting agony, drew no complaining comments from the artist, who must have walked the dark streets where people carried lanterns as they had in the middle ages, and seen the Red Cross flag at the portals of the theater where the royalty of Europe had applauded the cancan of Offenbach not long before. The foyer of the Théâtre-Francais, now a hospital, reeked of ether; the dark shapes of cannon loomed against the white statues in the gardens of the Tuileries; and families made homeless by the Prussians slept among the famous dead in the basements of the Pantheon. On the floor of the dismantled throne room lay the gilded cupids, the crowns and velvet draperies which would be carried off as souvenirs. The true collectors of thrones, said Jules Clarétie, were the people of Paris; and Daumier echoed that sentiment with a drawing of France as a housewife sweeping away the kings and princes. The statues of Goujon on the façade of the Louvre were given a protective coat of plaster; sandbags covered the stained glass of Sainte-Chapelle, and the Venus de Milo journeyed by night to the cellar of the Prefecture of Police. By the end of October rationed food was so scarce that Paris consumed dogs, cats and rats, and slaughtered the two pet elephants of the zoo for nourishment.

Aside from an occasional litho in which the Prussians watch Paris from a distance in the rain and sleet of November, Daumier seldom calls attention to specific events—the failure of the several sorties against the investing armies, the government's dispatch of Thiers to negotiate an armistice with Bismarck, the anger of Paris with leaders who can make neither war nor peace which provokes a near-revolution but is suppressed by the National Guard, the furious debates in the Assembly between Gambetta and the majority of frightened conservatives, the shells falling on Paris at the beginning of the new year, and toward the end of January the violent mob storming the Hôtel de Ville with cries of *"Long Live the Commune!"* to protest the imminent surrender. During these terrible weeks we have instead a pictorial chastisement of the Empire, an indictment for which Hugo needed thousands of words and Daumier only a few relentless blacks and whites. This mild man who had always refused to belabor a fallen

84. *A Page of History,* lithograph. Collection Benjamin A. and Julia M. Trustman, Brandeis University, Waltham, Mass.

enemy now releases the pent fury of twenty years not only as a judgment but as a warning to his people that men moved in public affairs who still intrigued for the third Napoleon and talked of another "return from Elba."

Those twenty years of Caesarism were neatly summed up in Daumier's *History of a Reign:* the figure of France, bound hand and foot, stands between the mouths of two cannons, one of which is labelled Paris, 1851, the other Sedan, 1870. "The crowning of the edifice"—Morny's phrase for the Liberal Empire—becomes under Daumier's hand the capping of the fortress of Sedan by a huge Prussian helmet. Another famous remark is quoted above the drawing of a burning village whose owners lie among the rubble, a remark which Hugo also turned against its maker in the lines:

85. *Peace, an Idyl*, lithograph. Museum of Fine Arts, Boston, Mass.

> O dead, the grass grows silently upon your catacombs,
> Sleep in your shrouds! Be quiet in your tombs!
>   The Empire means Peace.

Daumier borrows more than once from Hugo, whose *Chastisements* he doubtless read in smuggled form before its French publication in the second month of the siege. The exiled poet whose romantic posturing had once been mocked by Daumier returned on the fifth of September and noted in his diary at least two occasions when they dined or talked together in Paris. Hugo in *Expiation* had described the exiled first Napoleon bound to a rock while the British vulture tore out his heart; in a Daumier drawing it is France which now becomes Prometheus and the devouring bird is the Napoleonic eagle. The tempestuous author and the mild-mannered artist were fighting the same battle when the latter's *A Page of History* appeared on November sixteenth in 1870, a very dead eagle crushed beneath Hugo's verses, and the poet sent a copy of his book with the remark, "You have made so fine a frontispiece that now it belongs to you." (Fig. 84). And Daumier returned the compliment by borrowing a caption from his friend. Addressing Napoleon the Little in 1853, Hugo had mocked his vain wish to be a figure of history. Instead, the charnel house of kings and emperors would be denied this human scarecrow, this plucked bird, this dead creature; "you will remain outside, nailed to the door." In Daumier's magnificent and terrible drawing, an eagle's spread carcass is impaled on the cover of the Book of History, with Hugo's verse beneath, and the date of March first, 1871 when the National Assembly formally declared the end of the Empire. Five days after this decree, a skeleton with a flowered and beribboned bonnet pipes his threnody of death among the ruins (Fig. 85).

Although the best of Daumier is in these expressions of his grief and anger, he found other and equally effective ways of interpreting the events of day by day in what Hugo called the Terrible Year. When the Assembly signed an armistice and announced elections for a new body whose task would be the negotiation of a peace he drew a blasted tree with the caption, "Poor France! The trunk is shattered, but the roots still hold"; when that body met at Bordeaux with a minority of republicans and a dominant group who seemed eager to make peace at any price, he pictured them above the prostrate body of France, asking, "Who will take up the knife?" When they made Thiers Chief of the Executive Power he showed the little man strutting on the stage at Bordeaux with Bismarck as his invisible prompter. Neither Daumier nor any other draftsman had any image for the morning of March first, 1871, when the hussars in blue uniforms led the Prussian troops down the Champs-Élysées. No paper was published, no shops were open, no omnibuses ran in the streets where people watched in silence.

A fortnight later the government failed in its effort to seize the cannons which the National Guard had stored at Belleville and Montmartre and decided to quit a capital whose people still refused to concede the Prussian victory. On the twenty-eighth of March the country had two capitals: a ceremony in the square at the Hôtel de Ville installed the Commune of Paris, an alliance of the laboring classes with the more radical elements of the urban bourgeoisie; at Versailles sat an Assembly which, having come to terms with its conqueror, now prepared to destroy the "handful of bandits and assassins" which defied its power. Daumier's litho of March thirty was both a plea and a prophecy: The city of Paris confronts Monsieur Reactionary with the graves of the war's victims and reminds him that there are already enough dead.

Within a week French shells are falling in the city, and a month later the armies of Versailles are storming the fortifications at its edge. Within the Commune there is conflict aroused by the ruthless measures of its own Committee of Public Safety. On the twenty-first of May the troops force the gates and push back the Communards street by street in a week of vengeful slaughter whose toll of lives mounts into the thousands. Hasty court-martials are set up, the defenders of barricades mowed down, alleged revolutionaries lined up before a firing squad in Père Lachaise; and the vast muddy plain of Satory, with its prisoners cowering under machine guns, becomes "Hell in the open air." Remarking that Democracy has been bled for a generation, Thiers holds a review of his conquering army at Longchamps on the twenty-ninth of June.

What was Daumier's response to the Commune? He made few comments on its specific actions. When the guillotine was burned before a statue of Voltaire which had been dedicated while the Germans marched toward Paris, he sketched the figure of the man who had defended Calas and now rose from his marble chair to applaud the destruction of this symbol of ancient tyranny. His sympathies were clear in a litho published on the day when the Fortress of Issy was attacked, with its image of the chariot of State being driven in two directions by a noble Paris and a repulsive hag labelled Versailles. With or without his consent, Daumier was elected to a Committee of Artists, along with Courbet, Millet, Corot and others, to protect works of art from the bombs and also to liberalize the system by which artists were trained and works of art exhibited.

During May and June he made no drawings, and when the blood bath of the Commune was ended and men free to walk in the ravaged city, he did not join the chorus of recrimination. Théophile Gautier, emerging from a garret on the quai Voltaire in which he had lived out the siege, remarked that this revolution would be the end of him, as he observed the headless statues in the place de la Concorde, the ruins of the Ministry of Finance strewn in the rue de Rivoli, the fragments of the Vendôme Column lying on a bed of manure, the Tuileries a few blackened and smoking walls, the paintings of Ingres and Delacroix gone from the Hôtel de Ville, whose courtyard looked like the crater of a volcano. For him the Communards were gorillas lusting for fire and blood; for Villemessant, Thiers was a hero who failed to conquer the Prussians but at least gave the democrats of France the bloodiest of lessons; for the Goncourts, events had proven how evil and petty were the passions of the French populace, to whom

Liberty, Equality and Fraternity meant the enslavement and ruin of the superior classes. On the whole, one concludes that for Daumier, the Commune was a noble experiment which failed, "a good idea badly managed," as Hugo said, a hasty glimpse of social and political changes for which time was not ripe, a revolution impossible of fulfillment in one city encircled by a whole country of conservatives. He must have shared Hugo's horror of the butchery which followed its suppression. The real culprits were the too-clever statesmen, the unreconstructed monarchists, the priestly enemies of intellectual progress, the unrepentant Napoleonists and the summer soldiers of republicanism— all those, in short, whose plans for France could not contain the hopes nor satisfy the needs of her people. Against these obstacles he now waged his last battle.

In the summer of 1871 Thiers was once more the man of the hour. "He has turned many somersaults in his long life," wrote Veuillot, "and has always picked himself up. At present he is hurrying toward his last one." Nearly half of France was occupied by Germans; a huge ransom was to be somehow paid; the monarchists of Bourbon and Orleanist stripe formed the most aggressive group in the Assembly; the Ultramontaine party threatened to involve France in a crusade to restore the Pope's temporal power, which had been lost when French troops finally withdrew from Rome during the preceding autumn and the Italians marched into their rightful capital. Daumier represented the conservatives' idea of a republic as a statue of Venus without arms, The Republic of Milo; and the Colossus of Rhodes became under his crayon the figure of Thiers straddling the Right and the Left. As for the royalist clique, he causes the Ghost of Louis the Fourteenth to descend from his statue to listen at the keyhole of the Assembly, unhappy with "the way things are going for the Bourbons." For his attacks on the men who now dreamed of establishing the son of Napoleon the Third as ruler of France, the artist revives the sinister Ratapoil and shows the ex-Prime Minister Rouher trying to wash bloodstains from the soiled linen of the Empire. His most cruel irony is reserved for the black-robed clergy whose ranks march into the political scene as the Prussians leave—"One invasion replaces the other"—and for *Requiescat in Pace,* the funeral couch of the temporal power, published soon after King Victor Emmanuel made his formal entry into Rome. When the Church party threatens once more to take the educational system of the country into its hands his Basile prays to Saint Ignorance for protection against schools administered by laymen.

In May of 1872 Daumier shows in two lithographs both his negative fear and his positive hope for a republic. *If the workers fight, how shall the house be built?* is his call for unity among factions; in *The Sovereign*

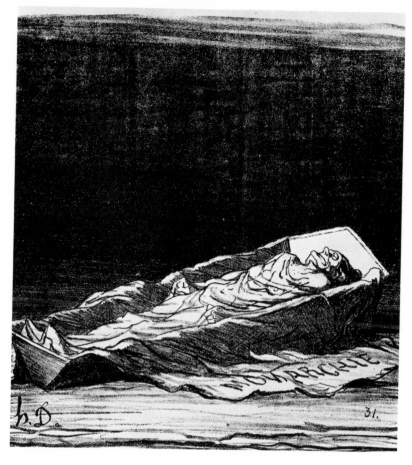

86. *And During that Time . . .* , lithograph
Museum of Fine Arts, Boston, Mass.

People he affirms in the face of previous disappointments that the
electoral urn is still the most potent instrument for ridding France
of its backward-looking elements. His faith is vindicated 'when the
June elections show that the masses of his countrymen have overcome
their fear of a republic, whose strength increases moreover week by
week as the monarchists waste their strength in bickering and the
extravagant claims of the Ultracatholics provoke an anticlerical reaction. In a drawing of July third "those ugly wrecks" Ratapoil and
Basile console each other for their failures; on September twenty-fourth,
he wraps the shriveled corpse of Monarchy in her shroud and lays her
in a coffin on his page (Fig. 86).

This was the last of Daumier's political drawings to be published,
and from the sidelines he could now watch the fulfillment of his
hopes. He must finally have thought better of his old enemy Thiers in
1873 for making sure that the indemnity would be paid and the
Prussians quit France by the fall; and he must have seen with an-

noyance the replacement of the little man by MacMahon, a royalist who could easily become the tool of the religious extremists. In 1874, on the other hand, republicans in the Assembly were clearly replacing their opponents, and Thiers made what Veuillot would have called his last somersault to join their cause. The national wish for this form of government was asserted more strongly than ever in the elections of 1877, and with the resignation of MacMahon the following year Jules Grévy became President of a full-fledged and democratic Third Republic. As a modern historian has said, "A new epoch in the history of France, the advent of which had been awaited since the fall of the Monarchy in 1792, though delayed for a hundred years by crises within and without, was now beginning."

No one could have seen this outcome with more relief and pleasure than the artist who for more than forty years had fought the republican campaign with so much wit and so much staunch conviction.

8: LA FONTAINE, MOLIERE AND CERVANTES

Students of Daumier's art have variously described its evolution. One of them calls its sequence Romantic-Naturalistic-Impressionistic. Surveying the lithographs Kurt Bertels contrasts the early analytical illustrations with the synthetic ones of the middle years and these with the symbolic character of the artist's last period. His water colors of the early 1860s, made with some concern for the purchaser's desire for pictorial completeness, were small masterpieces of descriptive illusion; but the naturalistic motive was not his only one, as the Goncourts realized. In 1860 they wrote that in his drawings "the trivial becomes the epic . . . the grotesque rises to the level of the frightful, the comical becomes a Juvenal-like chastisement." The events of the next decade sharpened the tragic sense which is here suggested, as Daumier explored the deeper implications of ordinary human actions.

How far he goes beyond the literal can be seen if one compares his painting *The Secret* with the *Witchcraft* of his friend Diaz. The latter presents a gay crowd of girls in a forest glade and in the foreground places a maiden and a witchlike old crone in obvious contrast. Two similar figures confront each other in Daumier's small canvas, but there is a tender subtlety in their relation, and the painter asks the observer to give his own meaning to an exchange between withered age and fresh youthfulness which has mysterious and troubling overtones.

Daumier is now a master of suggestion: in his lithograph, *European Equilibrium,* a few fluttering lines of drapery convey the flimsiness of peace in Europe; in his pen drawings the ballooning sleeves of lawyers are the visual counterpart of their windy orations; his wash drawing *Soup* has in its very lines the savage maternity of a working-class woman who nurses a child at her huge breasts; in his paintings of artists he needs only a drapery thrown over a stool or the glint of light on the edge of an easel to evoke the atmosphere of a studio.

The earlier pictures of amateurs and railway carriages had usually been scenes of contemplation, of quiet movement or of none at all, and his lawyers conversed in corners or pompously descended stairways; now there is a sense of urgency, a nervous intensity, a paroxysm of feeling in his lithographed woman who points with one finger at the ballot box and with the other at a field of corpses. That violent gesture reappears in drawings and water colors of side-show barkers and in the clown of the painting *The Strong Man,* whose outflung arm is a foil to the lumpy immobility of a carnival Hercules.

87. *Testimony Behind Closed Doors*, water color
Ny Carlsberg Glyptotek, Copenhagen, Denmark

Along with this intensity of life goes the image of mortality in the work of a man constantly reminded of its reality by the passing of old companions and by the events on which it was his task to comment—the deaths of his countrymen in the Emperor's reckless ventures, death in a Prussian mousetrap for the small German duchies, death by starvation at Metz. He presents that grim skeleton on many pages, now as a nightmare of Bismarck, now with a flowered bonnet on its head, playing the pipes of peace in a countryside which has become a desert, now driving the hearse of the year 1871. He gives us death by quarreling doctors in an illustration of La Fontaine and the fear of it on the face of Molière's imaginary invalid.

For other purposes, other means. In paintings of the decade which followed 1865 no sudden transformation of method is to be found; rather, certain tendencies of mind and hand which could be glimpsed on earlier occasions now assert themselves in a more compelling fashion. There is less dependence on the preliminary drawing and in his lighter passages, especially of heads and hands, a heavier pigment which may, as Rosen and Marceau have surmised, reflect the influence of Corot. The modeled forms emerge vividly from a somber and brooding background. Oil is no longer handled as though it were water color, but with a grasp of its own expressive powers.

In this sense one could think of certain works as transitional: *The Chess Players* with its rather heavily loaded lights; *The Theatre Box;* the *Three Lawyers* of Duncan Phillips; *The Painter,* in which the figure who stands poised before his *Deposition* is the same artist who appears in water colors of the early 1860s and is vigorously brought to life by the pigment itself. Daumier's procedure in *Advice to a Young Artist* is in marked contrast with that of the *Print Collectors* of the Hahnloser collection. In both works one man looks over the shoulder of another who is examining a print. In the former, which has been completed, one still sees the thin dark lines which served as a guide to the modeling and as final accents; in the latter, which never went beyond its first blocking out, a larger brush has roughed in the dark brownish background and broadly traced the contrasting shapes of light on heads and shoulders. A sense of the enveloping power of light which blots out details gives a new and limpid freedom to his washes in *Man Reading in a Garden. The Testimony Behind Closed Doors* is not a "finished" water color in the accepted sense, but he has fixed the essence of sinister and brutal justice with a single dark tone which throws into relief the three judges and plunges the courtroom into shadow behind the timid child who is testifying (Fig. 87).

Daumier gives to his drawings and paintings of street acrobats and clowns a poignant sense of their weariness, their drab existence behind the scenes, their valiant efforts to attract indifferent crowds. Three of them have finished their turn on a street corner and are stumbling homeward in a water color for which a preliminary drawing exists and which he traced on another sheet as though, K. E. Maison suggests, he wished to see how it looked in reverse (Color plate VI). These outdoor performers could no longer compete for patrons in the Boulevard of Crime, for that fabulous street had been destroyed by Haussmann; but in the 1860s Daumier watched them at the carnivals near Valmondois. His series of lithographs of 1865, *The Festival in the Neighboring Village,* included drawings of a side show at a country fair with merry-go-rounds and tents; and one surmises that here he found the theme of *The Strong Man,* which has the raucous tumult of a rural carnival and an almost brutal ruggedness of pigment in the form of the gesturing clown.

The fables of La Fontaine had been known by Daumier since his childhood, perhaps in Engelmann's edition which the brothers Vernet had illustrated. They were issued again in the 1820s with Devéria's plates and in 1839 their publication had wood engravings by many of Daumier's contemporaries. For his own canvas he had borrowed the miller and his son, and later the two thieves and the jackass. At Rousseau's farm in the mid-fifties he was one of the group who planned a new edition of the fables which would be illustrated also by Corot, Millet, Dupré, Delacroix and Rousseau, a project unhappily never carried out. Perhaps the great La Fontaine of 1867 with its hundreds of elaborate engravings after Gustave Doré reminded the caricaturist of the enduring wisdom of the old writer who called his own work "an ample comedy in a hundred acts whose stage is the universe," a wisdom which current happenings seemed to vindicate. One of his slight but witty drawings is of the beloved cat who was changed into a woman but reverted to her old form when the mice came. In 1867 Daumier made another fable contemporary with a Prussian wolf who disguised himself as a shepherd to guard the German sheep:

> Whoever is wolf, as wolf will act,
> This is the most assurèd fact.

A year later, when the Spaniards began their agitation for a monarch to replace Isabella, they appeared in *Charivari* as La Fontaine's frogs who, tired of their freedom, implore Jupiter to send them a king. And in a water color more macabre than humorous the fabulist's two doctors dispute the merits of their treatments while a smirking skeleton of Death carries away their defunct patient. One of them proudly asserts that he had predicted this outcome, while the other claims that the invalid would still be alive if they had followed his advice.

Even closer was the bond between the caricaturist and that other great satirist who had written *The Would-be Gentleman*. When the Director of the Comédie-Française once asked Daumier who had been his master in art, the answer was "Molière," and Houssaye adds that he often saw the man from *Charivari* in his audiences. In one of his Monday essays in 1863 Sainte-Beuve remarked how many new editions of the plays had recently appeared. To love Molière, he wrote, was to be immune to many vices of the mind, to be forever cured of that fanaticism which builds its bitter doctrine out of rancor, and of that softness of mind which cannot summon anger in the presence of wrong. The man who loved Molière would be hostile to all affectation, all false manners in thinking and in language; knowing the stuff of which humanity is made, he would neither idolize nor scorn it.

Sainte-Beuve might have been characterizing Daumier, who never drew Tartuffe but for nearly half a century exposed hypocrisy in general and that of false priests in particular, and whose mockery of Doctor Véron and of Joseph Prudhomme carried the would-be gentleman into the nineteenth century. The *Affected Young Ladies* of the actor-playwright lives again in Daumier's bluestockings and female socialists, and Robert-Macaire is Scapin in modern dress.

Common to both artists was their low opinion of the medical and the legal professions. When doctors gathered in Paris for the Universal Medical Congress, a Daumier lithograph presented them in the black robes of Molière's physicians with pointed hats on their bewigged heads and syringes in their hands. "Yesterday," the caption goes, "we had the new needle-gun, tomorrow we shall have these. Shall we gain anything by the change?" In *Men of the Law* and on dozens of other pages, the draftsman brought to life the species which, as the playwright's Monsieur de Bonnefois explained, specialized in finding indirect ways around the law. The Scapin of Molière listed the interminable procedures of a lawsuit: "You can see how many rapacious animals there are whose claws will be out for you"; and Sprigani's exchange with Monsieur de Pourceaugnac could serve as a caption for many a lithograph:

Here they begin by hanging a man and then bring him to trial.
But if he is innocent? . . .
It doesn't matter, they don't look into that.

On scraps of paper Daumier scribbled in pen and crayon his memories of what he had seen in the House of Molière, including a black chalk drawing with grey wash, perhaps of Sgagnarelle and Monsieur Purgon, and other notations of the players in action which his biographer found in the studio at Valmondois and gave to the younger Coquelin. On canvas in *Types of the Old Comedy* he was content to parade his players as though lined up for a curtain call—Scapin and Harpagon, Géronte, Rosine and the rest. The whispering rogues in the Louvre painting *Crispin and Scapin* seem to have been wrongly identified in that title, since the former character, the creation of the Italian comedians, makes no appearance in Molière; probably they are Scapin and the scheming valet Silvestre. Another painting, *Scene from the Theater,* also in the Louvre, gives in its incomplete state an even more violent effect of footlights on the sly face of Scapin, who has offered Géronte an alarming and fictional account of the kidnapping of the latter's son by Turks who have sailed for Algeria and are demanding ransom; he leans back to watch the effect of his tale on the distraught parent, who can only mutter the famous refrain, "But what the devil was he doing in that galley?"

Of all the great comedies Daumier seems to have been most obsessed with *The Imaginary Invalid,* where humor and pathos were as strangely blended as in his own late work. The finished water color in the Courtauld Institute, a masterfully controlled composition, frames the sick man between the curtains of his bed as he hears the pronouncement of the pompous doctor, behind whom lurks an assistant with the inevitable syringe (Fig. 88). In another version of the episode the artist contrives a more direct and poignant effect by placing Argan

88. *The Imaginary Invalid,* water color
Courtauld Institute of Art, London

in an invalid's chair directly facing the observer with the dread of
death in his features. The pose had been used on other occasions, in a
lithograph of a man in a dentist's chair and in the wash drawing of
The Music Lover, but never with so horrid an impact as now in a water
color where Doctor Diafoirus holds the patient's left wrist. In a
pen and ink study which has no trace of humor Daumier experiments
with the scheme of a seated invalid with Diafoirus at one pulse and
his son Thomas at the other:

> Thomas. Dico that Monsieur's pulse is the pulse of a sick man.
> Diafoirus. Good.
> Thomas. That it is rather hard . . . throbbing . . . just a little
> uneven.

Daumier gives us the haunting image of the man who sees death, not
the antiphonal pedantry of the dialogue (Fig. 89). Once more, on a
panel nine inches by seven (Fig. 90), the furiously indignant face of

89. *The Imaginary Invalid,* pen and wash
Collection Miss Edith Wetmore, New York

the Doctor appears as Daumier must have seen it in the full glare of
the footlights in the midst of his tirade against the rebellious Argan:

> I abandon you to your wretched constitution, to the intemperance
> of your intestines, the corruption of your blood, the bitterness of your
> bile and the feculence of your humors. . . .

The dramatic force of Molière's climactic scene is perhaps best caught
in the painted version in Philadelphia, where the frightened eyes of
Argan search the face of the quack who has seized his arm. The
radiographs of Rosen and Marceau have shown how, as he worked,
the artist changed his figures to achieve the forward thrust of Diafoirus
and the recoil of Argan and to make room for the background figure
of the apothecary in this confrontation of militant ignorance with
self-pity.

Among the thousands of images which lived together in the mind
of Daumier none was so persistent, so inexhaustible of variation as that

90. *Doctor Diafoirus,* oil
Collection Dr. and Mrs. Harry Bakwin, New York

of Don Quixote and his squire. The drawings, water colors and oils which he made of Cervantes' pair are too numerous and too different in style and feeling to belong in a single period; between the panel once owned by Aubry and the unfinished study of the Courtauld Institute one senses the span of a long career with its deepening insights and slow mastering of form.

The Spanish novel had become popular in France only a few years after its publication, and one translation had followed another as each generation read and interpreted it in its own fashion. La Fontaine delighted in the Knight of the Rueful Countenance; Coypel at the midpoint of the eighteenth century completed his designs for tapestries on the theme; Florian, who made his version during the Revolution, saw in the Don the embodiment of Reason; La Harpe could find no universal meaning in a work whose tone and form seemed to him extravagant and frivolous. This condescending attitude changed with the coming of Romanticism, although young writers whose minds dreamed of the cavaliers and ladies of the middle ages reproached Cervantes for attacking their delightful image of the age of chivalry. They soon managed, however, to transform Quixote from a figure of fun, a deluded fool, an instrument of his creator's satire on chivalric literature, into a tragic hero whose noble enthusiasm contends with a vulgar and prosaic world. Sancho, as Léon Bloy wrote, embodies the brutish appetite of the belly, "the coarse laughter of the multitude in the sad face of Poetry."

In Daumier's youth and early manhood *Don Quixote* became the saddest book ever written, a symbol to the romantic artist of his own rejection of common reality, his tilting against the bourgeois windmills, his substitution of the life of the imagination for that of the world around him. Chateaubriand reflects his own pessimism when he notes that this cruelly gay masterpiece is the work of a man who weighed life and was forced to laugh in order to forget how sad an enterprise it is. The ridicule of Cervantes, wrote Alfred de Vigny, cannot harm the image of the Don, who personifies that superiority which is forever scorned and ostracized.

Thanks to this revival and transformation the profiles of the lanky knight and his rotund companion took a thousand forms in France, in ballets, comedies and operas, in statuettes and on the carved bowls of pipes. When Jules Janin in an essay of 1834 asked why the artists had not made use of a book which offered so many fine subjects, Daumier's colleague Charlet had already made a series of illustrations; in 1836 the translation by Louis Viardot had rather banal vignettes by Tony Johannot. Sooner or later every artist of consequence tried his hand with the subject, among them Decamps, Rousseau and Daubigny. A *Don Quixote in Meditation* by Delacroix, finished in 1825, showed the knight sitting beside a book-laden table and two or three people, including a priest, watching him from the background, a scheme in all essentials like that of Daumier's paintings on this theme. A water color of Decamps places the two riders side by side as they amble toward us in a wide and arid landscape, describing both the figures and their setting in exquisite but humorless detail. In what seems a relatively early effort by Daumier, the scrawny old carriage horse now dignified as Rosinante and her rider "marvelously cheerful and content to see how easily he had started on his new career," are made to dominate the scene, their outline silhouetted against a sky streaked with sunrise; a small and distant Sancho jogs into sight on his ass

91. *Don Quixote and Sancho Panza,* oil. Private Collection, Boston
Photo Courtesy Boston Museum of Fine Arts

among boulders whose dark shapes are merely suggested (Fig. 91).

Another scene which Daumier attempted several times was the siesta of the travelers under a great tree. In one painting the knight awakes first and ponders how he may nourish his oblivious retainer and improve his lot; in another he stands guard on the horizon while Sancho sits up to sniff the odor of fried ham and listen to the sound of fiddles from the nearby wedding feast. These paintings, by no means his best, are content to be amusing illustrations. Perhaps his most successful version, said to have been painted in the late 1850s, has a bold but rather labored modeling of the sturdy tree, the emaciated Don and the crumpled rotundities of his sleeping retainer (Fig. 92).

92. *Don Quixote and Sancho Panza under a Tree,* oil
Ny Carlsberg Glyptotek, Copenhagen, Denmark

Daumier's fascination with these characters and their expressive possibilities may have been enhanced in 1864 by the new edition of the Viardot text for which Gustave Doré had designed three hundred and
seventy-five illustrations. Engraved on wood by the brilliant Pisan, the
large plates and the vignettes were crowded with authentic details of
costume and of place for which Doré had made a journey to Spain; the
episode of the windmills, which seems never to have tempted Daumier,
became an elaborate spectacle in a setting worthy of the Opéra. The
comments of Sainte-Beuve and others on this occasion indicate that with
the waning of the Romantic ego the work of Cervantes had acquired a
new and different interpretation. Even Hugo, in his volume on Shake-

93. *Don Quixote and Sancho Panza,* black chalk and water color
Musée des Beaux-Arts, Reims. Photo Bulloz

speare that year, praised the Spaniard not for presenting a tragic hero
but for revealing in the Don and Sancho the two faces of all mankind,
the sublime and the ridiculous, with no more pity for one than for the
other. In three of his "Mondays" Sainte-Beuve complained that his
contemporaries looked for "noon at fourteen o'clock" in this masterpiece,
and warned them not to overload its wit, its natural goodness with too
many and too subtle meanings.

Sainte-Beuve remarked that everybody could find what he wanted in
Don Quixote, and Émile Chasles in 1866 found in it a single aim, the
exposure of man's false ideas and his chimeras. In the beginning the
knight takes up his lance against the illusions of his own day, "the
miracle which is a lie, the platonic love which is an hypocrisy, the effemi-
nate novel which is poison." As the work proceeds its characters become
symbols and its satire universal, embracing the two great families which
share the world between them, the idealists and the realists, those who
see only ideas and those who see only things. For this critic the conversations between Quixote and Sancho were a continuous duel between
the poetry and the prose of life.

To Daumier, no man of words, these commentaries would have

94. *Don Quixote Rushing Upon the Sheep,* oil
Collection Mr. and Mrs. Charles S. Payson, New York
Photo courtesy M. Knoedler and Co., New York

seemed tiresome. For a long time he was content to draw and paint the
famous duo as a mildly comic antithesis, but his variations on this theme
grow simpler and stronger with the years (Fig. 93). On one of his canvases the riders emerge in silhouette from their flat background simply
through the notation of their dark shapes in monochrome. Perhaps it was
Daumier's close friendship with Corot, Daubigny and Rousseau which
suggested a few paintings of his later years in which the two figures are
subordinated to a rock-strewn mountainous landscape painted with bold
contrasts of tawny browns and near-blacks. They are based on the episode in Cervantes where the companions in their passage through the
Brown Mountains come suddenly upon the carcass of a dead mule half-
devoured by dogs and crows. We are told that Daumier visited Daubigny's studio at Auvers in the Spring of 1868 and painted a *Don
Quixote* on the bare wall, while Corot made a companion picture; there
exists a powerful brush drawing with a few indications of tone with a
dead mule in the foreground which was done not on a wall but on a tall
and narrow sheet of canvas. Corot's alleged pendant may be the painting on whose far horizon an area of foliage has been scraped out and the
diminutive figures of the two riders added. Two oils by Daumier present

the same episode in a horizontal composition, one of them painted in a manner suggestive of the landscapes of Daubigny, whose widow owned the work.

Daumier chose an unusually large canvas, twenty-two by thirty-three inches, for one of his most ambitious and successful Don Quixotes, (Fig. 94), from chapter eleven of the book:

> "Do you not see yon dust-cloud, Sancho? Know then that it is churned up by a mighty army composed of sundry and innumerable people that are marching this way." . . . As for the clouds of dust he had seen, they were raised by two large flocks of ewes and rams. "Do you not hear the neighing of the horses, the blaring of the trumpets, and the rattling of the drums?"
> "I hear nothing," answered Sancho, "but the bleating of sheep and lambs."
> "If you are so afraid, stand to one side and leave me to myself." . . . With these words he clapped spurs to Rosinante and, with lance couched, rode down the hillside like a thunderbolt.
> Sancho stood on the hillock watching his master's mad escapade, and tearing his beard and cursing the unlucky hour and moment when he first met him.

No illustrator of Cervantes had neglected this episode, from Johannot, who drew the knight in the act of spearing the frightened flock, to Doré whose vignette was a panorama of Spanish landscape with two small figures. As was his custom, Daumier worked out his essential scheme in a charcoal drawing accented with pen and ink; on its margin is a small diagram with two intersecting triangles which indicate the two opposing lines of movement which were to give the picture its force. Setting aside an oil in which the figure of Sancho did not satisfy him, he made a powerful study, again in oil, of this figure alone, its outlines firmly expressive, its tones laid in flatly and with no detail. Now he was ready for the final effort: in the foreground of a rocky plain under a wide and sunny sky stands the distraught servant on his ass, and away from him into the middle distance plunges a Don who is a skeleton in motion. The muted but luminous colors, the pervasive light, the balance-by-contrast of Sancho's recoil and Don Quixote's furious gallop, are the achievement of a master dramatist.

In catching the madness of the master's lunge and the consternation of the all-too-sane fat servant, Daumier has gone beyond mere illustration. The deeper implications of the Don Quixote theme were not lost on this crusader whose lance against the follies and self-deceptions of his time was a crayon. During his life he had seen the contrast which they symbolized take many forms—between the troublemaker and the safe citizen insulated from thought by prosperous fat, between the man who faces the political storm and the politician who sits it out serenely faith-

95. *The Painter at His Easel,* oil
Phillips Collection, Washington, D.C.

ful to the notion that the least action is the best action, between the
artist who charges forward and the one who leans against the academic
tree in the cool shade of accepted practice. As the artist grew old his
interpretations of the Don Quixote story seem to reflect his sense of the
mingled comedy and tragedy of life. The two riders lose their separate
identities and are fused in a single image of man himself, that part of
him which is his conscience and that part which clings to comfort and
dulls the edge of challenge by indifference. In a painting which must
surely be one of his last, the *Don Quixote* of the Courtauld Institute, he

96. *Woman Carrying a Child,* oil
Collection Frau Ch. Bührle-Schalk, Zürich

weaves the stalking pace of Rosinante and the plodding gait of Sancho's ass into a rhythm as complex as the movement of the mind (Color plate VII).

This transformation of the particularized image into a simpler and stronger symbol during the final years, so easily traced in the lithographs, is to be found in many panels and canvases whose conception reveals a final maturity, works not so much postponed as interrupted by illness, failing eyesight and death. One sees the culmination of his artistry in a *Don Quixote and Sancho Panza* which still shows the squares by which it was enlarged and in which a few dark blocks of shadow already convey his intention. In Duncan Phillips' *Two Sculptors,* the peering heads and the object of their admiration exist in space and light by virtue of a few bold strokes of the brush. In *The Painter Be-*

fore His Easel (Fig. 95) an elderly artist stands in a darkening room where it will soon be too late to paint, the glow from an unseen window striking only the top of his head and the edges of his jacket, arm and palette; Daumier has summoned the intent mind and the stout body firmly planted with only a few sketchily blocked-in masses and rippling threads of pigment.

These works are incomplete only in the sense that their maker probably would have wished to carry some of them further; but in them all the essentials of character and movement, of place, time and mood, have been established. And this is true of other paintings in which an unexpected lyricism appears, and a fluent poetry of the brush which some students attribute to the influence of Fragonard. We are told by Arsène Alexandre that Daumier visited the Louvre in 1869 to see a collection of the eighteenth-century master's work; and both the *Singing Pierrot* with its ribbonlike movements of the brush and the sketch, *Woman Carrying a Child,* may reflect this encounter (Fig. 96).

At this late moment the artist returned with a new sense of urgency to a theme which he had earlier explored, and painted the tragic flight of refugees heading into the wind under an angry sky. One of these *Fugitives* is in the Montreal Museum of Art; another and seemingly later one in Minneapolis (Color plate VIII) may represent the rout of French villagers before the Prussian advance, or the terrified people whom Edmond de Goncourt in 1871 saw "fleeing the bombardment, women and children, loaded down with bundles." With no distracting detail he gives us here the essence of despairing panic, a crescendo of scale and motion from distance to foreground in this surging mass.

In these oil studies and in the drawings of the 1870s the brush or the crayon and the pen not only define his figures but lash them into life and gesture. Out of a tangle of broken, tentative, interweaving lines, a kind of eloquent scribbling, emerge the faces of terrified men, the forward lurching of a horseback rider, a group of sad and patient people seen as through a mist, a wildly gesticulating clown whose companion beats a drum (Figs. 97, 98). These fragments put Daumier in the company of Guardi, Tiepolo and Rembrandt, with all the great draftsmen who have hinted more than they said and have resolved the smaller truths into a larger one.

People have called this final manner the "impressionism" of Daumier, noting its analogy with the work of that younger generation of painters battling for recognition in the 1870s. We do not know precisely what he thought of their experiments. On the one hand, it is said that he saw Monet's *Garden of the Princess* in the window of a dealer and urged that this "horror" be removed; on the other, we know that he frequented the shop of Pierre Martin along with Pissarro, Degas and other innovators.

98. *Study of a Man on Horseback*, pen and ink
Collection V. W. Van Gogh. Stedelijk Museum, Amsterdam, Holland

In February, 1870, when Manet and his friends drew up a list of candidates for the Salon jury whom they considered sympathetic to the work of the new men, Daumier's name was included. The Impressionists' dissolutions of form may well have startled a man who had long seen the world in so sculptural a fashion; but he cannot have ignored their challenge to the fixed contours, the separate and solid object, the contained local colors and the inert illumination of traditional painting. In a sense this new way of seeing paralleled his own. Some of the alleged impressionism of his last works was, however, probably involuntary; if his brush or crayon seemed to be groping for the forms, it was because there were times toward the end when he could not clearly see them. Their haunting quality, their mysterious emotional impact derive from the fact that they were seen with the mind's eye. In both a literal and a figurative sense, sight was replaced by insight.

97. *Sheet of Studies with a Group of Men*, pencil
The Art Institute of Chicago, Ill.

99. Portrait of Daumier by Nadar
George Eastman House, Rochester, N.Y.

VIGNETTE: LAST YEARS

He was broad and solid with a powerful head on a sturdy neck. Eyes which could be dreamy, could be searching and could be mischievous; a wide forehead framed in a long mane of fine white hair . . . a face which held both malice and a humorous good nature. . . . You should have seen him smoking his pipe with a vague expression, lost in idle thoughtfulness. . . .

Jules Clarétie thus recalled a Daumier whose image comes to us also through the photographs of Nadar and Carjat (Fig. 99). His last decade was to have its financial difficulties and its physical afflictions, but also its consciousness of work well done and warmly recognized by men whose friendship he cherished.

To those friends he first mentioned the failure of his eyes in 1872. This blindness, which for an artist must have been a kind of death in life, was partial and intermittent. The lithographs which he published between January and September of that year must have been drawn at the moment, since they dealt with current happenings. During most of 1873 no drawings appeared, and one supposes that this was the period of complete rest which his doctors had ordered; but his unpublished *The Witnesses* must have been done in the fall of that year, when the trial of Marshal Bazaine opened. This terrible indictment is one of his finest lithographs, without a trace of fumbling, in which the starved and mutilated ghosts of the siege of Metz storm the Council of War to testify to the Marshal's treason. In that year *Le Monde Illustré* mentioned an operation; still, the writing in his notebooks as late as 1877 was firm and clear.

His isolation from the world around him, however incomplete, must sorely have tried Daumier's spirit; and as the 1870's progressed he knew that other isolation which comes to older men with the passing of colleagues and companions. His old comrade in arms, Philipon, had died in 1862; Decamps, Rousseau and the sympathetic critic Thoré did not live to see the "terrible year"; Baudelaire, who had once compared him to Delacroix and Ingres, had gone, and so had the two great masters. Théophile Gautier, true to his own prediction that the revolution of 1871 would be the end of him, survived only a year. Millet in 1874 was followed in 1875 by Corot; in 1877 died Courbet, an exile in Switzerland for the part he had played in the civil war, and also Thiers, who had crushed the Commune. The little statesman, who boasted that he had been the butt of twelve hundred caricatures, had shaken hands not long before at an evening reception with the caricaturist who had heaped ridicule and scorn upon him in more than a hundred lampoons, sharp arrows which never punctured his self-esteem. Now even Hugo and Gambetta came to the funeral of the man who, as the latter said, had liberated France; and Flaubert was heard to say, "I never liked this King of the Prudhommes, but he was a giant compared to those around him—and a patriot."

207

Daumier in his sixties had his financial problems, but they have been exaggerated. His income from lithographs was sharply reduced; in 1871 his friend Daubigny loaned him seven hundred and fifty francs; Moreau-Nélaton records that the generous Corot, knowing his friend's difficulties, bought the property at Valmondois and gave Daumier the bill of sale. Recent scholarship, however, has shown that his situation improved between 1875 and 1877, when his pension from the State was raised through the pressure of his friends to twenty-four hundred francs and when his account books record the sale of his work to Dupré, Lemaire, Aubry, Jacquette and Madame Bureau (Fig. 100). This was no sadly impoverished Daumier, but a man who could live in reasonable security on an income which Jean Cherpin estimates as nearly seven hundred francs a month (about one hundred and thirty-five dollars).

When the artist's friends came together at a supper in Auvers to plan an exhibition, its purpose was not so much to provide funds as to demonstrate the quality of the work itself. Geoffrey-Dechaume believed that it would be received with joy, "a truly enlightening affair"; and when the show opened at the gallery of Durand-Ruel on the seventeenth of April, 1878, a list of thirty sponsors headed by Victor Hugo included Banville, Daubigny, Champfleury, Paul Meurice, Nadar, Pierre Véron and many other ardent champions. Of the ninety-four oils and one hundred and thirty-nine water colors and drawings in that exhibition, all but a few were loaned by collectors who had bought them or by owners who had received them as gifts from Daumier. A group of sculptors was included, and a sampling of the lithographs.

This modest man had approved the project only after much persuasion and his doubts were confirmed when the public largely ignored it, perhaps distracted by the great Exposition of that year, perhaps in some quarters still resentful and still reluctant to admit that a maker of lampoons could be an artist. The show resulted in a deficit of four thousand francs; yet Daumier could read reviews in which major critics now hastened to make up for previous neglect. Albert Wolff assured the readers of *Figaro* that this man was a great unknown, a great master of form; in *Le Rappel* Camille Pelletan wrote that his style had an almost classic nobility and grandeur; two articles by Duranty maintained that his lithographs were in no sense inferior as works of art to his canvases. "His talent," said Paul Foucher in *Le National*, "is made of indignation and of pity"; and Carjat headed his piece, *The People's Michelangelo*.

An artist who could no longer draw or paint had two consolations in this final year: after the fall of Sedan, the cruelties of the siege and the bloodbath of the Commune he was at last a free citizen of a Republic; after long years when the experts praised him as a graphic humorist but with some notable exceptions ignored his efforts as a painter, his full stature was beginning to be recognized.

These rewards came none too soon. An Act of Decease dated February eleventh, 1879, recorded Daumier's death the previous night after a stroke had suddenly felled him. Three days later his village neighbors were joined by his Parisian friends. The local curé had refused a funeral pall to this old disciple of Voltaire, and the flowers from country gardens covered his body as the men of Valmondois carried it the few steps from his studio to the grave. Standing beside it, Carjat said, "If all those were here today who have been helped by this man, himself so needy, this modest cemetery would be too small to hold them"; and it was fitting that Jules Champfleury, who had been one of the first to recognize his gifts, now spoke the valediction. Daumier, like all the great humorists, had been serious, thoughtful and profound:

His mission was to study the exterior man, to probe his internal life, and out of the crucible of his observations to cast his many medals. . . . He goes from blindness into light and rejoins his great contemporaries Delacroix, Corot and Millet.

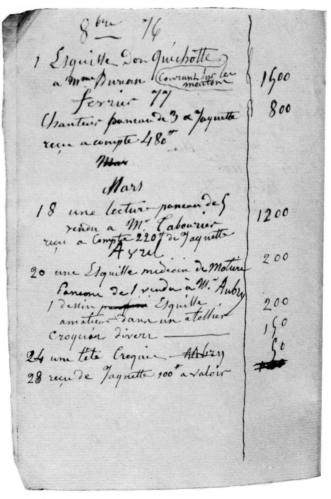

100. Page from Daumier's account book
Courtesy Jean Cherpin, Marseille

9: MAN OF HIS TIME AND OURS

What degree of power and what kind of meaning could the art of Daumier, so intimately related to the ideas and values of its own age, have for later generations? By what process do the reputations of a former time either dissolve or grow more solid? Is the status of an artist at the mercy of social and ideological change, or are there indestructible qualities which guarantee its survival? And what, given the prodigious body of this man's work on the one hand and ourselves on the other, is the significance of Daumier today?

One of the few remarks attributed to him, "One must be of one's time", suggests that it was important for him to live in the present, to immerse himself in its human drama, to assume responsibility for its problems, to celebrate its noblest and its worst. But this slogan, echoed by others in a period whose will to break with the past was unusually strong, has other implications. It assumes that each epoch in man's history has a definite character which is wholly its own. If, however, you had asked the men of the first half of the nineteenth century in France to define that "spirit of the time," you would have received a bewildering variety of answers. For some of them, as George Boas has pointed out, the central fact of the age was the return to Catholicism in faith and to Royalism in politics; for others the growth of industrialism, for still others the increasing importance of science. Courbet best expressed the age for Proudhon; to the ultraconservative Planche it was Ingres who best challenged the disruptive forces of the time; Baudelaire wrote that the painter of modern life must look the present in the face and discover beauty there; and in Daumier and Delacroix he found that "bitter and stoical wisdom" which he called heroic. Champfleury dedicated his book *The Eccentrics* to Daumier, praising his power to expose the egotism, the greed and the sordid ambition of the age, its vulgar cunning and its blindness to spiritual, moral and artistic values:

> You must often have smiled at the difficulty felt by the novelist who tries to sketch a physiognomy in words,—you who in a few strokes of the pencil give eternal life to creatures whom future historians will be glad to consult in order to learn what the bourgeois exterior of our century looked like.

Thus the timeliness of Daumier for one group among his contemporaries derived from the fact that his art corresponded to their own highly selective notion of their period, that his interpretation of man and his condition reinforced their own. The art of Daumier did not impose itself on more than a fraction of those around him, and then not by virtue of qualities which they considered absolute and timeless. Its place in their minds was the result of an interplay between the art itself and the beliefs and values of those who saw it. This interplay is what André Malraux has in mind when he writes that "every masterpiece keeps up a dialogue with time." That dialogue began for Delacroix, for example, when his *Liberty on the Barricades* was born into an age which alternately worshipped and rejected it and at last installed it in the Louvre when the passions it symbolized had been forgotten. As this exchange continues from one generation to the next, the history of an artist's reputation becomes a history of taste. The process is further complicated by the fact that a work of art can at once change and be changed by history; it alters men's thoughts and feelings, and at the same time these thoughts and feelings will change the degree and kind of importance the work is claimed to have or not to have.

These transformations become most striking when one compares the evaluations of a given artist by men who are separated by centuries of human history. When, for example, Vasari wrote his life of Piero della Francesca some sixty or seventy years after Piero's death, he praised the painter as a master of perspective, called him the best geometrician of his time, and emphasized his skill in reproducing the outward appearance of solid objects in space, his ability as a story teller. "Piero gives us to know," he wrote, "how important it is to copy things as they are; which he did so well that he enabled the moderns to attain, by following him, to that supreme perfection wherein art is seen in our own time." For this writer Piero's battle scene at Arezzo "most successfully represented fear, animosity, dexterity, vehemence and all the other emotions that can be imagined in men who are fighting together with almost incredible courage."

In contrast with these observations a writer of our time can bring to his study of Piero not only a wider knowledge than Vasari had of what had gone before Piero, but also standards of judgment which owe a good deal to what has happened in the four and one half centuries since his death. Aldous Huxley can see in the composition of the *Resurrection* not merely a success in three-dimensional representation but a magnificent symbol; he can compare the curious headdresses of Piero's women to those on the statues of Egyptian kings, and the folds of the Madonna's dress to the flutings on the robe of the archaic bronze charioteer in the Louvre. Huxley pays tribute to the artist's passion for "solidity as such," but finds his dominant quality to be "a natural, spontaneous and unpretentious grandeur, a worship of what is admirable in man." For this modern critic Piero was little concerned with the drama of life and religion; the battle scenes are not, as they were for Vasari, dramatic compositions, but superbly intellectual wholes. "It is as though Bach had written the *1812 Overture*."

Clearly, a work of art does not derive its power to withstand the "test of time" from qualities of form and content which are independent of place and circumstance. It would be a rash historian who prophesied that a painting or a sculpture long prized in the past and highly regarded in the present is sure to be held a masterpiece one or more centuries hence, or declared that the seemingly dead bodies of Frith, Alma-Tadema, Fortuny and Cabanel, whom we now regard as having failed the test of time, will never be brought to life. Perhaps it is wiser to say that some works of art possess to a greater degree than others the power to be enjoyed and prized for always new and always different reasons by successive generations who find in them the embodiment of their own concerns.

That power was in Daumier, whose posthumous dialogue with time began when picture dealers descended on his studio and carted away its contents in exchange for a few hundred francs, and when Arsène Alexandre came there to interview the widow in preparation for the first biography. Into that book went Madame Daumier's dismal and distorted version of her husband's later days, but also much precious information gathered from men who had known him. While it was being written, a large exhibition of French caricature at the École des Beaux-Arts threatened to obscure Daumier's merits as a painter, merits which Alexandre believed would some day "open wide the doors of the museums." He discussed the man's art as a whole and added an admittedly tentative list of Daumier's work in all media.

Alexandre was one of several admirers who acquired the work of Daumier while he was still living. The artist recorded in a notebook the sale of two paintings to Aubry in 1875 and 1877, and the receipt of fifteen hundred francs (two hundred and eighty-eight dollars) from Madame Bureau in 1876 for his *Don Quixote Rushing upon the Sheep*. Among the owners of works shown in 1878 were Jules Dupré, Count Doria, Lemaire, Henri Rouart and Dollfus. Even at this early date other hands than his own were producing fakes or adding to his unfinished sketches those touches which would make them more salable; indeed, he was startled one day in 1877 to find a false Daumier in a shop window in the rue de Seine.

The faith and foresight of these early collectors were more than justified. At the sale of Geoffroy-Dechaume in 1893 a version of *The Washerwoman* brought five thousand, four hundred francs (slightly over one thousand dollars), and the State paid twelve thousand, one hundred francs (about two thousand, three hundred and thirty-six dollars) for *The Thieves*. Ten years later the painting, *The Heavy Burden*, from the collection of Alexandre was sold for fourteen thousand francs (two thousand, seven hundred dollars). The Ottawa version of *The Third Class Carriage* was one of the fifteen oils which Count Doria had amassed by 1900, together with thirty-two drawings.

The large exhibition of Daumier's work, both genuine and spurious, which was held at the École des Beaux-Arts in 1901 raised the prices of his paintings but did not launch a flood of appreciation in his own country. One of the few books about him in these years was the "critical biography" of Henri Marcel in 1907, presenting a Daumier whose passion for painting left him in mid-career indifferent to his own graphic work, a reluctant slave to the task of castigating his generation by laughter, a man whose compelling motivation was neither social nor political but rather a sensuous, a joyously pagan response to the world, an intoxication with lines and masses, a passionate will to give an ample and vigorous expression to his own inner life and to that of his characters. In 1908 Burt Bertels published his *Daumier als Lithograph* and Erich Klossowski, a painter and critic of Munich, the first edition of his monograph. A legend was being created—the legend of an artist sacrificing his gifts to portray men he did not know and problems which did not deeply concern him. Élie Faure in 1921 evoked a lonely and tragic individual who lived in a world of his own, "content to possess the street and conquer the future." Ardengo Soffici portrayed him as a man forced in his caricatures to assume a lightness of spirit which was not in his true nature.

As this Daumier legend grew, France was losing some of his finest works to connoisseurs in other countries. The Rouart Collection, to be sure, held a superb group of his oils, including a *Painter in His Studio* which sold in 1913 for twenty-one thousand, five hundred francs (about four thousand, one hundred and fifty dollars) and the *Crispin and Scapin* of the Louvre, which fetched the French equivalent of eleven thousand, five hundred and eighty dollars at the same sale; among other rich collections were those of Claude Roger-Marx and of Mme. Esnault-Pelterie and Mme. Pierre Bureau, the widow of a man who had painted scenes in Daumier's neighborhood along the Oise. During the early 1900s, however, William Burrell of Scotland, Duncan Phillips of Washington, D. C., Sir William Van Horne of Canada, Eduard Fuchs and Otto Gerstenberg of Berlin and Oskar Reinhart of Winterthur in Switzerland were adding some of the finest oils, water colors and drawings to their collections. Of seventy-three oils which were part of a large Daumier show of 1926 in Berlin, the larger number were from private collections in Germany.

The sale of the Bureau collection in 1927 brought bidders from several countries to Paris and proved to be the sensation of the season.

Once more *The Washerwoman* went on the block and was acquired for the Louvre at the equivalent of one hundred and thirty-five thousand dollars, while the Bureau *Don Quixote* was knocked down for nearly two hundred and fifty thousand. The artist who had labored over the water colors for which he asked one hundred francs would have been astounded to see his *Imaginary Invalid* sold on that occasion for four thousand times that amount, or a fine proof print of his litho, *Yes, Madame Fribochon*, bought at another sale for ten thousand, one hundred francs.

Perhaps he would also have been amused by the written comments which accompanied these soaring prices. In 1923 a Daumier exhibition at the Maison Victor Hugo was the signal for several new monographs, including the first of five studies by Raymond Escholier. In this year André Fontainas asserted that the lithographs expressed only the superficial thought of the artist, and Klossowski in a revised edition of his work explained that he had no interest in reviving political passions which had long been dead. The caricatures, although they revealed a great draftsman, were in his opinion mere bastards in comparison with the oils and water colors which were Daumier's true children. These latter could only be understood when the great artistic revolution of the late nineteenth century had been accomplished. "He owes his rebirth," wrote the German critic, "to eyes whose aesthetic feeling was developed through Manet, Degas, even Cézanne, Lautrec and Van Gogh."

To this narrowing image of Daumier's achievement three English commentators made their contributions. For Michael Sadleir in 1924 he had become a kind of noble simpleton, "a garret revolutionary" whose uncritical goodness had been warped by the partisanship of his editors and whose ultimate significance is due to qualities in his paintings which anticipate Post-Impressionism. The Daumier of Roger Fry and Clive Bell was the creation of sensitive and militant spirits whose aim was to interpret the Post-Impressionists to the enlightened few. A true artist was in their minds the natural enemy of social man and his work could have no appeal to a crass and unredeemably ignorant public. Comparing the revolutionary changes in art to those which occurred in society, Fry could see no significant relation between the two, and for Bell there was only a vague parallel between the curves and depressions of aesthetic creativity and those of human faith and enthusiasm.

Fry's picture of Daumier is that of a split personality torn between the demands of illustration and those of formal design. One suspects that this split personality was a projection of Fry's own problem as a critic, a problem never quite resolved by him, of the relation between form and content in a work of art. Fry's reservations on Daumier reflect his own notion that no artist ought to be diverted from his task by considerations of moral, social or political responsibility; that his mission is to create forms which can be enjoyed for their own sake. The caricaturist in his opinion was betrayed by his own revolutionary ardor and his generous indignation at injustice and oppression. "What a great artist Daumier just missed being," he cries, "by his too precipitate moral indignation!"

Clive Bell is even more severe. The critic concedes the man's power as a draftsman and, on a few occasions, as a painter, but blames his poverty, his democratic illusions and the pressures of time and propaganda for his failure to consummate his powers. "So he produced," Bell sadly concludes, "a few masterpieces, a mass of mere hackery, and innumerable drawings . . . splendid but imperfectly elaborated or in part sacrificed to the lamentable exigencies of illustration and emphasis."

During these same years, however, a very different Daumier was presented to their readers by historians and critics with other notions of the relation between art and life. The German Daumierists, Fritz Stahl and Eduard Fuchs, were citizens of the short-lived Weimar Republic and their social and political idealism is reflected in their word picture of Daumier. Stahl disputes the legend of an unhappy and penniless artist and refuses to think it a tragedy that he could not make painting his profession, since what he had to say was richly said in black and white, a belief shared with the American Duncan Phillips, who observed that the lithographs more fully and freely expressed the artist than a lifetime wholly given to painting would have done. Fuchs had amassed a huge group of lithos, drawings and paintings when he published four volumes of the master's graphic work and in his volume *Der Maler Daumier* reproduced over three hundred oils, water colors and drawings, many of which, one regrets to add, were either doctored originals or complete fakes.

Far from being the weary and frustrated hack drawn by Fry and Bell, Daumier emerges from the pages of Fuchs as the creator of forms in which the ideology of the French middle class could be expressed, its revolutions and its counterrevolutions, and as a democrat whose best talent was in the caricatures which nobly embodied his belief in social and political progress, even though he sometimes misunderstood the more radical forces of his time. And Stahl made the same point. "What stunted minds the purists must have," he said, "to ignore the fact that Daumier labored all his life for a free and happy society." He might have reminded the purists, on the evidence of the drawings themselves, that no half-willing fellow traveler of democracy could have achieved the silent eloquence of the early print, *Rue Transnonain,* or the scornful and angry denunciation which Daumier compressed into a few lines in the work of his last years.

This social and political relevance of Daumier seemed in the prewar years to be increased rather than diminished by events: the march on Rome which made Mussolini a dictator; the sordid scandal of Teapot Dome; the general strike in England; the ordeal of Sacco and Vanzetti; the Reichstag fire; the collapse of the American economy and the emergence of the New Deal; the formation of a socialist government in France and the outbreak of a civil war in Spain. Jean Charlot, who had known the Mexican revolution at first hand, declared it both paradoxical but true that "siding with one's own moment, country, party or hamlet, diving into the social turmoil, using pencil and brushes to club your opponents, is one of the surest ways to remain in posterity's consciousness." The pictorial campaign waged by a group of American artists against current wrongs in the 1930s—the Rollin Kirbys, the William Groppers, the Ben Shahns—was to a degree inspired by the example of Daumier, whose image in their minds owed less to Cézanne than to George Grosz, to Käthe Kollwitz, to the indictments of Orozco and the outraged humanity of Picasso's *Guernica*.

These two concepts of the meaning of Daumier still confronted each other when a great retrospective show of his works at the Orangerie in 1934 proved that he belonged with the masters. In the wave of critical appraisal inspired by this exhibition one finds a Daumier who is once more being generalized. Claude Roger-Marx, one of the artist's most perceptive admirers, praises his power to transcend literal content and to recreate the life of man in epic proportions. For Paul Valéry he has become the great moralist whose work is a chastisement of all forms of self-satisfied mediocrity, of high pretenses and low passions, of human error and rascality, a "next-to-the-Last Judgement."

Further transformations of Daumier's image have been wrought by men of our time, in a quarter century which has seen several exhibitions of his work, notably that of the Philadelphia Museum in 1937 and a superb show of oils, water colors and drawings at the Tate Gallery in London during the summer of 1961. His art has become familiar at second hand through a series of picture books with a minimum of text which have reproduced Daumier with more profusion than with faithfulness of color. The flood of published comments in French, in English, in German, in Italian and in Russian has risen to alarming proportions, much of it repeating what has been said before, some of it the work of careful scholars. Thanks to these latter we can now base our notions of the man's life and art not on legend but on solid fact.

With the aid of the X ray and of infrared photography David Rosen and Henri Marceau have helped us to understand his painting method. An enterprising Daumierist of Marseille, Jean Cherpin, has published new documents to supplement the story of his life as it appears in Alexandre and in the monographs of Raymond Escholier. K. E. Maison has enriched our knowledge and appreciation of the drawings in a series of articles and has undertaken the thorny task of compiling a catalogue of these and of the paintings. To Jean Adhémar belongs the credit for having written a comprehensive critical biography and for his attempt to date the paintings. Others, including Bernard Lemann, have worked out a chronology which might help us to understand the evolution of his style, but Adhémar first published his scheme, and his book of 1954 reproduces a good many oils and water colors in what he believes to be their order of creation.

But our current idea of Daumier is no mere scholarly correction or amplification of those held by our predecessors; it has been shaped by the preoccupations of the postwar world. This world has seen many of its most precious political and social visions dimmed or shattered by war and by that relapse into indifference and complacency, into those forms of coercive intolerance and of ruthless materialism which have been war's aftermath. In such a world many sensitive artists and critics have come to believe that the painter or sculptor of integrity is forced to isolate himself from the common concerns of man and to regard with suspicion or with scorn those forms of art which are intended to convey a "message." The responsibility of the artist, they feel, is wholly to his personal vision, his task the making of a completely individual, anarchic gesture, his method to dispense partly or completely with visual references to the objective world and through massive blocks of color or through intricately swirling lines to express his instinctive response to the universe, hoping but not believing that his letter to the world will be legible to others.

André Malraux sees Daumier as a transitional figure who appeared at the moment when the anecdote was about to be rejected in favor of an art whose values were purely those of painting. "The distinguishing feature of modern art," writes the author of *The Voices of Silence*, "is . . . that it never tells a story. . . . Before the art of our time could come into its own, the art of historical fiction had to pass away—and it died hard"; nevertheless, the anecdotal "subject" was bound to give way to a new subject, which Malraux defines as "the presence of the artist upon his own canvas." The first true modern was Manet, who broke with anecdote and boldly proclaimed the new values; and the importance of Daumier lies in a few works, *The Washerwoman* and *The Soup* for example, in which the suffering of poverty, the life of everyday, are sublimated onto a higher plane, are raised above mere illustration by "the boldness of their style, their disdain of illusive realism, and a layout that is unmistakably modern."

This image would seem to be the prevalent one of our time. For

Joseph Sloane in 1961 the most striking feature of *The Washerwoman* is a certain monumental impersonality, "as though the artist were relaxing from the necessity of being significant"; in the painter's best work he sees "a retreat into artistry after a lifetime of almost forced labor in a less grateful medium, a delight in painting for its own sake." In 1960 Philippe Jones devotes his essay on Daumier to those lithographs and drawings whose analysis and suggestion of light prefigure Impressionism; and E. H. Gombrich maintains that it is rather the Expressionists whom he anticipates. Reviewing the Tate show the following year, Lawrence Gowing explains how the painter looks forward across the epoch of Impressionism to the twentieth century; how magnificent form is achieved by a man groaning in agony at the terrible sentence which chained him to the stone three times a week for a lifetime, but managing now and then to rid his mind of description and of indignation, finally to paint "not a subject so much as a process, the process by which form materializes out of feeling." In a similar mood David Sylvester in the *New Statesman* emphasizes Daumier's enormous capacity for absolute empathy, a complete identification of himself with the figures he paints, which enables him to set forth "what it feels like to do something, not what somebody looks like doing it." Sylvester chooses to discuss not the more finished works at the Tate exhibition but a study of Don Quixote which the painter had scarcely begun and which reveals only his general intention. The Don on his horse is as yet only a dark shadow-shape, and the critic observes that the shape does not describe the knight rushing but is rather the embodiment of headlong rushing. He concludes that Daumier's forms are not a description of visual situations but the visual projection of motor sensations; "hence they come to acquire a degree of autonomous life which gives them both the immediacy and ambiguity of impact which are characteristic of . . . twentieth century painting."

These critics, often preferring the unfinished to the completed painting and the intention to the deed, make of Daumier a modernist unaware of his modernism. We can be grateful to men whose eyes have seen Picasso and Klee, Mondrian and Kandinsky, De Kooning and Pollock, for reminding us that the shapes and colors of Daumier go beyond literal description and that his appeal for us today owes much to his power of transforming an ordinary incident into a very special occasion, his gift for endowing lines, contours, masses, light, shadow and color with an enduring life of their own on paper and on canvas. But we must ask whether his gift to us is limited to the expressive power of his forms as such, and whether the new critics take the full measure of his meaning for our time.

Need we assume that the social satire of Daumier, since it had its origin in the acts and situations of his own day, has lost its relevance to ours? When the owner of the firetrap tenement in Chicago is haled into court we see that the battle between the space merchant and his victims has not essentially changed since Daumier portrayed it in his *Tenants and Landlords*. The rapt and vacuous faces of his audiences at cheap melodramas are like those of a televised "western." A farmer and his wife stand beside their farmhouse and see Paris pushing toward them; not otherwise does the dweller in Levittown watch the spreading blight of Manhattan. When a newspaper reports the eloquent pleas of the defense lawyer in a murder trial we seem to see Daumier's fat and sobbing barrister and the all-too-obvious guilt of the pretty woman who smirks beside him.

Even in the political drawings we are constantly reminded that the issues to which he gave his keen analysis, his sturdy common sense, his angry commitment, have not been resolved and that his battle is the one for which men in our time have been driven from one continent to another, have gone to prison or died behind barbed wire. That fable of opportunism, *The Thieves*, may have been understood in his time as a sly reference to Napoleon's coup d'état; but that Prince was not the last would-be dictator to mount the jackass while his opponents wrangled among themselves. The relations between Church and state in education are not less troubled today than when he attacked the Falloux Law. His drawing of a rigged plebiscite by which a whole nation condemned itself to destruction reminds us that this device is not a modern invention. His alarm at the ever-mounting budgets for war strikes a familiar chord today, nor could our present situation be more effectively symbolized than in his *Equilibrium*.

Again, when an American Governor tells a group of students that "the attack on freedom of speech and freedom of inquiry is frequently masked as a crusade against subversion," the *Red Spectre* of Daumier rises before us in a new context. In an exchange of views between the heads of two great powers, each of them declares that, if nuclear tests begin again, full blame will rest upon the other; Daumier's litho is still relevant, with its caption, *After You!*

On more than one occasion, both in sculpture and in pigment, Daumier created the haunting image of men, women and children in huddled flight from their homes, the victims of war and of political reprisal. On the Île Saint-Louis, only a few steps from the studio where some of these images were created, one sees today a tablet on the façade of a large building with the inscription:

To the memory of the one hundred and twelve tenants of this house, including forty small children, who were deported and who died in the German camps in 1942.

More recent events in Hungary and in Berlin have given a tragic significance to Daumier's human displacements.

It is not unimportant that images created so long ago can still nudge our consciences and stir our compassion, and that importance is increased by our awareness that we have no such courageous draftsman today. We can only imagine how this child of the Enlightenment would chastise a nation which spends each year four times as much in legalized gambling as on its higher schools. We can only guess what scathing imagery he would invent for the distinguished scientist who blandly asserts that the danger of atomic fallout has been exaggerated by ignorant laymen, and that only a few million Americans would be killed outright in a nuclear attack. If we have no Daumier today, is it because the price of *lèse-majesté* has become prohibitive? Is it, as one writer suggests, because the horrors of total war and dictatorship have set a boundary to all satire, that a world so distorted cannot be further subjected to distortion? Or is it that our wish not to be dislodged from our assumptions brooks no painful challenge; that the crust of our complacency has no crevice through which the point of an impertinent and doubting pencil can be thrust?

When we turn from the lithographs to the paintings do we not see a richer and more profoundly penetrant expression of Daumier's commitment to man's struggle? In many respects a painting by Daumier is an extension of his lithographic method: it begins with a drawing, and its forms as they come into existence are supported and clarified by lines; its tones suggest color without exploiting actual color contrasts; its action is likely to occupy a small format and to take place within a relatively restricted and clearly defined space; light is an active force which searches out and concentrates upon the essential. His painted figures are given a bodily existence by the same sculptural modeling which called his black-and-white effigies to vigorous life in three dimensions, and their power to move compellingly in space is also to be seen in the rhythms of his best caricatures of the 1860s. With no daily pressure to complete the oils Daumier could proceed in careful stages from the rough drawing to the sharper definition in outlines to be enlarged for his canvas or panel. As he worked, those details which in the lithographs made his point more obvious were sacrificed for greater intensity of utterance.

From early to late one follows his growing concentration upon the essential—from *The Washerwoman,* whose silhouetted form derives its strength from his experience as a lithographer, to *The Third Class Carriage,* where a more complex technique gives his figures a livelier existence and more subtlety of character, and later to *The Painter Before His Easel,* more summary and more mysteriously suggestive and at the same time more purely painterly, a panel which has been called a self-

portrait but could more aptly be called the portrait of a life. In his paintings of Don Quixote, Daumier was content at first to present the knight
and his companion simply as a droll contrast, but his later visions of the
pair gained in force what they lost in descriptive detail until they stood
for the unending conflict between the generous dream and the harsh
reality, the lean and the fat in man's existence.

How inadequate to speak of such canvases as "an excursion into
artistry"! Daumier turned to painting not as "a relief from being significant," but in his search for deeper significance. And the significance is
there for people who can see Daumier whole, who do not need to blind
themselves to the relevance of his images of man in order to perceive
their formal excellence.

In our present world, where Sancho more often represents our mood
than his venturesome companion, where individuals often feel helpless
in the mass, where men begin to doubt their own capacity to think and
to act their way through the injustices, the impasses, the threat of total
disaster, we can ill afford to take any but the broadest and most comprehensive view of Daumier, whose luminous common sense can still in the
context of our time lay bare our small meannesses, our misplaced ambitions, our stupidly false values, our moral ambiguities. Nor by the same
token can we dispense with his constant reminder, in hundreds of drawings and paintings, of his unshakable belief in the strength, dignity and
wisdom of the human creature.

NOTES

General References

The principal studies of Daumier's life and work: Alexandre, Arsène, *Honoré Daumier, l'Homme et l'Oeuvre*, Paris, 1888; Marcel, Henry, *Daumier*, Paris, 1907; Klossowski, Erich, *Honoré Daumier*, Munich, 1908, revised edition 1923; Escholier, Raymond, *Daumier, Peintre et Lithographe*, Paris, 1923; Sadleir, Michael, *Daumier the Man and the Artist*, London, 1923; Escholier, *Daumier*, Paris, 1930; Grass-Mick, A., *La Lumière sur Daumier*, Marseille, 1931; Fosca, François, *Daumier*, Paris, 1933; Escholier, *Daumier*, 1934 and 1938; Scheiwiller, Giovanni, *Honoré Daumier*, Milan, 1936, useful for its bibliography; Courthion, Pierre (ed.), *Daumier Raconté par Lui-même et par ses Amis*, Geneva, 1945; Adhémar, Jean, *Honoré Daumier*, Paris, 1954; Besson, George, *Daumier*, Paris, 1959; Escholier, *Daumier et son Monde*, 1965. In preparation by Jean Cherpin, *Le Citoyen Daumier;* by Howard Vincent, *Daumier and His World;* by K. E. Maison, a catalogue raisonné of the paintings and drawings.

Daumier's painted work is most fully reproduced (with many falsely attributed pictures) in Fuchs, Eduard, *Der Maler Daumier*, Munich, 1927, supplement 1930; see also Fontainas, André, *La Peinture de Daumier*, Paris, 1923, and Lassaigne, Jacques, *Daumier*, translated by Eveline B. Shaw, New York, 1938.

Delteil, Loys, *Le Peintre-Graveur Illustré*, Paris, 10 vols., 1925–1930, (to be cited below as Delt.) attempts to reproduce the complete body of Daumier's lithographs, with the dates of their publication. More selective is Fuchs, Eduard, *Honoré Daumier: Lithographien*, 3 vols., Munich, n.d. See also Bertels, Kurt, *Daumier als Lithograph*, Munich and Leipzig, 1908; Laran, Jean, *Cent Vingt Lithographies d'Honoré Daumier*, Paris, 1929; Stahl, Fritz, *Honoré Daumier*, Berlin, 1930; Lemann, Bernard, *H. Daumier*, New York, 1946.

On the sculptures: Bouvy, Eugène, *Trente-Six Bustes de H. Daumier*, Paris, 1932; Gobin, Maurice, *Daumier Sculpteur*, Geneva, 1952 (the most complete study); *Daumier Scultore*, a catalogue of sculptures and related prints at the Museo Poldi Pezzoli, Milan, 1961, with introduction by Dario Durbé.

The wood engravings are catalogued by Rümann, Arthur, *Honoré Daumier, sein Holtzschnittwerk*, Munich, 1914, and by Bouvy, Eugène, *Daumier: L'Oeuvre Gravée*, 2 vols., Paris, 1933. See also Fuchs, Eduard, *Honoré Daumier: Holtzschnitte*, Munich, n.d.

On drawings and water colors by Daumier: Adhémar, Jean (ed.), *Honoré Daumier, Drawings and Watercolours*, translated by Eveline Winkworth, New York, 1954; K. E. Maison, *Daumier Drawings*, London and New York, 1960.

Portraits of Daumier in various media are listed by Jean Cherpin in "Iconographie de Daumier," in *Arts et Livres de Provence*, numéro spécial 8, 1948, pp. 84–92.

References to other books and articles are given below under the appropriate chapter headings.

Vignette: Rebellious Young Man

Bernard Lemann discusses the artist's early years in "Daumier Père and Daumier Fils," in *Gazette des Beaux-Arts*, vol. 27, May, 1945, pp. 297–316. Three letters from Alexandre Lenoir were published by Jean Cherpin in *Arts et Livres de Provence*, Bulletin no. 18, Jan., 1950, pp. 30–32; see also "Les Logis de Daumier" in the same, p. 37. Rousseau is here quoted from "The Creed of the Savoyard Priest" in Book IV of *Émile*. On the problem of Daumier's first prints, see Lemann in the above cited article and Edwin Bechtel, "Les Lithographies de Jeunesse" in *Arts et Livres de Provence*, numéro spécial 8, 1848, pp. 50–56. *Passe ton Chemin, Cochon!* is Delt. no. 1; *Gargantua*, no. 34; *Les Blanchisseurs* is no. 39. On life at Sainte-Pélagie prison, see Nerval, Gerard de, *Oeuvres Complètes*, 1926, vol. 2. A litho by Daumier, *Souvenir de Sainte-Pélagie*, is Delt. no. 192. His letter from prison was published in Alexandre, *op. cit.*, pp. 54–55.

1: The First Republican Campaign

Michelet is quoted from *Le Peuple*, in *Oeuvres Complètes*, vol. 6, p. 306.

On the events and issues of the period: Bourgeois, Émile, *History of Modern France*, Cambridge University, vol. 1, 1919, pp. 115–288; Weill, Georges, *La France sous la Monarchie Constitutionnelle*, Paris, 1912; La Gorce, Pierre F. G. de, *Louis Philippe*, Paris, 1931; Weill, Georges, *Histoire du Parti Républicain en France de 1814 à 1870*, Paris, 1900; Lucas-Dubreton, J., "Les Trois Glorieuses," in *Revue Hébdomadaire*, Feb. 8, 1930, pp. 131 ff. On the attitude of the Romantics, see Picard, Roger, *Le Romantisme Social*, New York and Paris, 1944. Michelet on the clergy is quoted from Heinrich Heine, *French Affairs*, London, 1893 ,vol. 2, p. 433. Heine's picture of revolutionary activity is in the same, ch. 4.

Thackeray on Philipon versus the régime: "Caricatures and Lithography in Paris," in *Paris Sketch Book*, Boston, 1882, pp. 156–174.

On caricature: Champfleury, Jules, *Histoire de la Caricature Moderne*, Paris, 1878; Dayot, Armand, *Les Maîtres de la Caricature Française au 19e Siècle*, Paris, 1888; Deberdt, Raoul, *La Caricature et L'Humour Français au 19e Siècle*, Paris, n.d. On the republican newspapers, see Avenel, Henri, *Histoire de la Presse Française*, Paris, 1900, and Galtier-Boissière, Jean, *Histoire de la Presse*, Paris, 1934.

Lithography and its practitioners: Hullmandel, C., *The Art of Drawing on Stone*, London, 1824; Pennell, Joseph, *Lithography and Lithographers*, London, 1898; Bersier, Jean E., *La Lithographie en France*, vol. 2, *L'Époque du Romantisme*, Mulhouse, 1947. On the decline of lithographs, see Bouchot, Henri, *La Lithographie*, Paris, 1895, and Introduction to vol. 1 of Delteil, *op. cit.* The poem on lithography is from Charles Blanc, *Grandville*, Paris, 1855, pp. 8–9. References to Philipon's associates: Blum, André, "La Caricature Politique sous la Monarchie de Juillet" in *Gazette des Beaux-Arts*, period 5, vol. I, Mar.-Apr., 1920, pp. 257–277; Goncourt, Edmond and Jules, *Gavarni, l'Homme et l'Oeuvre,* Paris, 1925; Champfleury, *Henry Monnier,* Paris, 1879; Dayot, *op. cit.*

Daumier lithographs on the King: Delt. Nos. 61, 73, 83, 85, 86, 111, 134.

On Daumier's sculptured busts of legislators, the most complete discussions are in Gobin, *op. cit.* and in the Catalogue of the Milan exhibition of 1961. The attribution of several works catalogued by Cherpin has been questioned; it is hard to see in the figurines, nos. 40–58, the same hand which modeled the busts. For the later history of the busts, see Berthe. Le Garrec, "Les Bronzes des Parlementaires," in *Arts et Livres de Provence,* numéro spécial 8, 1948, pp. 101–102. On the relation of Daumier's busts to the work of Dantan, see Seligman, Janet, *Figures of Fun,* Oxford University Press, 1957.

The bust-length lithographed portraits made with the help of the sculptures are Delt. nos. 43, 45, 48, 51, 144, 147, 148–154, 156, 162, 164, 165, 168, 170, 171, 173, 175. The full-length portraits are nos. 52–60, 62–64, 68–70, 72, 74, 75. Other lithos here mentioned are nos. 35, 118, 20, 71, 133. The massacre in the rue Transnonain: Ledru-Rollin, Alexandre, *Mémoire sur les Événements de la rue Transnonain,* a pamphlet, Paris, 1834, here quoted; Daumier's lithograph is Delt. no. 135.

The April trials: *Le Fantôme* is Delt. no. 115; dialogue from the trial is quoted from the *Gazette des Tribunaux.* Daumier's series on the judges are Delt. nos. 117, 121, 123, 125, 128, 298. Daumier's final comment on the defeat of republicanism is no. 130.

2: Daumier's Human Comedy

On French life: see references for Chapter I; also Croisset, François de, "Le Paris de 1830," in *Revue Hébdomadaire,* Feb. 22, 1930. Michelet describes the bourgeois of this time in *Le Peuple,* pp. 140–143, and Balzac in *Grandeur et Décadence de César Birotteau,* p. 161. Balzac's purpose is stated in his *Avant-Propos,* in vol. 1 of the *Comédie Humaine.* On the peasant, see Balzac, preface to *Les Paysans,* and drawings by Daumier, Delt. 1391, 1392.

On the vignette, see Champfleury, *Les Vignettes Romantiques,* Paris, 1883. On wood-engraved illustrations, see Bouvy and Rümann, *op. cit.* Daumier's woodcut for *Némésis Médicale* is Bouvy no. 340.

On Macaire: Banville's description is in *Contes, Souvenirs et Portraits,* Paris, n.d., pp. 122–132; see also Osiatovski, Stanislav, "History of Robert Macaire and Daumier's Place in It," in *Burlington Magazine,* vol. 100, Nov., 1958, p. 388 ff. The Macaire lithos of Daumier are Delt. 354–455 and 866–885. Thiers is portrayed as Macaire in no. 124.

The principal series of social satires in Delteil: *Types Français,* nos. 260–270; *Plaisirs de l'Hiver,* 283–288; *Galerie Physionomique,* 326–350; *La Chasse,* 302–317 and 1072–1083; *Croquis d'Expressions,* 466–522; 571 *bis,* 571 *ter; Journée du Célibataire,* 607–618; *Moeurs Conjugales,* 624–683; *Émotions Parisiennes,* 635, 684, 728, 754–759; *Les Baigneurs,* 760–790; *Types Parisiens,* 502, 503, 559–606; *Bohémiens de Paris,* 822–849; *Scènes Parlementaires,* 1018–1022; *Les Chemins de Fer,* 1043–1058; *Les Beaux Jours de la Vie,* 1088–1188; *Les Philanthropes du Jour,* 1292–1326; *Les Pastorales,* 1388–1437, 1563;

Les Bons Bourgeois, 1477–1567, 1571, 1572; *Les Papas*, 1568–1593; *Locataires et Propriétaires*, 1594–1628.

Briffault on the politician is quoted from *Les Français Peints par Eux-mêmes*, Paris, 1840–42, vol. 1, p. 186. Daumier on the new shops is Delt. 1288. Two lithos on Véron, nos. 990 and 1310. Satires on the National Guard: nos. 575, 601, 728, 742, 1479, 1520, 1697.

Satires on the professions: *Professeurs et Moutards*, Delt. 1438–1469; *Gens de Justice*, 1337–1377; on artists, 146 (*Le Bois est Cher*), 269, 719, 1334, 1495, 1721–1728.

On the feminists, see Barbey d'Aurévilly, Jules, *Les Bas-Bleus*, Paris, 1878. The Daumier series, *Les Bas-Bleus*, is Delt. 1221–1260; *La Lune* is no. 1228; *Les Divorçeuses* is nos. 1769–1774; *Les Femmes Socialistes*, 1918–1931.

On French theaters: Weill, Georges, *La France sous la Monarchie Constitutionnelle*; d'Alméras, H., *La Vie Parisienne sous le Règne de Louis-Philippe*, Paris, 1911; de Croisset, *op. cit.*; Beaulieu, Henri, *Les Théâtres du Boulevard du Crime*, Paris, 1905. Gautier describes the opening night of *Hernani* in *Histoire du Romantisme*, Paris, 1911, ch. 10; for his comments on plays and authors of his time, see Patch, Helen E., *The Dramatic Criticism of Théophile Gautier*, Bryn Mawr, 1922. Thackeray on the theater is here quoted from "French Dramas and Melodramas," in Paris *Sketch Book*, p. 269. Daumier caricatures of classical drama are Delt. 512, 516, 518, also 890–904 and 1740–1742. Portraits of Odry are 352, 353; *Bobêche et Gallimafré* is 457; *Bernard Léon* is 1269; *Un Pierrot Déplumé*, 1655; *Une Maîtresse à l'Opéra*, 1149; *Le Parterre de l'Odéon*, 1237; *Le Cinquième Acte à la Gaîté*, 1674; on Hugo and *Les Burgraves*, 1004; on *Lucrèce*, 1010; on *Diogène*, 1471.

The series *Histoire Ancienne* is Delt. 925–974. See Gigoux, Jean, *Causeries sur les Artistes de Mon Temps*, Paris, 1885, on Daumier's use of the Iliad and the Odyssey, and of the *Télémaque* of Fénelon. Baudelaire's comment on this series is in "Some French Caricaturists," in *The Mirror of Art*, translated by Jonathan Mayne, London, 1955. The series *Physionomies Tragico-classiques* is Delt. 840–904. Baudelaire's remarks on Daumier's picture of bourgeois life are in *The Mirror of Art*, p. 166 and were probably written in the 1840s.

3: The Artist

Léon Rosenthal surveys movements in painting in "Les Conditions Sociales de la Peinture sous la Monarchie de Juillet," three articles in *Gazette des Beaux-Arts*, vol. 43, 1910, pp. 93–114, 217–241, and 332–354; see also his *La Peinture Romantique*, Paris, n.d., and *Du Romantisme au Réalisme*, Paris, 1914. The comments of Diderot are in his Salons of 1763 and 1765, in *Oeuvres Complètes*, Paris, 1875–77, vol. 10. The relation of Berlioz, Hugo and Delacroix is suggested by Jacques Barzun in *Berlioz and His Century*, New York, 1956. Gautier is quoted from *Histoire du Romantisme*, p. 230 ff. On the vicissitudes of the *Liberté* of Delacroix, see article by Hélène Adhémar in *Gazette des Beaux-Arts*, vol. 43, Feb. 1954, pp. 83 ff. Gautier sets forth the doctrine of art for art's sake in the preface to *Mademoiselle de Maupin*, Paris,

1835. On social romanticism, see Picard, *op. cit*. Champfleury comments on the young republican artists in *Souvenirs et Portraits de Jeunesse*, Paris, 1872. For Baudelaire on the art of his time, see *The Mirror of Art*, p. 38. The letter of Delacroix to Daumier is in Escholier, Raymond, *Daumier*, Paris, 1923, pp. 185–186. On Alexandre Decamps, see du Colombier, P., *Decamps*, Paris, 1928. On Barye, see Théophile Gautier's article of 1866, reprinted in *Histoire du Romantisme*. On Préault, see article by Ernest Chesneau in *L'Art*, vol. 17, 1879, pp. 3–15.

Daumier's progress as a draftsman: *Le Bois est Cher* is Delt. 146; *Quand on a Brûlé son Dernier Chevalet* is 1334. For Baudelaire's comparison of Daumier with Ingres and Delacroix as draftsmen, see *Mirror of Art*, p. 8. On Daumier's difficulty in finishing, see Delacroix *Journal* for Feb. 5, 1849, in the Walter Pach translation, New York, 1937, p. 182.

The problem of dating Daumier's paintings: Adhémar presents his scheme in *Honoré Daumier*, 1954, differing in many respects from my own. A general theory of the painter's development is suggested in articles cited below by David Rosen and Henri Marceau, whose laboratory examination of his technical procedure exposed some false works and led them to question the authenticity of paintings which other students consider genuine.

Some early paintings: Adhémar reproduces a photo of the lost painting alleged to be a copy of Rubens' *Kermesse*, in *op. cit.*, plate 27; *L'Aquafortiste* was in the Rouart collection; *Nocturnal Strollers* and *Workmen in a Street* are in the National Museum of Wales, Cardiff; *Le Tireur de Bateau* (*Le Haleur*) is in a private collection, Germany. Other early oils: *Oedipus and the Shepherd* (J. K. Thannhauser); *Two Men Drinking* (Metropolitan Museum); *The Water Carrier* (Barnes Collection, Merion, Pa.); *The Horsemen* (Boston Museum of Fine Arts); *The Watering Place* (Miss M. S. Davies); *Bather at the Watering Place* (Lord Wharton); *Le Bain des Jeunes Filles* (Pierre Lévy, Troyes); *Le Premier Bain* (Oskar Reinhart); *The First Bathe* (J. E. Hanson); *The Bathers* (Burrell collection, Corporation of Glasgow); *Children Under a Tree* (Toledo Museum of Art); *La Sortie de l'École* (Alfred Daber, Paris). Among the more obviously doctored works are *Retour du Marché* (O. Reinhart) and *The Good Samaritan* (Glasgow Art Gallery). *To the Street* (Duncan Phillips) seems to be a work of the 1840s.

On the iconography of *La République*, see Renouvier, Jules, *Histoire de L'Art pendant la Révolution*, Paris, 1863; also Lemann, Bernard, "Daumier and the Republic," in *Gazette des Beaux-Arts*, vol. 27, Feb., 1947, pp. 105–120. Barbier's verses are from his *Iambes*, Paris, 1832. A drawing in the collection of Claude Roger-Marx has been called a study for the painting. The remarks of Champfleury on the competitive sketches appeared in *Revue des Arts et des Ateliers*, Aug. 6, 1848, and are reprinted in his *Oeuvres Posthumes*, Paris, 1894, pp. 97–99.

Vignette: Family Man

For Daumier's financial problems, see Quintaine, André, "Peines d'Argent," in *Arts et Livres de Provence*, numéro spécial 8, Marseille,

1948, pp. 93–96; also Cherpin, Jean in the same, pp. 74–76.

Zola's description of the Île Saint-Louis is in *La Curée,* ch. 2.

Letters from Daumier to his wife at the seashore were published by Cherpin in *Arts et Livres de Provence,* Bulletin no. 27, May, 1955, pp. 35–42.

For the Goncourts on Daumier, see *Journal,* integral edition, Monaco, 1956–58, vol. I, p. 66. Gavarni's description of the studio is in Escholier, *op. cit.,* 1923, p. 78. Champfleury's description of his visit to Daumier is reprinted in *Daumier Raconté par Lui-même et par ses Amis,* Geneva, 1945, pp. 77–78; see the same, pp. 145–148 for Baudelaire's description of the artist.

The lithographed portrait-caricature of Daumier by Benjamin Robaud was published Jan. 18, 1839. A wood engraving by Gavarni in Adhémar, *op. cit.,* opposite p. 15, shows a similar figure.

The anecdote of the window blind, from the Goncourts, is quoted by Escholier, *op. cit.,* 1923, p. 78.

4: The Republican Honeymoon

On the Revolution of 1848 and the Second Republic: Bourgeois, *op. cit.,* vol. 1; Seignobos, Charles, vol. 6 in Lavisse, Ernest, *Histoire de France Contemporaine;* Schmidt, Charles, *Les Journées de Juin 1848,* Paris, 1926; Weill, Georges, *Histoire du Parti Republicain en France.* See also the Goncourt *Journal,* vol. VII, p. 229 and VIII, p. 89. Delacroix is quoted from his *Correspondance Générale,* Paris, 1936, vol. 2, p. 347. *Le Dernier Conseil des Ex-ministres* is Delt. 1746; *Le Gamin de Paris aux Tuileries* is 1743. The series, *Les Alarmistes et les Alarmés* is 1761–1768. The letter of Decamps to Daumier, Oct. 20, 1848, is published by Escholier, 1923, p. 185. Jean Cherpin prints two letters on commissions for a religious painting in *Arts et Livres de Provence,* no. 8, 1948, pp. 74–92.

Paintings of this period: *Marie-Madeleine Pénitente* (private collection); *The Miller, His Son and the Ass* (Glasgow Art Gallery); *Two Nymphs Pursued by Satyrs* (Montreal Museum of Fine Arts); *La Marche de Silène* (drawing, Musée de Calais); *The Uprising* (Duncan Phillips), which has later retouches, perhaps by another hand. A vertical composition on the same theme was once owned by Daubigny, later by Gerstenberg, and is now lost. *Famille Sur la Barricade* (Národny Museum, Prague), has been drastically retouched; a charcoal study for the head of the principal figure is privately owned, and a superb oil sketch for the same is in the National Museum of Wales, Cardiff. A study for the boy's head is in Toledo Museum of Art. Jean Adhémar believes that the *Don Quixote* of the Salon of 1850–51 has been lost; Maison identifies it as the painting once owned by Aubert, and now in a private collection, Boston. The two reliefs of *Fugitifs* or *Émigrants,* which I place at this time, have been variously dated. On their history see Gobin, *Daumier Sculpteur,* under nos. 64, 65. Alexandre saw the casts from the Trajan Column in Daumier's studio; see his *Honoré Daumier,* p. 332. The painting, *Les Émigrants,* in the Petit-Palais seems to be of this time.

Daumier caricatures on political figures: *Les Représentants Représentés,* Delt. 1796–1903; *Physionomie de l'Assemblée,* 1947–1978; *Idylles Parlementaires,* 2050–2076.

On Hugo's politics see Grant, Elliott M., *Victor Hugo During the Second Republic,* Northampton, Mass., 1935. The endorsement of Louis-Napoleon is quoted by the same, p. 22. *La Paquebot Napoléonien* is no. 1754.

The Roman question: Bourgeois, Émile, *Rome et Napoleon III,* Paris, 1907; Debidour, Antonin, *Histoire des Rapports de l'Église et de l'État en France de 1798 à 1870,* Paris, 1898. Montalembert is described by the Goncourts in *Journal,* vol. II, p. 8. He appears in Delt. 1932, 1984, 2007, 2088, 2098, 2100, 2105, 2119, 2133, 2141, 2148.

Daumier and Hugo: the portrait-litho of Hugo is Delt. 1861; Hugo's anticlerical speech is in *Actes et Paroles,* vol. 1, Paris, 1937, pp. 178–188. *Une Gloire Éteint l'Autre* is Delt. 1755 (unpublished).

Lithos on the collapse of the Republic: Universal Suffrage as Gulliver, Delt. 2010; *Le Festin de Baltasar-Véron,* 1997; *Le Révérend Père Gorenflot,* 2091; *Les Moucherons Politiques,* 2012; *Alliance des Bonapartistes et des Capucins,* 2093; *Renouvelé du Serment des Horaces,* 2095. On Louis Veuillot, see Lemaître, Jules, *Les Contemporains,* Paris, 1897–1899, vol. 6. The litho, *Un Auto-da-fé,* is Delt. 2100; other lithos on Veuillot are 2088, 2105, 2147, 2148. Romieu is quoted from *Le Spectre Rouge de 1852,* Paris, 1851. Lithos on Romieu are Delt. 1990, 2090, 2105, 3752. Hugo's speech on "Napoleon the Little" is in *Actes et Paroles,* p, 257.

Daumier creates *Ratapoil:* on the statuette, see Gobin, *op. cit.,* pp. 294–299; Ratapoil appears in lithos 2029–2031, 2033, 2035, 2045, 2085, 2093, 2104,· 2106, 2108, 2111, 2117, 2118, 2123, 2126, 2128, 2137, 2138, 2139, 4647, 4652, 4653, 4658.

The coup d'état: Proudhon's interpretation is in *La Révolution Sociale,* in *Oeuvres Complètes,* 1936, vol. 13. Hugo's *Histoire d'un Crime,* completed in 1852, was published in 1877. He is here quoted from pp. 154 and 210, and from *Napoléon le Petit,* published in London in 1852, pp. 131 and 133. The meeting of Hugo and Proudhon is described by the former in *Oeuvres Complètes,* vol. 28, p. 378. The letter of Michelet to Daumier is in Alexandre, *op. cit.,* p. 302.

5: The Human Comedy, Act Two

The background: Guedalla, Philip, *The Second Empire,* New York, 1928; Seignobos, Charles, *Le Second Empire,* vols. 6, 7 in Lavisse, Ernest, *Histoire de France Contemporaine,* Paris, 1920–22; Gooch, C. P., *The Second Empire,* London, 1960; Sonolet, Louis, *La Vie Parisienne sous le Second Empire,* Paris, 1929; Bellesort, André, *La Société Française sous Napoleon III,* Paris, 1932. See also *Mémoires du Comte Horace de Viel-Castel,* 6 vols., Paris, 1883; *The Journal of Eugène Delacroix,* translated by Walter Pach, New York, 1937, pp. 463–464.

Daumier on Veuillot: Delt. 2248, 2264.

Les Cosaques pour Rire is Delt. 2472–2490. *Chargeons les Russes* is 2491–2505 and 2506–2563. *Ces Bons Autrichiens* is 3158–3183.

On the "Gillotages," see Prouté, Paul, "Le Procédé Gillot," in *Arts et Livres de Provence*, no. 8, 1948, pp. 113–114.

On Haussmann's work: Chapman, J. M. and Brian, *The Life and Times of Baron Haussmann*, London, 1957; Pinckney, David H., *Napoleon III and the Rebuilding of Paris*, Princeton, 1958. Champfleury is quoted from *Souvenirs de Jeunesse*, pp, 124–125; Banville from *Occidentales*, p. 299. Daumier lithos on this theme are Delt. 2275–2278, 2305, 2361, 2429, 2564, 2570–2580, 2585, 2586, 2630, 2775, 2837–2842.

Macaire and Bertrand as statues at the Bourse: Delt. 2024, 2569. The verses of Hugo are from *Les Châtiments*, Book 3, Poem One, *Apothéose*.

Satires on Louis Véron: Delt. 1912, 2249, 2252, 2254, 2255–2259. Taine's comments on theaters and audiences are in *Vie et Opinions de M. Frédéric-Thomas Graindorge*, Paris, 1889.

On Joseph Prudhomme: Champfleury, *Henry Monnier, Sa Vie, Son Oeuvre*, Paris, 1879; Gautier, *Fusains et Eaux-fortes*, Paris, 1907, pp. 23 ff. Gautier is here quoted from his essay on Monnier in *Portraits Contemporains*, Paris, 1911. Daumier lithos: *Henry Monnier dans le Rôle de Joseph-Prudhomme*, Delt. 2347; also Delt. 2593, 2654, 2779, 2938, 3549, 3748, and others.

Caricatures on recreations and fads: *Croquis Aquatiques*, Delt. 2411–2423, 2591–2596 and 2715, 2716; *Croquis de Chasse*, 2436, 2451, 2471, 2720, 2992–2995, 3211–3217, 3232, 3304–3309, 3338–3343, 3456, 3467, 3468; *Croquis d'Été*, 2410, 2581–2583, 2710–2714, 2843–2877, 3200–3203, 3457–3462; *Émotions de Chasse*, 2601–2615, 2878–2896; *Paris Qui Boit*, 2307–2312; *Les Bons Bourgeois*, 2324–2395, 2598–2600; *Croquis Musicaux*, 2229–2245; *La Fluidomanie*, 2397–2408; *La Potichomanie*, 2643, 2650; on crinolines, 2916, 2917, 2626, 2627, 2676, 2758, 2759, 2968–2973, 2976, 2977, 3063, 3289.

Daumier on artists and public: *Les Artistes*, Delt. 1725–1728; *Scènes d'Ateliers*, 1721–1724; *Le Public au Salon*, 2292–2302; *Le Salon de 1857*, 2959–2965; *L'Exposition de 1859*, 3135–3143. See also Champfleury, "M. Prudhomme au Salon" in *Contes Vieux et Nouveaux*, Paris, 1852.

On railway travel: *Physionomies des Chemins de Fer*, 2279–2288; *Les Trains de Plaisir*, 2325, 2339; *Les Chemins de Fer*, 2729–2732 and 3002, 3003; *Les Agréments des Chemins de Fer*, 2823, 2824.

On plays, actors and audiences: see Cherpin, Jean, *Daumier et le Théâtre*, Paris, 1958; *Physionomies Tragiques*, Delt. 2175–2184 and *Croquis Dramatiques*, 2348–2351, 2897–2911, 3279–3281. Persigny's strictures on the theater are quoted by Houssaye, Arsène, *Les Confessions*, Paris, 1885, vol. 4, p. 237; on Daumier at the Comédie-Française, see the same, p. 284. The wood engravings on *Ulysse* are in Bouvy, *op. cit.*, nos. 774–785. *Souvenirs de Richard III* is Bouvy, nos. 804–816. *Boulevard du Temple à Minuit* is Bouvy no. 924. The Goncourts are here quoted from *Journal*, vol. IV, p. 175. *Une Première Représentation de la Bourse* is Delt. 2763. Lithos of the Opera: Delt. 2220, 2764, 2806, 2903, 2905, 2910. The water color, *A Box in the*

Theater, is in the Ernest Rouart collection. On Offenbach, see Kracauer, S., *Orpheus in Paris,* translated by Gwenda David and Eric Mosbacher, New York, 1938; also the Goncourt *Journal,* vol. 14, p. 92. On amateur dramatics, see Clarétie, Léo, *Histoire des Théâtres de Société,* Paris, n.d. Daumier's series is *Comédiens de Société,* Delt. 3031–3046. Backstage scenes: Delt. 2406, 2432, 2809, 2926, 2847, 2849, 2897, 2902, 2903, 2906, 3281. Ludovic Halévy is quoted from *Les Petites Cardinal,* Paris, 1889. Lithographs of audiences: Delt. 2628, 2764, 2844, 2911, 3083, 3262, 3263, 3264, 3407.

6: Citizen-Painter

The notes of Poulet-Malassis on his visit to Daumier are in Adhémar, *op. cit.,* pp. 44–45. Some paintings which he may have seen: *Nous Voulons Barabbas!* (Museum Folkwang, Essen); *Sancho Panza sous un Arbre* (Kunsthistorisches Museum, Vienna); *A Waiting Room* (Albright Art Gallery, Buffalo); *Washerwomen on the Steps of the Quay* (private collection, New York); *On a Bridge at Night* (Duncan Phillips); *Les Émigrants* (Petit-Palais). Gobin speculates on the "bacchanal" in *Daumier Sculpteur,* p. 146. Maison thinks that the "martyrdom" may be the *Mise au Tombeau* described by Klossowski, p. 52.

Jean Gigoux on Daumier's procedure: see his *Causeries sur les Artistes de Mon Temps,* pp. 53–56. Alexandre notes the repainting of the *Nymphs* in *op. cit.,* p. 344.

The statuette and paintings of *The Heavy Burden:* Rosen, David and Marceau, Henri, "A Terra Cotta by Daumier," in *Journal of the Walters Art Gallery,* vol. XI, 1948, pp. 77 ff.; Maison, K. E., "Daumier's Painted Replicas," in *Gazette des Beaux-Arts,* vol. 57, June, 1961, pp. 369–377 (a discussion of six known versions).

The artistic situation: Baudelaire compares Ingres and Delacroix in his review of the Exposition of 1855, in *Mirror of Art,* pp. 191 ff. The group at Fontainebleau is described by Taine in *op. cit.,* ch. 19.

Daumier as draftsman and painter: *Un Léger Zéphir* is Delt. 2622. *Oui, Madame Fribochon* is here compared with two drawings, *Three Gossiping Women* in Chicago Art Institute and Victoria and Albert Museum, with the water color (Wildenstein Gallery, 1961) and with the litho, *La Comète de 1857,* Delt. 2925. The litho, *Les Amis,* is Delt. 1387; two drawings of the thieves are in the Roger-Marx collection; the painting, *Les Voleurs et l'Âne* is in the Louvre. The litho made from the painting is Delt. 3253.

Some drawings and water colors mentioned here: *Child Running* (Lessing J. Rosenwald); *Centaure Enlevant une Femme* (Claude Roger-Marx); *The Connoisseurs* (Cleveland Museum of Art); *The Market* (Mrs. John D. Rockefeller, Jr., New York); *Corot Drawing at Ville d'Avray* (M. Loncle); and a larger and more complete version of the same called *Man Reading in a Garden,* in Metropolitan Museum; two nearly identical versions of *Politics in a Beer Garden* (*La Politique*) owned by Oskar Reinhart, Winterthur, and Albert Nussbaumer, Lugano; *The Advocate* (Corcoran Gallery, Washington, D.C.)

K. E. Maison discusses Daumier's preparatory drawings for his paintings in *Burlington Magazine,* vol. 96, Jan., 1954, pp. 13–17 and March, 1954, pp. 82–86; also vol. 98, June, 1956, pp. 199–203. The wash drawing *The Thin Woman and the Colossus (The Side Show),* dedicated to Jules Dupré, is in the Burrell Collection, Corporation of Glasgow; the finished water color is in Philadelphia Museum of Art. The notes of Philippe Burty on his visit to Geoffroy-Dechaume in 1862 are reprinted by Adhémar in *Honoré Daumier: Drawings and Watercolours,* New York and Basel, 1954, p. 7. Some water colors presumably of this period: *L'Attente* (Victoria and Albert Museum); *Joueurs de Dominos* (Dr. Fritz Nathan); *Le Réquisitoire* (Dr. Z. Bruck, Buenos Aires); *Three Gossiping Women.* See Agnes Mongan, "Six Aquarelles Inédites de Daumier," in *Gazette des Beaux-Arts,* vol. 17, April, 1937, pp. 245–253, and Marvin Ross in *Journal of the Walters Art Gallery,* vol. II, 1948, pp. 84–85.

Daumier's water colors of lawyers: The Goncourts are quoted from the *Journal,* vol. VII, p. 60; their descriptions of trials seen by them are in the same, vol. VIII, p. 182 and pp. 189–192. Related works: *After the Trial* (Philadelpia Museum of Art); *Stairway of the Palais de Justice* (Baltimore Museum of Art); *Lawyer with a Woman Client* (National Museum of Wales, Cardiff); *A Famous Case* (Phila. Museum of Art), with related drawings (A. Strolin, Neuilly, and Maurice Gobin).

Other water colors of the period: *The Drinking Song* (Phila. Museum of Art); two water colors in Fogg Museum, Harvard University, of butchers at work, a subject which appears in lithos of 1857–58, Delt. 3010–3013, 3015, 3016, 3018–3021; *The Critics in the Theatre* (once in Gerstenberg collection, reproduced in Maison, *Daumier Drawings,* London and New York, 1960, no. 105.

Daumier's work in oils: Rosen and Marceau analyze his methods in "Technical Notes on Daumier" in the catalogue of the exhibition at Philadelphia in 1937; also in "Daumier: Draftsman-Painter," in *Journal of the Walters Art Gallery,* vol. III, 1940, pp. 19–23 and 33–41. Paintings here assigned to his middle period: *Le Liseur* (Paul Rosenberg, Paris, in 1959); *The Washerwoman (La Blanchisseuse),* in three versions (Albright Gallery, Buffalo, the Louvre, and Metropolitan Museum, New York). The first of these is probably the one shown in 1861. Théophile Thoré comments on the exhibited version in *Salons de W. Bürger,* 1861 à 1868, Paris, 1870, vol. 1, p. 116. Also *The Third Class Carriage,* the unfinished painting in the Metropolitan Museum, a more finished one in the National Gallery of Art, Ottawa. Arthur Stevens' letter is published by Quintaine, André, in *Arts et Livres de Provence,* no. 8, 1948, pp. 93–96. Other works mentioned here: *Crispin et Scapin* (Louvre); *Le Drame* (Staatsgalerie, Munich) and a related litho, Delt. 3280; *Print Collectors* (Clark Institute, Williamstown, Mass.); *Les Amateurs* (Museum Boymans-Van Beuningen, Rotterdam); *The Curious Ones* (private collection, U.S.A.); *The Print Collector* (Burrell Collection, Corporation of Glasgow); *L'Amateur d'Estampes* (Petit-Palais); *The Print Collector* (Phila. Museum of Art); *Le Couple Chantant* (Stedelijkmuseum, Amsterdam); *Head of a*

Buffoon (Mr. Emery Reves); *The Game of Draughts* (Phila. Museum); *Three Lawyers* (Duncan Phillips).

Contemporary criticisms of art: Baudelaire discusses the "spoiled children" of art in his Salon of 1859, in *Mirror of Art*, p. 217 ff.; the comments of Thoré are in his *Salons de W. Bürger;* Zola's reviews of the Salon of 1866 are in *Mes Haines,* Paris, 1879; see also Hennings, F. W. J. and Neiss, Robert, *Émile Zola, Salons,* Geneva and Paris, 1959, especially pp. 49–80. For the satire of the humorous press on the innovators, especially Manet, see Philippe Roberts-Jones, *De Daumier à Lautrec,* Paris, 1960. Daumier refers to Manet's *Olympia* in Delt. 3446.

On the role of the observer, see E. H. Gombrich, *Art and Illusion,* London and New York, 1960, Ch. VI.

The Meissonier, *A Painter Showing His Drawings,* is in the Wallace Collection, London.

Vignette: Time of Crisis

The absence from *Charivari:* Baudelaire and Burty are quoted from Escholier, 1923, pp. 162–63; Philipon's remarks were in *Le Journal Amusant,* Sept. 21, 1861.

On financial problems: Tavernier and Jules Dupré are quoted in Escholier, *op. cit.,* pp. 188 and 191.

For the gatherings at the Café de Madrid and the Divan, see Dreyfous, Maurice, *Ce que Je Tiens à Dire,* Paris, n.d., p. 51.

The litho-portrait by Carjat was published in *Le Boulevard,* Dec. 1, 1861. The Goncourts mention their meeting with Daumier in *Journal,* vol. V, pp. 54 and 206. On the artists' colony at Valmondois and Barbizon, see Sensier, A., *Souvenirs Sur Théodore Rousseau,* Paris, 1872, esp. pp. 232–233 and 247–248.

The notice of Daumier's return to *Charivari* is given under Delt. no. 3255.

Champfleury's letter on the testimonial dinner is in Troubat, Jules, *Sainte-Beuve et Champfleury,* Paris, 1908, pp. 226–229.

On the house at Valmondois, see Cherpin in *Arts et Livres de Provence,* no. 8, 1948, pp. 81–84.

7: The Republic Victorious

Some satires of bourgeois life in 1864–65: *Les Bons Bourgeois,* Delt. 3282, 3416; *Croquis de Chasse,* 3304, 3309, 3338–3343, 3456, 3467, 3468; *Baigneurs,* 3318–3327; *Plaisirs de la Campagne,* 3365–3370; *Croquis pris au Théâtre,* 3261–3268.

On the Liberal Empire of the 1860s, see previously cited works by Bourgeois, Seignobos, Gooch, Sonolet and Bellesort. Bourgeois is quoted from vol. 2, p. 75; Persigny, from Guedalla, p. 317. Sainte-Beuve on Hugo's underground popularity: Goncourt *Journals,* vol. VI, p. 180. Lafargue on the new generation is quoted by Bourgeois, vol. 2, p. 77.

The rising opposition: Daumier refers to the republican press in *La Grande Marée de 1868*, Delt. 3681. Assolant is quoted by Bellesort, p. 300; Rogeard and Rochefort by the same, pp. 323 and 341. For Gambetta's oration at the trial of *Le Réveil*, see *Discours et Plaidoyers de M. Gambetta*, Paris, 1880, pp. 15–17.

The opera bouffe as satire: Weiss, J. J., "Les Moeurs et le Théâtre," in *Revue des Deux Mondes*, Feb. 1, 1866. Daumier's litho, *L'Histoire Revue et Corrigée par l'Opérette* is Delt. 3679. The speech of the Augur is from act one, scene two of Meilhac and Halévy, *La Belle Hélène*. Francisque Sarcey is quoted by Kracauer, *op. cit.*, p. 181.

Daumier resumes political work: two lithos on Émile Ollivier, Delt. 3482, 3484 (unpublished); anti-clerical drawings, Delt. 3562, 3563, 3737, 3741 (on Père Hyacinthe), 3801; on the Italian question, 3496, 3511, 3520, 3525, 3530, 3603 (*Le Jésuite*), 3620 (*Dur à dénouer*). Anti-Prussian caricatures: 3503, 3504, 3508, 3514, 3523, 3567, 3569, 3570, 3575, 3588, 3592, 3599, 3602, 3607, 3626, 3639 *bis*, 3684, 3740. For the metaphor of the two locomotives, see Guiral, Pierre, *Prévost-Paradol*, Paris, 1955, pp. 503–504.

The great lithos on peace and war are Delt. 3499, 3535, 3548, 3556, 3540, 3660, 3094, 3505, 3517, 3518, 3537, 3547, 3566, 3595, 3640, 3659, 3683. Two lithos on the Peace Congress of 1869: Delt. 3691, 3693.

On the elections of May, 1869: Delt. 3696, 3700, 3705, 3713, 3717, 3755. *Recevant ses Sujets* is 3707; Michelet's letter about this litho is in Escholier, 1923, Appendix, p. 190.

Flaubert on Thiers: see Reclus, Maurice, *Monsieur Thiers*, Paris, 1929, p. 279.

The revision of the Constitution in 1869: Delt. 3730, 3721, 3731, 3733, 3738.

The Ecumenical Council: Delt. 3744, 3749, 3783 (*La Nouvelle Assomption*).

Daumier and Hugo on the Red Menace: Delt. 3752, and Hugo, *Oeuvres Complètes*, vol. 28, p. 107 (in *Napoléon le Petit*). Some lithos on the situation in 1870: 3758 (*L'Arène Parlementaire*), 3765 (*Place aux Jeunes!*), 3764, 3767, 3769, all on Thiers; 3780 (on the plebiscite). Daumier contrasts the Prussian and French mobilizations in 3803 and 3804.

On the Siege and the Commune, see Kranzberg, Melvin, *The Siege of Paris*, Ithaca, New York, 1950; also Gautier, Théophile, *Tableaux de Siège*, Paris, n.d.; Clarétie, Jules, *Paris Assiégé*, 1871; Mason, Edward S., *The Paris Commune*, New York, 1930; Jellinek, Frank, *The Paris Commune of 1871*, Oxford, 1937. Related lithos by Daumier: 3810, 3813.

Daumier's indictment of the Empire, and Hugo's imagery: lithos 3803, 3811, 3814 (related to Hugo's poem, *Aux Morts du 4 Décembre*, in *Les Châtiments*); 3847 (France as Prometheus, see Hugo's poem *L'Expiation*, in *Châtiments*); 3820 (*Page d'Histoire*), see letter of Hugo to Daumier in Escholier, *Daumier*, 1923, p. 490. Other lithos of this time: Delt. 3843, 3848, 3850 (Thiers at Bordeaux), 3858, 3864, 3867 (*Le Char de l'État en 1871*). Hostile reactions to the Commune: Villemessant, Jean de, *Mémoires d'un Journaliste*, Paris, 1872–1884, vol. 4, p. 364; Goncourts, *Journal*, vol. IX, p. 185. Veuillot on Thiers is quoted in Halévy, Daniel, *La Fin des Notables,* Paris, 1930, pp. 231–232.

From the fall of the Commune to the founding of the Third Republic: see Soltau, Roger, *French Parties and Politics, 1871–1921,* Oxford, 1930; see also Bourgeois, vol. 2, p. 268. Some lithos of 1871 and 1872: Delt. 3870, 3871, 3877, 3908, 3910, 3925, 3928, 3935, 3937.

8: La Fontaine, Molière, Cervantes

The Goncourts are here quoted from an article in *Le Temps,* July 8, 1860. On the influence of Corot in the late paintings, see Watkins, Franklin C. and Henri Marceau in "Beneath the Paint and the Varnish," in *Magazine of Art,* vol. 37, April, 1944, pp. 128–134. Some paintings discussed here: *The Strong Man* (Duncan Phillips); *Le Secret* (Leonard C. Stein, Geneva), contrasted here with Diaz' *Le Maléfice* (Musée des Beaux-Arts, Lyon); *Les Joueurs d'Échecs* (Petit-Palais); *Le Peintre* (Musée de Reims). Water colors: *La Soupe* (Louvre); *Huis Clos* (Ny Carlsberg Glyptotek, Copenhagen); *Mountebanks Changing Place* (Wadsworth Atheneum, Hartford, Connecticut); preliminary drawings for the same reproduced by Maison in *Daumier Drawings,* nos. 75 and 76. The series of lithos, *La Fête du Village Voisin,* is Delt. 3371–3377.

Daumier and La Fontaine: the drawing of the cat changed into a woman is reproduced by Escholier, *Daumier,* 1938, p. 70; the litho, *Renouvelé de La Fontaine,* is Delt. 3599; *En Espagne* is 3675. The water color, *Les Deux Médecins et la Mort,* is in the Oskar Reinhart collection.

Daumier and Molière: for Daumier at the Comédie-Française, see Houssaye, *op. cit.,* vol. 2, p. 284. Sainte-Beuve discusses Molière in *Nouveaux Lundis,* vol. V, 1872. Daumier's litho on the doctors is Delt. 3577. Scapin and Sprigani are quoted from *Les Fourberies de Scapin,* Act 2, Scene 5, and *Monsieur de Pourceaugnac,* Act 2, Scene 10. Maison in *Daumier Drawings* reproduces a sketch of Molière characters from the Burrell collection, Glasgow Art Gallery, no. 96, and a study of a scene from Molière in a private collection, no. 87. Oil paintings mentioned: *Crispin et Scapin* (Louvre); *Types of the Old Comedy* (Phila. Museum of Art); *Scène de Molière* (Louvre); *Doctor Diafoirus* (Dr. and Mrs. H. Bakwin, New York); *The Imaginary Invalid* (Philadelphia). Water colors and drawings on this last theme: a water color in the Courtauld Institute, London; a pen and ink drawing (Miss Edith Wetmore, New York).

Daumier and Cervantes: on *Don Quixote* in France, see Chasles, Émile, *Michel de Cervantes,* Paris, 1866; Hazard, Paul, *Don Quichotte de Cervantes,* Paris, n.d.; Sainte-Beuve in *Nouveaux Lundis,* vol. 8, Paris, 1867, pp. 1–65; Hugo in *William Shakespeare,* 1864; Chateaubriand in *Memoirs,* translated by Alexander Teixeira de Mattos, London, 1902, vol. 1, p. xxiv and p. 151; Vigny, Alfred de, in *Journal,* 1839, p. 141 and in preface to *Daphné,* 1837. See also Ashbee, H. S., *Iconography of Don Quixote,* London, 1895 and Faure, Élie, *Les Don Quichotte de Daumier,* Paris, 1934. Some Daumier oils on this theme: *Don*

Quixote in the Mountains (private collection, Boston); *Don Quixote and Sancho Panza Under a Tree* (Ny Carlsberg Glyptotek, Copenhagen), shown according to Adhémar at the Martinet Gallery in 1861; a grisaille, *Don Quixote and Sancho Panza* (Van Beuren collection, Newport, Rhode Island), probably the work seen by Goncourt and mentioned in *Journal,* vol. XIX, p. 163. The story of the painting on Daubigny's wall is in Moreau-Nélaton, Étienne, *Histoire de Corot,* Paris, 1905, p. 226. Philip Adams suggests that Daumier inserted the two figures into Corot's *Don Quixote;* see *Cincinnati Museum Bulletin,* May, 1952. The oil sketch of Don Quixote and the dead mule (Kroller-Müller Gallery) is probably a study for the painting in the Metropolitan Museum, New York; Maison discusses a charcoal drawing for the same in *Burlington Magazine,* vol. 96, Jan., 1954, pp. 13–17.

The episode of Quixote and the sheep is in chapter eleven of the novel. The finished oil is now in the C. S. Payson collection, New York. Related to it: an unfinished oil in Hugh Lane Bequest, National Gallery, London; an oil study of Sancho alone, privately owned in Paris and reproduced by Maison in his article, "Some Unpublished Works by Daumier," in *Gazette des Beaux-Arts,* vol. 51, May-June, 1958, p. 344; a preliminary drawing (Claude Roger-Marx, Paris). Two late and unfinished oils of Don Quixote are in a private collection, Zürich, and in the Courtauld Institute, London.

Other late works: *The Painter Before His Easel,* in two nearly identical versions (Duncan Phillips and Clark Institute); *Pierrot Chantant* (Oskar Reinhart); *Woman Carrying a Child* (private collection, Zürich); *The Fugitives* (Minneapolis Institute of Arts). Edmond de Goncourt is quoted from *Journal,* vol. IX, p. 153. Daumier's quasi-impressionistic drawings include a study of five terror-stricken men (Maurice Gobin, Paris), a sketch in pen and ink of a man on horseback (Ing. Van Gogh collection, Amsterdam); a sheet of studies with a group of men (Chicago Art Institute); *A Clown and a Drummer* (Metropolitan Museum).

The anecdote of Daumier's hostility to the work of Monet: see Rewald, John, *The History of Impressionism,* New York, 1961, p. 150 and note. The nomination of Daumier for the jury list is reprinted in the same, pp. 230–40.

Vignette: The Last Years

The description of Daumier by Jules Clarétie is reprinted in *Daumier Raconté,* pp. 109–110. The litho, *Les Témoins,* dated by Delteil 1872, was probably done late in 1873. On the many satires of Thiers, see Cherpin, Germaine in *Arts et Livres de Provence,* numéro spécial 8, 1948, pp. 35 ff. On Daumier's financial position toward the end of his life, see Cherpin, Jean, in *Marseille,* series 3, no. 29, May-July, 1956, pp. 35–42. On Corot's purchase of the house at Valmondois, see Moreau-Nélaton, *op. cit.,* pp. 327–328. A somewhat different version of the episode is given by Jean Gigoux in *Causeries sur les Artists de Mon Temps.*

The exhibition of Daumier's work opened April 17, 1878: see Cherpin, Jean, "Autour de la Première Exposition des Peintures de Daumier," in *Gazette des Beaux-Arts,* vol. 51, 1958, pp. 329 ff. For the comments of Wolff, Pelletan and others see Lassaigne, Jacques, *Daumier,* translated by Eveline B. Shaw, New York, 1938, pp. 161–165.

The remarks of Carjat at the funeral are quoted by Escholier, 1923, p. 171. The speech of Champfleury is reprinted in *Daumier Raconté,* p. 125.

9: Man of His Time and Ours

George Boas discusses the phrase, "one must be of one's time," in *Wingless Pegasus,* Baltimore, 1950, Appendix I. Champfleury is quoted from *Les Excentriques,* Paris, 1852, p. 8. Giorgio Vasari on Piero della Francesca is in the *Lives,* translated by Gaston de Vere, London, 1912–1915, vol. 3, pp. 12–23; Aldous Huxley on the same is in *On Art and Artists,* New York, 1960, pp. 196–202.

On the early collectors of Daumier paintings and drawings: Adhémar, *Daumier,* pp. 83–86; Cherpin, "Le Dernier Carnet de Comptes de Daumier," in *Marseille,* 3rd series, no. 29, May-July, 1956, pp. 35–42; *L'Amour de l'Art,* vol. 8, 1927, pp. 149 ff.; *Bulletin de l'Art Ancien et Moderne,* no. 734, Paris, 1927, pp. 166–173 and pp. 202, 203; *Kunst und Künstler,* vol. 10, June, 1912, pp. 449–464; *Gazette des Beaux-Arts,* vol. 44, July, 1910, pp. 11–25; *Les Arts,* vol. XI, Dec., 1912, pp. 1–32; *International Studio,* vol. 49, April, 1913, pp. 188 ff.

Interpretations of Daumier: Faure, Élie, *History of Art,* translated by Walter Pach, New York and London, vol. IV, 1924, pp. 320–326; Soffici, Ardengo, "Daumier Pittore," in *Dedalo,* II, 1921–22, pp. 405–419; Fontainas, André, *La Peinture de Daumier,* Paris, 1923, p. 15; Klossowski, *Honoré Daumier,* revised edition, 1923, pp. 2–4; Sadleir, Michael, *Daumier, the Man and the Artist,* London, 1924, Introduction; Fry, Roger, *Characteristics of French Art,* New York, 1933, pp. 113–116; Bell, Clive, *Landmarks in Nineteenth Century Painting,* London, 1927, pp. 118 ff.; Stahl, Fritz, *Honoré Daumier,* Berlin, 1930, pp. 5–13; Fuchs, Eduard in *Cahiers d'Art,* nos. 5–6, 1928, pp. 187–188 and Introduction to *Honoré Daumier: Lithographien,* Munich, n.d.; Phillips, Duncan, *Honoré Daumier,* New York, 1922, p. 15; Charlot, Jean, *Art from the Mayans to Disney,* New York, 1939, p. 190; Roger-Marx, Claude, preface to catalogue of 1934 exhibition at the Orangerie, Paris; Valéry, Paul, *Daumier,* Paris, 1938, Introduction; Malraux, André, *The Voices of Silence,* translated by Stuart Gilbert, New York, 1953, Part One, Section 5; Sloane, Joseph, *French Painting Between the Past and the Present,* Princeton, 1951, p. 124; Jones, Philippe, "Daumier et l'Impressionisme," in *Gazette des Beaux-Arts,* vol. 55, April, 1960, pp. 247–250; Gombrich, Ernst H., *Art and Illusion,* New York, 1960, pp. 352–355; Gowing, Lawrence in London *Observer,* June 18, 1961; Sylvester, David in *New Statesman,* London, June 23, 1961.

On the decline of caricature, see Hofmann, Werner, *Caricature from Leonardo to Picasso,* New York, 1957, pp. 52–57.

INDEX

Actor of the Funambules, litho, 55, Fig. 25

Adhémar, Jean, 134, 146, 217

Advice to a Young Artist, oil, 153, 156, Fig. 74

After the Trial, water color, 148

After You!, litho, 172, 219, Fig. 82

Alarmists and Alarmed, lithos, 86

Alexandre, Arsène, 77, 88, 135, 203, 212, 213, 216, 217

Alliance of the Bonapartists and the Capuchins, litho, 100

Amateur theatricals, lithos on, 128, 129, Fig. 56

Ancient History, lithos, 60, 61, 128, 165, Figs. 26, 27

And During That Time . . . , litho, 185, Fig. 86

April riots and trials of 1835, 27, 28, 29, Fig. 10

Aquatic Sketches, lithos, 119

Argout, Comte d', 23, 31

Artists, lithos on, 46, 47, 122

Assolant, Eugène, 163, 164, 166

Auber, Daniel, 51, 127, 177

Audebrand, Philibert, 158

Augier, Émile, 127

Auto-da-fé, litho, 100

Balzac, Honoré de, 6, 14, 33, 34, 37, 40, 43, 61, 80, 114, 115

Banville, Théodore de, 37, 81, 109, 112, 165, 171, 208

Barbès, Armand, 11, 85

Barbizon painters, 137, 138, 160

Barye, Antoine-Louis, 71, 86, 160

Bathers, lithos, 48, 161, Fig. 23

Baudelaire, Charles, 11, 15, 27, 61, 63, 67, 68, 69, 70, 73, 80, 81, 84, 122, 134, 137, 149, 155, 156, 157, 158, 207, 210

Baudry, Paul, 155

Behold Our Nuptial Chamber, litho, 112, Fig. 47

Bell, Clive, 214, 215

Bellini, Vincenzo, 51, 127

Benjamin, 82, Fig. 34

Béranger, Pierre-Jean, 3, 5, 7, 12, 25, 109

Berlioz, Hector, 66, 159

Bertels, Kurt, 187, 213

Bigger and Bigger Shops, litho, 43

Bismarck, Otto von, 162, 177, 178, 182, 188

Blanc, Charles, 67, 86, 87

Blanc, Louis, 11, 95

Blanqui, Auguste, 11

Bluestockings, lithos, 48, 190

Boas, George, 210

Bonvin, François, 81

Bouguereau, Adolphe, 155

Boulevard, Le, 157, 158

Bourbon Restoration, 9

Bourgeois, Émile, 84, 85, 161

Bourgeoisie, evolution of, 31, 32, 33, 115

Box at the Opera, water color, 127

Box at the Théâtre Ventadour, litho, 103, Fig. 58

"Burgraves," 97, 98, 99

Burty, Philippe, 146, 157

Bust portraits, sculptures and lithos, 19, 20, 21, 23, Figs. 4, 5, 7

Butcher at Work, water color, 148

Cabat, Louis, 70

Cabet, Étienne, 12, 48

Café de Madrid, radicals of, 158, 163

Caraguel, Clément, 110, 160

Caricature, development of, 14, 15, 16, 17

Caricature, La, 6

Carjat, Étienne, 157, 158, 159, 207, 208, 209, Fig. 75

Carpeaux, Jean Baptiste, 116, 167

Cavaignac, General Eugène, 86, 95, 96

Centaur and Woman, drawing, 143, Fig. 67

Cervantes, Miguel de, *Don Quixote,* 193, 194, 195, 196, 197, 198, 199, 200, 201

Cham, 110, 157

Champfleury, Jules, 10, 67, 69, 79, 81, 84, 87, 112, 118, 157, 158, 208, 209, 210

Charivari, 14, 110, 157, 160

Charlet, Nicolas-Toussaint, 16, 157, 195

Charlot, Jean, 216

Charms of Railway Travel, litho, 123, Fig. 54
Cherpin, Jean, 208, 216, 217
Chess Players, oil, 189
Child Running, drawing, 143
Cholera Morbus, wood engraving, 37, Fig. 13
Church, The, 12, 13, 84, 85, 109, 161, 162, 163; lithos on, 25, 98, 99, 100, 110, 166, 167, 168, 169, 175, 184, Figs. 43, 44, 77
Clarétie, Jules, 145, 179, 207
Collectors of Daumier, 208, 212, 213
Comet of 1857, lithos, 142
Commune of Paris, 179, 182, 183
Condorcet, Marquis de, 8, 10
Conference of London, litho, 24
Conjugal Mores, lithos, 47, 80, Fig. 22
Connoisseur, water color, 146
Connoisseurs, oil, 151
Considérant, Victor, 12
Constitutionnel, Le, 17, 44, 58, 116
Corneille, Pierre, 53, 60, 127
Corot, Jean-Baptiste Camille, 86, 153, 159, 160, 183, 188, 190, 199, 207, 208
Cossacks to Laugh At, lithos, 110
Country Pleasures, lithos, 160, 161
Coup d'état of 1851 and Second Empire, 103, 104, 105, 106, 107, 108, 109, 110
Courbet, Gustave, 67, 81, 86, 109, 122, 137, 155, 158, 183, 207, 210
Crimean War, lithos on, 110
Crinolines, lithos on, 120, Fig. 51
Crispin and Scapin, oil, 150, 153, 191, 213, Fig. 73
Critics in the Theater, water color, 148
Curious Ones, oil, 152

Dantan, Jean-Pierre Édouard, 21, 23
Daubigny, Charles, 80, 90, 137, 160, 195, 199, 208
Daumier, Jean-Baptiste, 3
Daumier, Marie-Alexandrine, 80, 212
David, Jacques Louis, 3, 27, 57, 61, 64, 65, 77
David d'Angers, 67, 71, 81
Deburau, Charles, 126
Deburau, Jean-Baptiste Gaspard, 54, 55
Decamps, Alexandre-Gabriel, 18, 71, 72, 86, 195, 207

Decamps, Maurice-Alexandre, 67
Delacroix, Eugène, 15, 65, 66, 67, 68, 69, 70, 72, 73, 77, 81, 84, 109, 136, 137, 156, 183, 190, 207, 210, 211
Delaroche, Paul, 65, 66, 157
Delescluze, Louis Charles, 158, 163, 164
Demimondaines, litho, 142, Fig. 51
Departure for Spain, litho, 24, 25
Devéria, Eugène, 16, 65, 189
Dialogue of the Dead, litho, 167
Diaz, Narcisse-Virgile, 68, 70, 77, 137, 160, 187
Diderot, Denis, 8, 57, 64
Divorcing Women, lithos, 50, 84
Doctor Diafoirus, oil, 192, 193, Fig. 90
Doctor Véron at Auteuil, litho, 116, Fig. 48
Don Quixote, paintings and drawings, 88, 135, 195, 196, 199, 200, 201, 202, Figs. 91, 92, 93, 94, Color Plate VII
Donizetti, Gaetano, 51, 127
Don't Meddle With It!, litho, 35, Fig. 12
Doré, Gustave, 142, 159, 190, 197, 200
Drama, oil, 150, 151
Dramatic Sketches, lithos, 124
Drinking Paris, lithos, 120
Drinking Song, water color, 148
Dumas, Alexandre, père, 53, 54, 55, 57, 58, 126
Dumas, Alexandre, fils, 53, 127
Dupin senior, 23, Fig. 7
Dupré, Jules, 145, 190, 208, 212
Duranty, Louis Edmond, 208

Ecumenical Council, lithos on, 175
Emigrants, see *Fugitives*
Emotions of the Hunt, lithos, 119, 120
Enfantin, Pére, 48, 109
Escholier, Raymond, 214, 217
Etcher, oil, 74
European Equilibrium, litho, 172, 187, 219, Fig. 81
Even So, It Is Flattering, litho, 122, Fig. 53
Exhibitions of Daumier, 208, 213, 214, 216
Expositions, 122, 137, 172

Falloux, Comte de, 97, 98, 99, 163

Family on the Barricade, oil, 90, 91, Fig. 39

Famous Case, water color, 148

Faure, Élie, 213

Favre, Jules, 162, 176

Feast of Belshazzar-Véron, litho, 99

Female Socialists, lithos, 50, 190

Feminist movement, lithos on, 48, 50, 189, Fig. 24

Festival in the Neighboring Village, lithos, 189

Feuchère, Jean, 7, 71, Fig. 2

Final Council of the Ex-Ministers, litho, 84, Fig. 35

First Bathe, oil, 76

First Class Carriage, water color, 147

Flaubert, Gustave, 27, 28, 48, 174, 207

Fontainas, André, 214

Fourier, Charles, 12, 48

Fragonard, Jean Honoré, 203

Franco-Prussian War, lithos on, 177, 178, 179, 182, Figs. 83, 85

French Revolution, 4, 8, 9

Frémy, Arnould, 110

Friends, litho, 35, Fig. 11

Fruitless Search for the Planet, litho, 47, Fig. 21

Fry, Roger, 214, 215

Fuchs, Éduard, 213, 215

Fugitives, bas-reliefs, 91, 92, 134, Fig. 40; oils, 91, 92, 93, 135, 203, Fig. 41, Color Plate VIII

Gambetta, Léon, 163, 164, 165, 166, 174, 176, 178, 179, 207

Game of Draughts, oil, 153

Gamin of Paris, litho, 84

Gargantua, litho, 7

Garibaldi, Giuseppe, 161, 162, 169

Gautier, Théophile, 11, 13, 53, 57, 58, 66, 67, 71, 90, 109, 118, 125, 127, 137, 165, 183, 207

Gavarni, Chevalier Sulpice, 16, 17

Geoffroy-Dechaume, Adolphe-Victor, 71, 80, 146, 160, 208, 212

Gérard, François, 65

Géricault, Théodore, 15, 65, 72

Gérôme, Jean-Léon, 155

Gigoux, Jean, 134, 135

Gillotypes, 111, 161

Girardin, Émile de, 6, Fig. 42

Girodet, Anne Louis, 65

Gobin, Maurice, 134

Gombrich, Ernst, 156, 218

Goncourt, Edmond and Jules de, 71, 83, 84, 87, 98, 109, 112, 126, 128, 147, 148, 159, 183, 187, 203

Good Bourgeois, lithos, 34, 47, 84

Good Samaritan, oil, 77

Grandville, Charles, 17

Gros, Baron, 65

Guérin, Pierre-Narcisse, 65, 71

Guizot, Guillaume, 10, 19, 26, 33, 48, 83, 112

Halévy, Ludovic, 128, 129

Handsome Narcissus, litho, 60, Fig. 27

Haussmann, Baron, 111, 112, 113, 114

Head of a Buffoon, oil, 153

Heavy Burden, sculpture, 135, 136, Fig. 61; oils, 135, 136, 212, 213, Fig. 62

Heine, Heinrich, 13

High Tide of 1868, litho, 163

History as Revised by Operetta, litho, 166

History of a Reign, litho, 180

Horsemen, oil, 76, Color Plate I

Huart, Louis, 157, 160

Huet, Paul, 68, 70

Hugo, Victor, 11, 53, 55, 57, 65, 66, 95, 98, 99, 100, 104, 106, 115, 126, 163, 164, 165, 172, 176, 181, 182, 184, 197, 198, 207, 208, Figs. 42, 84

Human Pyramid, litho, 169

Hunt, lithos, 47, 48

Huxley, Aldous, 211, 212

Hyacinthe, Père, 168

I Wanted to Smear Him, litho, 168, Fig. 77

If the Workers Fight, litho, 184, 185

Île Saint-Louis, 80, 81, 82, Fig. 33

Imaginary Invalid, paintings and drawings, 188, 190, 191, 192, 193, Figs. 88, 89, 90

Impressionist painters, 203, 205

Ingres, Jean-Auguste-Dominique, 15, 60, 61, 65, 67, 69, 70, 81, 136, 137, 183, 207, 210

Italian question, 98, 161, 162, 163; lithos on, 169, 172, 175, 184, Figs. 78, 80

Jeanron, Philippe-Auguste, 7, 70, 77, 86

Johannot, Tony, 36, 195, 200

Jones, Philippe, 218

Jordaens, Jakob, 87

Journal Amusant, 157, 161

Judges of the April Defendants, lithos, 28, 29

Klossowski, Erich, 213, 214

Lady of the Eggs, litho, 172, Fig. 80

Lafargue, Paul, 163

La Fontaine, Jean de, 3, 5, 160, 188, 189, 194

Lamartine, Alphonse de, 11

Lamennais, Félicité-Robert de, 12, 13

Lawyers, lithos and paintings of, 44, 45, 142, 144, 146, 147, 148, 191, Figs. 19, 70, 87

Ledru-Rollin, Alexandre, 12, 13, 27, 28, 95, 96

Legislative Paunch, litho, 23, 24, Fig. 8

Lemaître, Frédérick, 37, 54, 125, 126, Fig. 14

Lemann, Bernard, 217

Lenoir, Alexandre, 3

Leroux, Pierre, 11, 48

"Liberal Empire," 161, 162

Light Breeze, litho, 141

Literary Discussion in the Second Balcony, litho, 133, Fig. 60

Lithography, development of, 15, 16, 17, 111, 161

Louis-Napoleon, 95, 96, 98, 99, 100, 105, 106, 108, 161, 164, 177, 178, 180, 184

Louis-Philippe, 10, 18, 19, 24, 25, 26, 55, 84, 116, Fig. 3

Lower the Curtain, litho, 19, Fig. 3

Lucas, George A., 146, 147, 149

Lucian, 57, 61, 128

Macaire, Robert, lithos on, 37, 39, 51, 115, 190, Fig. 15

MacMahon, Marshal, 177, 186

Magdalen in the Desert, oil, 87, 134

Maison, K. E., 91, 135, 143, 145, 217

Malraux, André, 211, 217

Man on Horseback, drawing, 203, Fig. 98

Man Reading in a Garden, water color, 143, 189

Manet, Édouard, 155, 205

Marceau, Henri, 148, 149, 150, 188, 193, 216

Marcel, Henri, 213

Marivaux, Pierre, 32, 57, 61

Meilhac, Henri, 128

Meissonier, Ernest, 122, 155, 156

Men of the Law, lithos, 45, 46, 191, Fig. 19

Meyerbeer, Giacomo, 51, 127

Michelangelo, 70, 72

Michelet, Jules, 8, 12, 13, 32, 100, 107, 174

Miller, His Son and the Ass, oil, 87, 135, 140, 142, Color Plate II

Millet, Jean-François, 76, 109, 137, 138, 155, 160, 183, 190, 207

Molé, Comte de, 99, 100

Molière, 188, 190, 191, 192, 193

Monde Illustré, 157, 207

Monet, Claude, 155, 203

Mongan, Agnes, 147

Monnier, Henry, 16, 17, 116, 117, 118, 119, Fig. 49

Montalembert, Charles de, 98, 99, 100, 103, 109, 110, 163, Fig. 43

Montalivet, Comte de, 24

Montesquieu, Charles Louis, 8

Morning After the Battle, litho, 174

Morny, Duc de, 108, 127, 162, 180

Motto for the Year 1850, litho, Fig. 43

Mountebanks Changing Place, water color, 189, Color Plate VI

Music Lover, water color, 192

Nadar (Félix Tournachon), 120, 122, 141, 159, 179, 207, 208, Fig. 52

Napoleonic Steamboat, litho, 96

National Guard, lithos on, 44, Fig. 18

New Assumption, litho, 175

New Cinderella, litho, 169, Fig. 78

Nieuwerkerke, Comte de, 109, 138

Nocturnal Strollers, oil, 74

Nymphs Pursued by Satyrs, oil, 87, 135, 140, Fig. 36

O Moon, Inspire Me, litho, 48, Fig. 24

Odry, Jacques, 52, 55

Oedipus and the Shepherd, oil, 76

Offenbach, Jacques, 125, 128, 165, 166, 179

Ollivier, Émile, 162, 166, 174, 176, 177
On a Bridge at Night, oil, 135
On Your Way!, litho, 6
One Glory Quenches the Other, litho, 99

Page of History, litho, 182, Fig. 84
Painter, oil, 189
Painter at His Easel, oil, 202, 203, 220, 221, Fig. 95
Papas, lithos, 47, 84
Parisian Emotions, lithos, 56
Parisian Types, lithos, 32
Parliamentary Arena, litho, 176
Parliamentary Idyls, lithos, 94
Pascal, Michel, 158
Pastorals, lithos, 34, 47, 73, Fig. 21
Peace, an Idyl, litho, 182, Fig. 85
Peace Conferences, lithos on, 98, 168, 172
Penelope's Nights, litho, 60, Fig. 26
Persigny, Duc de, 108, 124, 125, 162
Phantom, litho, 28
Philanthropists of the Day, lithos, 77
Philipon, Charles, 6, 14, 17, 18, 31, 83, 110, 157, 207
Phillips, Duncan, 215
Physiognomy of the Assembly, lithos, 93, 94
Pixérécourt, René, 53
Planche, Gustave, 67, 137, 210
Plebiscite of 1870, 176, 177, 187
Politics in a Beer Garden, water color, 143, Fig. 68
Ponsard, François, 58, 59, 125, 127
Pope Pius IX, 98, 162, 175
Poulet-Malassis, Paul Auguste, 134, 135, 142
Préault, Auguste, 5, 59, 71, 72, 81, 86, 134
Press, republican, 12, 13, 14, 26, 30, 31; opposition in Second Empire, 160, 163, 164
Prévost-Paradol, Lucien, 164, 170
Print Collector, oil, 152, 153, Color Plate V
Print Collectors, oils, 151, 189
Procession of Silenus, drawing, 87, Fig. 37
Proudhon, Pierre-Joseph, 104, 105, 106, 210

Prudhomme, Joseph, 17, 51, 116, 117, 118, 119, 127; lithos, 119, 122, 123, 190, Figs. 49, 50
Prunelle, Clément, 23, 24, Figs. 5, 6
Prussian question, lithos on, 162, 169, 170, 172, Figs. 79, 80
Public at the Salon, lithos, 122
Pyat, Félix, 60, 158, 163

Queen Preparing for a Grand Tirade, litho, 129, Fig. 57

Rachel, 52, 59, 60, 61, 108, 109, 125
Racine, Jean, 53, 60
Railway travel, lithos on, 47, 123, 124, Fig. 54
Ratapoil, sculpture, 72, 103, 107, Fig. 45; lithos, 103, 106, 184, Fig. 46
Recalled with Enthusiasm, litho, 128, Fig. 56
Reader, oil, 149
Red Spectre, litho, 176, 219
Re-entry of the Capuchins, litho, 98
Refugees, see *Fugitives*
Rehearsal for the Council, litho, 175
Rembrandt, 72, 74
Rentier, Little, litho, 39, Fig. 16
Representatives Represented, lithos, 93
Republic, oil, 77, 81, Fig. 32
Republic Calls Us, litho, 179
Republic of Milo, litho, 184
Requiescat in Pace, litho, 184
Revolution of 1830 and July Monarchy, 9, 10
Revolution of 1848 and Second Republic, 83, 84, 85, 86
Rochefort, Henri, 157, 160, 164, 166, 174, 176
Rogeard, Louis-Auguste, 164
Roger-Marx, Claude, 73, 213, 216
Romantic movement in art and literature, 10, 11, 13, 57, 58, 59, 65, 66, 67
Romieu, Auguste, 100, 109, Fig. 44
Rosen, David, 148, 149, 150, 188, 193, 216
Rossini, Gioachino, 51, 127
Rousseau, Jean-Jacques, 3, 4, 5, 10
Rousseau, Théodore, 68, 137, 155, 157, 160, 189, 190, 195, 199, 207
Rubens, Peter Paul, 65, 72, 87

Rue Transnonain, litho, 27, 28, 215,
Fig. 9

Sadleir, Michael, 214
Saint-Simon, 11
Sainte-Beuve, Charles-Augustin, 109,
163, 190, 197, 198
Sainte-Pélagie Prison, 7, 73
Salon exhibitions, 64, 65, 66, 73, 86, 87,
122
Sand, George, 48, 159
Sarcey, Francisque, 166
Sardou, Victorien, 127
Scene from the Theater, oil, 191
Scribe, Eugène, 53, 127
Second Class Carriage, water color, 147
Secret, oil, 187
Séjour, Victor, 126
Sheet of Studies with a Group of Men,
drawing, 203, Fig. 97
Side Show, water color, 145, 146, Fig.
69
Silhouette, La, 6
Singing Couple, oil, 153
Singing Pierrot, oil, 203
Sketches Made at the Theater, lithos,
161
Sloane, Joseph, 218
Sniffing the Merchandise, litho, 42, Fig.
17
Society Actors, lithos, 128, 129, Fig.
56
Soffici, Ardengo, 213
Soup, drawing, 187, 217
Souvenir of Youth, litho, 47, Fig. 22
Souvenirs of Richard III, wood engrav-
ings, 126, Fig. 55
Sovereign People, litho, 185
Speech for the Prosecution, water color,
146
Stahl, Fritz, 215
Stairway of the Palais de Justice, water
color, 148
Strong Man, oil, 187, 189
Summertime Sketches, lithos, 119

Taine, Hippolyte, 116, 137, 160
Teachers and Brats, lithos, 44
Tenants and Landlords, lithos, 39, 84,
219

Testimony Behind Closed Doors, water
color, 189, Fig. 87
Thackeray, William M., 14, 54, 60
Theater in July Monarchy, 37, 50, 51,
52, 53, 54, 55, 56, 57, 58, 59, 60; in
Second Empire, 116, 117, 118, 119,
124, 125, 126, 127, 128
Theater, lithos and wood engravings on,
54, 55, 56, 57, 60, 61, 124, 125, 126,
127, 128, 129, 133, 161, 165, 166, Figs.
14, 25, 28, 29, 49, 55, 56, 57, 58, 59,
60; paintings, 127, 148, 150, 151, 191,
192, 193, Figs. 73, 88, 89, 90
Theater Box, oil, 189
*They Say the Parisians are Hard to
Please,* litho, 133, Fig. 59
Thiers, Louis-Adolphe, 10, 19, 24, 27,
31, 33, 39, 40, 99, 100, 104, 108, 110,
118, 133, 166, 170, 174, 176, 177, 179,
182, 183, 184, 185, 186, 207, Fig. 4
Thieves and the Ass, litho, 142; draw-
ing, 142, 212, Fig. 65; oil, 142, 219,
Fig. 66
Third Class Carriage, oils, 149, 150, 213,
220, Figs. 71, 72; water color, 149
This Morning Before Sunrise, litho, 47,
Fig. 20
Thoré, Théophile, 67, 68, 69, 71, 155,
156, 207
*Those Who are About to Die Salute
You!,* litho, 177, Fig. 83
Three Gossiping Women, water color,
142, 146, Fig. 64
Three Lawyers, oil, 153, 189
Three Little Saints, litho, 98
Towman, oil, 76, 140, Fig. 30
Tragedy, lithos, 61, 84
Tragical-classical Physiognomies, lithos,
61, Figs. 28, 29
Tragical Physiognomies, lithos, 124
Traviès, Charles, 17
Tristan, Flora, 48
Triumph of Paganism, litho, 110
'Twas Not Worth the Trouble, litho, 30
Two Future High Dignitaries, litho, 100,
Fig. 44
Two Men Drinking, oil, 76, 140
Two Print Collectors, water color, 77
Two Sculptors, oil, 202
Types of the Old Comedy, oil, 191

Ulysses, or the Pigs Avenged, wood engravings, 125
Uprising, oil, 88, 90, Fig. 38

Valéry, Paul, 216
Valmondois, 138, 160, 189, 191, 208, Fig. 76
Vernet, Horace, 15, 66
Véron, Louis-Désiré, 44, 99, 100, 115, 116, 190, Figs. 44, 48
Véron, Pierre, 157, 160, 161, 208
Veuillot, Louis, 100, 103, 109, 110, 163, 166, 167, 168, 169, 184
Victor Hugo and Émile de Girardin, litho, 95, 96, Fig. 42
Viel-Castel, Comte de, 109, 127
Vignettes, 36
Vigny, Alfred de, 11, 109, 195
Visitors in an Artist's Studio, water colors, 146, Color Plate III
Voltaire, 8, 10, 60, 168, 183, Fig. 77

Waiting Room, oil, 135; water color, 146

Washermen, litho, 7
Washerwoman, oils, 134, 149, 152, 212, 214, 217, 218, 220, Color Plate IV
Washerwomen on the Steps of the Quay, oil, 135
Water Carrier, oil, 76, Fig. 31
We Want Barabbas!, oil, 134
Weill, Georges, 32
Weiss, Jean-Jacques, 165
Witnesses, litho, 207
Woman Carrying a Child, oil, 203, Fig. 96
Wood engravings, 36, 37, 125, 126
Wood is Dear . . . , litho, 47, 73
Workmen in a Street, oil, 74

Yes, Madame Fribochon, litho, 142, 214, Fig. 63
You Have the Floor, litho, 29, Fig. 10
Young Girls Bathing, oil, 76

Zola, Émile, 80, 82, 111, 112, 114, 115, 155, 156

LIST OF ILLUSTRATIONS

Portrait of Daumier by the photographer Nadar, frontispiece

1. Street of the Iron Pot, Paris 4
2. Daumier at 22, lithograph by Jean Feuchère 6
3. Lower the Curtain, the Farce is Ended, lithograph 18
4. Thi . . . (Thiers), lithograph 20
5. Bust portrait of Prunelle, bronze 21
6. Mr. Prune (Prunelle), lithograph 22
7. Dup . . . (Dupin), lithograph 24
8. The Legislative Paunch, lithograph 25
9. Rue Transnonain, lithograph 26
10. You Have the Floor, Explain Yourself, lithograph 29
11. The Friends, lithograph (detail) 34
12. Don't Meddle with It, lithograph 35
13. Cholera Morbus, wood engraving 36
14. Lemaitre as Robert-Macaire, from a contemporary photo 38
15. Ladies and Gentlemen! (Robert-Macaire), lithograph 40
16. The Little Rentier, lithograph 41
17. Sniffing the Merchandise, lithograph 42
18. Yes, Dear Friend . . . , lithograph 43
19. True, You Have Lost Your Case . . . , lithograph 45
20. This Morning before Sunrise, lithograph 46
21. Fruitless Search for the Planet . . . , lithograph 49
22. A Souvenir of Youth, lithograph 50
23. Come, Make the Plunge, Père Goutout, lithograph 51
24. O Moon, Inspire Me . . . , lithograph 52
25. The Actor of the Funambules, lithograph 56
26. Penelope's Nights, lithograph 58
27. The Handsome Narcissus, lithograph 59
28. Yes, Since I Find So Faithful a Friend, lithograph 62
29. Rodrigue, Have You Courage?, lithograph 62
30. The Towman, oil 74
31. The Water Carrier, oil 75
32. The Republic, oil 78
33. The quai d'Anjou 81
34. Portrait of Daumier by Benjamin, lithograph 82
35. Final Council of the Ex-Ministers, lithograph 85
36. Nymphs Pursued by Satyrs, oil 88
37. The Procession of Silenus, chalk with gouache 89
38. The Uprising, oil 90
39. Study, Head of a Man, oil 91
40. The Refugees, bronze relief 92
41. The Emigrants, oil 94
42. Victor Hugo and Émile de Girardin, lithograph 96
43. Motto for the Year 1850 (Montalembert), lithograph 97
44. Two Future High Dignitaries (Romieu and Véron), lithograph 101
45. Plaster cast of Ratapoil 102
46. Ratapoil Making Propaganda, lithograph 105
47. Behold Our Nuptial Chamber, lithograph 113
48. Doctor Véron at Auteuil, lithograph 114
49. Henry Monnier in the Role of Prudhomme, lithograph 117
50. I Want to Leave a Monument, lithograph 118
51. Ladies of the Demi-Monde, lithograph 120
52. Nadar Elevating Photography, lithograph 121
53. Even So, It Is Flattering, lithograph 123
54. The Charms of Railway Travel, lithograph 124
55. Wood engraving from Souvenirs of Richard III 126
56. Recalled with Enthusiasm, lithograph 128
57. A Queen Preparing for a Grand Tirade, lithograph 129
58. A Box at the Théâtre Ventadour, lithograph 130
59. They Say the Parisians are Hard to Please, lithograph 131
60. A Literary Discussion in the Second Balcony, lithograph 132
61. Terra cotta figurine, The Heavy Burden 135
62. The Heavy Burden, oil 136
63. Yes, Madame Fribochon, lithograph 138
64. Three Gossiping Women, water color 139
65. Study for The Thieves, charcoal drawing 140
66. The Thieves and the Ass, oil 141
67. Centaur and Woman, pen and wash 143
68. Politics in a Beer Garden, pen and wash 144
69. The Side Show, water color 145
70. Lawyer with a Woman Client, water color 147
71. The Third Class Carriage, oil 150
72. The Third Class Carriage, oil 151
73. Crispin and Scapin, oil 152
74. Advice to a Young Artist, oil 154
75. Étienne Carjat, Caricature-portrait of Daumier 158
76. Daumier's House at Valmondois 159
77. I Wanted to Smear Him, lithograph 167
78. The New Cinderella, lithograph 168
79. Let Us Embrace, lithograph 170
80. The Lady of the Eggs, lithograph 171
81. European Equilibrium, lithograph 173
82. After You!, lithograph 175
83. Those Who Are about to Die . . . , lithograph 178
84. A Page of History, lithograph 180
85. Peace, an Idyl, lithograph 181
86. And During that Time . . . , lithograph 185
87. Testimony Behind Closed Doors, water color 188
88. The Imaginary Invalid, water color 192
89. The Imaginary Invalid, pen and wash 193
90. Doctor Diafoirus, oil 194
91. Don Quixote and Sancho Panza, oil 196
92. Don Quixote and Sancho Panza under a Tree, oil 197
93. Don Quixote and Sancho Panza, black chalk and water color 198
94. Don Quixote Rushing upon the Sheep, oil 199
95. The Painter at His Easel, oil 201
96. Woman Carrying a Child, oil 202
97. Sheet of Studies with a Group of Men, pencil 204
98. Study of a Man on Horseback, pen and ink 205
99. Portrait of Daumier by Nadar 206
100. Page from Daumier's account book 209

COLOR PLATES (following page 70)

I. The Horsemen, oil
II. The Miller, His Son and the Ass, oil
III. Visitors in an Artist's Studio, water color
IV. The Washerwoman, oil
V. The Print Collector, oil
VI. Mountebanks Changing Place, water color
VII. Don Quixote and Sancho Panza, oil
VIII. The Fugitives, oil